HUMAN VALUES AND SOCIAL CHANGE

INTERNATIONAL STUDIES
IN
SOCIOLOGY AND SOCIAL ANTHROPOLOGY

EDITED BY

Tukumbi Lumumba-Kasongo,
Rubin Patterson and Masamichi Sasaki

VOLUME LXXXIX

HUMAN VALUES AND SOCIAL CHANGE

Findings from the Values Surveys

EDITED BY

RONALD INGLEHART

BRILL
LEIDEN · BOSTON
2003

This book is printed on acid-free paper.

Die Deutsche Bibliothek - CIP-Einheitsaufnahme

Bibliografische Information der Deutschen Bibliothek
Die Deutsche Bibliothek verzeichnet diese Publikation in der
Deutschen Nationalbibliografie; detaillierte bibliografische Daten
sind im Internet über http://dnb.ddb.de abrufbar.

Library of Congress Cataloging-in-Publication Data

The Library of Congress Cataloging-in-Publication Data is also available

ISSN 0074-8684
ISBN 90 04 12810 7

Contents

Human Values and Social Change: Findings from the Values Surveys

Edited by Ronald Inglehart

vii   *Notes on Contributors*

1   RONALD INGLEHART
Introduction

5   PIPPA NORRIS and RONALD INGLEHART
Islamic Culture and Democracy: Testing the 'Clash of Civilizations' Thesis

35   YILMAZ ESMER
Is There an Islamic Civilization?

69   MANSOOR MOADDEL and TAQHI AZADARMAKI
The Worldviews of Islamic Publics: The Cases of Egypt, Iran, and Jordan

91   RONALD INGLEHART, PIPPA NORRIS and CHRISTIAN WELZEL
Gender Equality and Democracy

117   EPHRAIM YUCHTMAN-YA'AR
Value Priorities in Israeli Society: An Examination of Inglehart's Theory of Modernization and Cultural Variation

139   RUSSELL J. DALTON, PHAM MINH HAC, PHAM THANH NGHI and NHU-NGOC T. ONG
Social Relations and Social Capital in Vietnam: Findings from the 2001 World Values Survey

157 NEIL NEVITTE and MEBS KANJI
Authority Orientations and Political Support: A Cross-national
Analysis of Satisfaction with Governments and Democracy

183 HENNIE KOTZÉ and KARIN LOMBARD
Revising the Value Shift Hypothesis: A Descriptive Analysis
of South Africa's Value Priorities between 1990 and 2001

209 THORLEIF PETTERSSON
Individual Values and Global Governance: A Comparative
Analysis of Orientations towards the United Nations

235 JUAN DÍEZ-NICOLÁS
Two Contradictory Hypotheses on Globalization: Societal
Convergence or Civilization Differentiation and Clash

265 ALEJANDRO MORENO
Corruption and Democracy: A Cultural Assessment

279 *Index*

Notes on Contributors

TAGHI AZADARMAKI is Associate Professor in Sociology, Tehran University. He has published 13 books on social theory, social and cultural issues in Iran and social thought. Two of his major works are *Sociology of Sociology in Iran* and *The Idea of Modernization in Iran*. During the last seven years he has done research on cultural changes in Iran, partially with Mansoor Moaddel and Ronald Inglehart.

E-mail: tazad@chamran.ut.ac.ir

RUSSELL J. DALTON is Professor of Political Science and Director of the Center for the Study of Democracy at the University of California, Irvine. His interests include comparative political behaviour, political parties, social movements, and empirical democratic theory. Recent publications: *Critical Masses*, *The Green Rainbow*, and *Citizen Politics*; he also edited *Parties without Partisans*, and *Germans Divided*.

E-mail: rdalton@uci.edu

YILMAZ ESMER, Ph.D., is Professor of Political Science at Boğaziçi University in Istanbul, Turkey. His most recent publications include *Politics, Parties and Elections in Turkey*, coedited with Sabri Sayari (Colorado: Lynne Rienner, 2002), and *Devrim, Evrim, Statuko* (Istanbul: Tesev 1999). He is the principal investigator in Turkey of the World Values and European Values Surveys as well as the Turkish post-election studies.

E-mail: esmer@boun.edu.tr

RONALD INGLEHART is Professor of Political Science and program director at the Institute for Social Research at the University of Michigan. He helped found the Euro-Barometer surveys and directs the World Values Surveys. He has authored over 170 publications.

E-mail: rfi@umich.edu

MEBS KANJI is a post-doctoral fellow in the department of Political Science at the University of Toronto. His research interests are in Canadian and comparative politics, focusing on the study of political values and behaviour. He has published articles in the *International Journal of Public Opinion Research*, the *International Journal of Comparative Sociology* and the *American Review of Canadian Studies*.

HENNIE KOTZÉ is a Professor in Political Science at the University of Stellenbosch, South Africa. His two most recent publications relevant to value research are *Unconventional Political Participation and Political Confidence in South Africa: A Longitudinal analysis using data from the World Values Study* (Social Dynamics, Vol.27:2, 2001), and *Elite Perspectives on Policy Issues in South Africa*, (University of Stellenbosch, 2001). Currently he is working on a project comparing elite and mass values in a number of African countries.

E-mail: HJK@sun.ac.za

KARIN LOMBARD is a post-graduate student from the Department of Political Science, University of Stellenbosch. She is a researcher at the Institute for Justice and Reconciliation, Cape Town, South Africa. She is currently involved in a project on justice and reconciliation in South Africa.

E-mail: Karin@grove.uct.ac.za

MANSOOR MOADDEL, Professor of Sociology, Eastern Michigan University. He recently published *Jordanian Exceptionalism: An Analysis of State-Religion Relationship in Egypt, Iran, Jordan, and Syria* (New York: Palgrave, 2002), and *The Study of Islamic Culture and Politics: An Overview and Assessment*, (Annual Review of Sociology, August 2002, 28:359-86). In recent years, Moaddel has been carrying out comparative national surveys of the attitudes and value orientations of the Islamic publics in Egypt, Iran, Jordan, and Morocco.

E-mail: soc-moaddel@online.emich.edu

ALEJANDRO MORENO, Ph.D., is Professor of Political Science at the Instituto Tecnológico Autónomo de México, ITAM, and director of surveys at Reforma newspaper, both in Mexico City. He is the author of *Political Cleavages: Issues Parties and the Consolidation of Democracy* (1999), and co-author of *Human Values and Beliefs: A Cross-Cultural Sourcebook* (1998). He is currently working on a book about voting behaviour in Mexico.

E-mail: amoreno@itam.mx

NEIL NEVITTE is Professor of Political Science at the University of Toronto. His research interests are in public opinion and voting behaviour and he is co-investigator of the Canadian Election Study and principal investigator of the Canadian World Values Surveys. Nevitte's most recent publications include: *Value Change and Governance* (2002; editor); *Anatomy of a Liberal Victory* (2002).

E-mail: Nnevitte@epas.utoronto.ca

JUAN DÍEZ-NICOLÁS is Prof. of Sociology at Complutense University in Madrid. His publications include: "La Escala de Postmaterialismo como Medida del Cambio de Valores en las Sociedades Contemporáneas" (2000), in F. Andrés Orizo and J. Elzo, *España 2000, entre el Localismo y la Globalidad. La Encuesta Europea de Valores en su Tercera Aplicación, 1981-1999*, and in M.J. Ramírez-Lafita (2001), *La Inmigración en España: Una Década de Investigaciones* (Madrid: IMSERSO). He is currently working on the analysis of value preferences in different types of societies according to social position, as well as on the general comparison of values between Spain and Morocco.

E-mail: 100613.2721@compuserve.com

PIPPA NORRIS is the McGuire Lecturer in Comparative Politics at the John F. Kennedy School of Government, Harvard University. Her research compares election and public opinion, political communications, and gender politics. Recent books involve *Democratic Phoenix: Reinventing Political Activism* (2002), *Rising Tide: Gender Equality and Cultural Change* (with Ronald Inglehart 2003), and *Institutions Matter: Electoral Rules and Voting Choices* (2003).

E-mail: Pippa_Norris@harvard.edu

NHU-NGOC T. ONG is a Democracy Fellow and Ph.D. student in Political Science at University of California, Irvine.

E-mail: nong@uci.edu

PHAM MINH HAC, Dr. of Sciences, Professor of Psychology, National Centre for Social Sciences and Humanities, Vietnam. His publications include: *Vietnam Education in Threshold of 21st Century* (National Political Publishing House, Hanoi 1999), and *Human Studies and Human Resources in Entering Industrialisation and Modernisation* (National Political Publishing House, Hanoi 2001). He is currently working on several National Research Programs.

E-mail: ihsvn@hn.vnn.vn

PHAM THANH NGHI, Ph.D., Senior Researcher, National Centre for Social Sciences and Humanities, Vietnam. His publications include *Psychology applied in Higher Education* (Education Publishing House, Hanoi, 1992), and *Quality Management in Higher Education* (Vietnam National University Publishing House, Hanoi, 2000). He is currently working on Research projects on industrialisation and modernisation.

E-mail: ptnghi@fpt.vn

THORLEIF PETTERSSON, Ph.D., is Professor of Sociology of Religion at Uppsala University, Sweden. His major publications in the field of his contribution to Comparative Sociology are found in *Mot denna framtid* (Stockholm, Carlssons 1994), and *Religion in Secularizing Society* (Leiden: Brill 2003). Thorleif Pettersson is currently working on the World Values Survey.

E-mail: Thorleif.Pettersson@teol.uu.se

CHRISTIAN WELZEL, Ph.D., is Associate Professor of Political Science at the International University Bremen. His recent publications include *The Theory of Human Development: A Cross-Cultural Analysis*, in: *European Journal of Political Research* 42(2): 2003 (co-authors Ronald Inglehart and Hans-Dieter Klingemann), and *Democratic Institutions and Political Culture: Misconceptions in Addressing the Ecological Fallacy*, in: *Comparative Politics* 32(1): 2003 (co-author Ronald Inglehart). Based on the World Values Surveys, Christian Welzel currently works with Ronald Inglehart on *Foundations of Democracy: Modernization, Emancipative Values, and Effective Democracy in 80 Nations*.

E-mail: c.welzel@iu-bremen.de

EPHRAIM YUCHTMAN-YA'AR, Ph.D., is Professor of Sociology and Social Psychology and former Dean at Tel Aviv University. Since 1995 he has been the Head of the Tami Steinmetz Center for Peace Research. He is also the incumbent of the Rapoport Chair in Sociology of Labour. He has published several books and numerous articles in the areas of Israeli society, public opinion, the Israeli-Arab conflict, social inequality and the sociology of work and organizations.

E-mail: eppie@ccsg.tau.ac.il

Introduction

This volume presents findings based on a unique data-base, the World Values Survey (WVS) and the European Values Surveys (EVS). These surveys provide data from almost 80, societies containing over 80 per cent of the world's population and covering the full range of variation, from societies with per capita incomes as low as $300 per year, to societies with per capita incomes one hundred times that high; and from long-established democracies with market economies, to authoritarian states and ex-socialist states. These surveys make it possible to compare the values and beliefs of people throughout the world, and they reveal large and coherent cross-national differences in what people want out of life.

The World Values Surveys grew out of a study launched by the European Values Survey group (EVS), which carried out surveys in ten West European societies in 1981; the project evoked such widespread interest that it was replicated in 14 additional countries. Findings from these surveys suggested that predictable cultural changes were taking place. To monitor possible changes, a new wave of surveys was carried out in 1990-91, building on findings from the first wave, but this time designed to be carried out globally. Successive waves of surveys were carried out in 1995-96 and 1999-2001. In every case, we work with colleagues from the given society, and in most cases these surveys are supported by internal funding.

In the first three waves of surveys, the WVS covered most of the world's major cultural zones except for Africa and the Islamic region, where we were able to carry out only a few surveys in each region. In planning the fourth wave, the WVS association set a high priority on attaining substantially better coverage of these regions; and the 2000-2001 WVS includes eight African countries and ten predominantly Islamic societies (including three overlapping cases). As a result, we have an unprecedentedly broad range of Islamic societies, extending geographically from Morocco to Indonesia. Taking advantage of this rich source of insight, the present issue includes three articles analyzing Islamic worldviews. The findings demonstrate that a distinctive Islamic culture does exist. But, while Islamic publics reject some key aspects of Western society, they do not reject democracy — quite the contrary, the democratic ideal is endorsed by solid majorities of the public throughout the Islamic world. We were also able to extend the survey to previously neglected countries such as Vietnam. For many countries, the 2000-2001 WVS was the first time that their society had been included in a cross-national survey (and in some cases, the World Values Survey was the first representative national survey *ever* carried out in that country). We are grateful to the Bank of Sweden Tercentenary Foundation, the Swedish Agency for International Development, and the U.S. National Science Foundation for making these surveys possible.

We owe a large debt of gratitude to the following WVS and EVS participants for creating and sharing this valuable dataset: Anthony M. Abela, Q.K. Ahmad, Rasa Alishauskene, Helmut Anheier, W.A. Arts, Jose Arocena, Soo Young Auh, Taghi Azadarmaki, Ljiljana Bacevic, Miguel Basanez, Olga Balakireva, Josip Balobn, Elena Bashkirova, Abdallah Bedaida, Jorge Benitez, Jaak Billiet, Alan Black, Sheila Bluhm, Rahma Bourquia, Ammar Boukhedir, Fares al Braizat, Augustin Canzani, Marita Carballo, Henrique Carlos de O. de Castro, Pi-Chao Chen, Pavel Campeanu, Pradeep Chhibber, Mark F. Chingono, Hei-yuan Chiu, Margit Cleveland, Russell Dalton, Andrew P. Davidson, Juan Diez Nicolas, Jaime Diez Medrano, Herman De Dijn, Karel Dobbelaere, Peter J.D. Drenth, Javier Elzo, Yilmaz Esmer, P. Estgen, T. Fahey, Nadjematul Faizah, Georgy Fotev, James Georgas, C. Geppaart, Renzo Gubert, Linda Luz Guerrero, Peter Gundelach, Jacques Hagenaars, Loek Halman, Sang-Jin Han, Mustafa Hamarneh, Stephen Harding, Mari Harris, Bernadette C. Hayes, Camilo Herrera, Virginia Hodgkinson, Nadra Muhammed Hosen, Kenji Iijima, Ljubov Ishimova, Wolfgang Jagodzinski, Aleksandra Jasinska-Kania, Fridrik Jonsson, Stanislovas Juknevicius, Jan Kerkhofs SJ, Johann Kinghorn, Zuzana Kusá, M. Legrand, Noah Lewin-Epstein, Ola Listhaug, Hans Dieter Klingemann, Hennie Kotze, Noah Lewin-Epstein, Marta Lagos, Bernard Lategan, Dr Abdel-Hamid Abdel-Latif, Dr. Carlos Lemoine, Jin-yun Liu, Brina Malnar, Mahar Mangahas, Mario Marinov, Felipe Miranda, Robert B. Mattes, Carlos Matheus, Mansoor Moaddel, Jose Molina, Rafael Mendizabal, Alejandro Moreno, Gaspar K. Munishi, Elone Nwabuzor, Neil Nevitte, F.A. Orizo, Dragomir Pantic, Juhani Pehkonen, Paul Perry, Thorleif Pettersson, Pham Thanh Nghi, Pham Minh Hac, Gevork Pogosian, Bi Puranen, Ladislav Rabusic, Angel Rivera-Ortiz, Catalina Romero, David Rotman, Dr. Rajab Sattarov, Sandeep Shastri, Shen Mingming, Renata Siemienska, John Sudarsky, Tan Ern Ser, Farooq Tanwir, Jean-Francois Tchernia, Kareem Tejumola, Larissa Titarenko, Miklos Tomka, Alfredo Torres, Niko Tos, Jorge Vala, Andrei Vardomatskii, Malina Voicu, Alan Webster, Friedrich Welsch, Christian

Welzel, Toru Takahashi, Ephraim Yuchtman-Yaar, Brigita Zepa, Josefina Zaiter, and P. Zulehner.

For more information about the World Values Survey, see the WVS web sites http://wvs.isr.umich.edu/ and http://www.worldvaluessurvey.com. The European surveys used here were gathered by the European Values Survey group (EVS). For detailed EVS findings, see Loek Halman, *The European Values Study: A Sourcebook Based on the 1999/2000 European Values Study Surveys*. Tilburg: EVS, 2001. For more information, see the EVS website, http://evs.kub.nl.

Ronald Inglehart
President
World Values Survey Association

Islamic Culture and Democracy: Testing the 'Clash of Civilizations' Thesis

PIPPA NORRIS[*] AND RONALD INGLEHART[**]

ABSTRACT

In seeking to understand the root causes of the events of 9/11 many accounts have turned to Samuel P. Huntington's provocative and controversial thesis of a 'clash of civilizations', arousing strong debate. Evidence from the 1995-2001 waves of the World Values Survey/European Values Survey (WVS/EVS) allows us, for the first time, to examine an extensive body of empirical evidence relating to this debate. Comparative analysis of the beliefs and values of Islamic and non-Islamic publics in 75 societies around the globe, confirms the first claim in Huntington's thesis: culture *does* matter, and indeed matters a lot, so that religious legacies leave a distinct imprint on contemporary values. But Huntington is mistaken in assuming that the core clash between the West and Islamic worlds concerns democracy. The evidence suggests striking similarities in the political values held in these societies. It is true that Islamic publics differ from Western publics concerning the role of religious leadership in society, but this is not a simple dichotomous clash — many non-Islamic societies side with the Islamic ones on this issue. Moreover the Huntington thesis fails to identify the most basic cultural fault line between the West and Islam, which concerns the issues of gender equality and

[*] John F. Kennedy School of Government, Harvard University, Cambridge.
[**] Institute for Social Research, University of Michigan, Ann Arbor.

sexual liberalization. The cultural gulf separating Islam from the West involves Eros far more than Demos.

In seeking to understand the causes of the events of 9/11 many popular commentators have turned to Samuel P. Huntington's provocative and controversial thesis of a 'clash of civilizations.' This account emphasized that the end of the Cold War brought new dangers. *"In the new world,"* Huntington argued (1996:28), *". . . the most pervasive, important and dangerous conflicts will not be between social classes, rich and poor, or other economically defined groups, but between people belonging to different cultural entities. Tribal wars and ethnic conflicts will occur within civilizations. . . And the most dangerous cultural conflicts are those along the fault lines between civilizations. . . For forty-five years the Iron Curtain was the central dividing line in Europe. That line has moved several hundred miles east. It is now the line separating peoples of Western Christianity, on the one hand, from Muslim and Orthodox peoples on the other."* For Huntington, Marxist class warfare, and even the disparities between rich and poor nations, have been overshadowed in the twenty-first century by Weberian culture. This influential account appeared to offer insights into the causes of violent ethno-religious conflicts exemplified by Bosnia, the Caucuses, the Middle East, and Kashmir. It seemed to explain the failure of political reform to take root in many Islamic states, despite the worldwide resurgence of electoral democracies around the globe. The framework seemed to provide a powerful lens that the American media used to interpret the underlying reasons for the terrorist attack on the World Trade Center. Commentators often saw 9/11 as a full-scale assault on the global hegemony of America, in particular, and a reaction by Islamic fundamentalists against Western culture, in general. Nevertheless, the Huntington thesis has been highly controversial. The claim of rising ethnic conflict in the post-Cold War era has come under repeated and sustained attack (Gurr 2000; Russett, O'Neal and Cox 2000; Fox 2001; Chirot 2001; Henderson and Tucker 2001; Fox 2001). Many scholars have challenging the existence of a single Islamic culture stretching all the way from Jakarta to Lagos, let alone one that held values deeply incompatible with democracy (Kabuli 1994; Esposito and Voll 1996; Shadid 2001). What has been less widely examined, however, is systematic empirical evidence of whether the publics in Western and Islamic societies share similar or deeply divergent values, and, in particular, whether any important differences between these cultures rest on democratic values (as Huntington claims) or on social values (as modernization theories suggest).

This study seeks to throw new light on this issue by examining cultural values in seventy-five nations around the globe, including nine predominately Islamic societies, utilizing the World Values Survey/European

Values Survey (WVS/EVS) 1995-2001. *Part I* briefly outlines the Huntington thesis and the response by critics. *Part II* lays out the study's research design including the core hypothesis, comparative framework, and survey data. *Part III* analyzes the evidence. The conclusion summarizes the results and reflects on their implications. The evidence confirms the first claim in Huntington's thesis: culture *does* matter, and matter a lot: religious legacies leave a distinct and lasting imprint on contemporary values. But Huntington is mistaken in assuming that the core 'clash' between the West and Islamic societies concerns *political* values: instead the evidence indicates that surprisingly similar attitudes towards democracy are found in the West and the Islamic world. We do find significant cross-cultural differences concerning the role of religious leaders in politics and society, but these attitudes divide the West from many other countries around the globe, not just Islamic ones. The original thesis erroneously assumed that the primary cultural fault line between the West and Islam concerns government, overlooking a stronger cultural divide based on issues of gender equality and sexual liberalization. Cohort analysis suggests that as younger generations in the West have gradually become more liberal on these issues, this has generated a growing cultural gap, with Islamic nations remaining the most traditional societies in the world. The central values separating Islam and the West revolve far more centrally around Eros than Demos.

Part I: The 'Clash of Civilizations' Debate

The 'clash of civilizations' thesis advances three central claims. First, Huntington suggests that 'culture matters'; in particular that contemporary values in different societies are path-dependent, reflecting long-standing legacies associated with core 'civilizations.' The concept of 'civilization' is understood by Huntington as a 'culture writ large': *"It is defined both by common objective elements, such as language, history, religion, customs, institutions, and by the subjective self-identification of people."* (Huntington 1996:41-43). Of these factors, Huntington sees religion as the central defining element (p. 47), although he also distinguishes regional sub-divisions within the major world religions, such as the distinct role of Catholicism in Western Europe and Latin America, due to their different historical traditions and political legacies.

Second, the 'clash' thesis claims that there are sharp cultural differences between the core political values common in societies sharing a Western Christian heritage — particularly those concerning representative democracy — and the beliefs common in the rest of the world, especially Islamic societies. For Huntington, the defining features of Western civilization include the separation of religious and secular authority, the rule of law and social pluralism, the parliamentary institutions of representative government, and the protection of individual rights and civil liberties as the buffer between citizens and the power of the state: *"Individually almost none of these factors was unique to the West. The combination of them was, however, and this is what gave the West its distinctive quality."* (1996:70-71) Other accounts have commonly stressed that the complex phenomenon of 'modernization' encompasses many additional social values that challenge traditional beliefs, notably faith in scientific and technological progress, belief in the role of economic competition in the marketplace, and the diffusion of modern social mores, exemplified by sexual liberalization and equality for women (Inglehart 1997; Inglehart and Baker 2000; Inglehart and Norris 2003). But Huntington's claim is that the strongest distinguishing characteristic of Western culture, the aspect which demarcates Western Christianity most clearly from the Muslim and Orthodox worlds, concerns the values associated with representative democracy. This claim is given plausibility by the failure of electoral democracy to take root in most states in the Middle East and North Africa (see Midlarsky 1998). According to the annual assessment made by the Freedom House (2002), of the 192 countries around the world, two-thirds (121) are electoral democracies. Of the 47 countries with an Islamic majority, one quarter (11) are electoral democracies. Furthermore, none of the core Arabic-speaking societies in the Middle East and North Africa falls into this category. Given this pattern, in the absence of survey evidence concerning the actual beliefs of Islamic publics, it is commonly assumed that they have little faith in the principles or performance of democracy, preferring strong leadership and rule by traditional religious authorities to the democratic values of pluralistic competition, political participation, and political rights and civil liberties.

Lastly, Huntington argues that important and long-standing differences in political values based on predominant religious cultures will lead to conflict between and within nation-states, with the most central problems of global politics arising from an ethno-religious 'clash.'[1] It remains unclear whether Huntington is claiming that the core cleavage concerns Western democratic values versus the developing world, or whether the main contrast lies as a fault line between the West and Islam, but the latter has been the primary popular interpretation of the thesis, and the one which has aroused the most heated debate.

Middle Eastern area studies specialists, scholars of the Koran, and students of Islamic law have contested a series of issues about the 'clash' thesis. Critics have challenged the notion of a single Islamic

---

[1] International relations scholars have strongly challenged the evidence for Huntington's claim that ethnic inter-state conflict has increased during the 1990s (Gurr 2000; Russett, Oneal and Cox 2000; Fox 2001; Chirot 2001; Henderson and Tucker 2001), although this body of work is not central to the argument presented here.

culture, pointing to substantial contrasts found among one billion people living in diverse Islamic nations, such as Pakistan, Jordan, Azerbaijan, Indonesia, Bangladesh, and Turkey, and the differences between Muslims who are radical or moderate, traditional or modern, conservative or liberal, hard-line or revisionist (Hunter 1998; Esposito 1997; Fuller 2002). Observers stress the manifold differences within the Islamic world due to historical traditions and colonial legacies, ethnic cleavages, levels of economic development, and the role and power of religious fundamentalists in different states, claiming that it makes little sense to lump together people living in Jakarta, Riyadh, and Istanbul. Along similar lines, the idea that we can recognize a single culture of 'Western Christianity' is to over-simplify major cross-national differences, even among affluent postindustrial societies as superficially similar as the United States, Italy, and Sweden, for example the contrasts between Catholic Mediterranean Europe and Protestant Scandinavia, as well as among social sectors and religious denominations within each country.

Moreover, setting this issue aside for the moment, even if we accept the existence of a shared 'Islamic' culture, scholars have also argued that the core values and teaching of the Koran are not incompatible with those of democracy (Kabuli 1994; Esposito and Voll 1996; Shadid 2001). Edward Said (2001) decried Huntington's thesis as an attempt to revive the 'black-white,' 'us-them,' or 'good-evil' world dichotomy that had been so prevalent during the height of the Cold War, substituting threats from 'Islamic terrorists' for those from 'Communist spies.' Western leaders, seeking to build a global coalition against the followers of Osama Bin Laden, took pains to distance themselves from the clash of civilizations thesis, stressing deep divisions within the Islamic world between the extreme fundamentalists and moderate Muslims. Leaders emphasized that the events of September 11th arose from the extreme ideological beliefs held by particular splinter groups of Al-Qaeda and Taliban fundamentalists, not from mainstream Muslim public opinion. Just as it would be a mistake to understand the 1995 bombing in Oklahoma City as a collective attack on the federal government by all Christian fundamentalists, rather than the work of a few individuals, it may inappropriate to view the attack by Al-Qaeda terrorists on symbols of American capitalism and financial power as a new 'clash of civilizations' between Islamic and Western cultures.

As well as challenging the basic premises of the 'clash of civilizations' thesis, alternative explanations of radical Islamic fundamentalism suggest that the underlying root causes lie in deep disparities between rich and poor within societies, buttressed by the pervasive inequalities in political power in Middle Eastern regimes (Chirot 2001). Structural or neo-Marxist theories suggest that the best predictors of radical disaffection lie in uneven patterns of modernization around the world and the existence of pervasive inequalities *within* many Muslim societies. The most important cleavage may be between middle class, more affluent, educated and professional social sectors on the one hand, — the teachers, doctors, and lawyers in Cairo, Beirut and Islamabad — and the sub-strata of poorer, uneducated, and unemployed younger men living in Saudi Arabia, Libya, and Syria who, if disaffected, may become willing recruits to Islamic fundamentalist causes. Huntington distinguishes certain demographic characteristics of Islamic societies, notably the phenomena of the 'youth bulge,' but does not pursue the consequences of this generational pattern, in particular whether younger men from poorer sectors of society are particularly prone to political disaffection.

Yet there are plausible alternative theories about the major cultural contrasts we could expect to find between Islam and the West. In work presented elsewhere (Inglehart and Norris 2003) we document how the modernization process has transformed values by generating a rising tide of support for equality between women and men in post-industrial societies, and greater approval in these societies of a more permissive and liberal sexuality, including tolerance of divorce, abortion and homosexuality. The version of modernization theory developed by Inglehart (1997) hypothesizes that human development generates changed cultural attitudes in virtually any society, although values also reflect the imprint of each society's religious legacies and historical experiences. Modernization brings systematic, *predictable* changes in gender roles. The impact of modernization operates in two key phases:

i) Industrialization brings women into the paid work force and dramatically reduces fertility rates. Women attain literacy and educational opportunities. Women are enfranchised and begin to participate in representative government, but still have far less power than men.

ii) The postindustrial phase brings a shift toward greater gender equality as women move into higher status economic roles in management and the professions, and gain political influence within elected and appointed bodies. Over half of the world has not yet entered this phase; only the more advanced industrial societies are currently moving on this trajectory.

These two phases correspond to two major dimensions of cross-cultural variation: (i) A transition from traditional to secular-rational values; and (ii) a transition from survival to self-expression values. The decline of the traditional family is linked with the first dimension. The rise of gender equality is linked with the second. Cultural shifts in modern societies are not sufficient by themselves to guarantee women equality across all major dimensions of life; nevertheless through underpinning structural reforms and women's rights they greatly facilitate this process (Inglehart and Norris 2003). If this theory is applied to cultural contrasts between modern and traditional societies, it suggests that we would expect one of the key differences between the Western and Islamic worlds to focus around the issues of gender equality and sexual liberalization, rather than the democratic values that are central to Huntington's theory.

Part II: Hypotheses, Comparative Framework, and Data

To summarize, many issues arising from the 'clash' thesis could be considered, but here we focus upon testing two alternative propositions arising from the theoretical debate. Huntington emphasizes that the political values of democracy originated in the West with the separation of church and state, the growth of representative parliamentary institutions, and the expansion of the franchise. As such, he predicts that, despite the more recent emergence and consolidation of 'Third Wave' democracies in many parts of the world, democratic values will be most deeply and widely entrenched in Western societies. If true, we would expect to find *the strongest cultural clash in political values would be between the Western and Islamic worlds*. In contrast, Inglehart's modernization theory suggests that a rising tide of support for women's equality and sexual liberalization has left a particularly marked imprint upon richer postindustrial nations, although traditional attitudes continue to prevail in poorer developing societies. Accordingly, given this interpretation, we also test the alternative proposition that *any deep-seated cultural divisions between Islam and the West will revolve far more strongly around social rather than political values, especially concerning the issues of sexual liberalization and gender equality*.

The issues of cultural conflict and value change have generated considerable controversy but, as yet, almost no systematic survey data has been available to compare public opinion towards politics and society in many Middle Eastern and Western societies. Interpretations by area scholars and anthropologists have relied upon more qualitative sources, including personal interviews, observations and direct experience, and traditional textual exegesis of the literature, religious scriptures, and historical documents (see, for example, Lewis 2002). Recently commercial companies have started to conduct opinion polls that are representative of the public in a limited range of Muslim nations;[2] Gallup's survey examined

---

[2] The main exceptions are the first-ever Gallup survey in nine predominately Islamic societies which was carried out to monitor reactions to the events of 9/11. Gallup surveyed 10,000 people in December 2001 and January 2002, with researchers conducting hour-long, in-person interviews in Saudi Arabia, Iran, Pakistan, Indonesia, Turkey, Lebanon, Kuwait, Jordan and Morocco. For details see

attitudes towards other countries in nine Middle Eastern societies and the United States (Moore 2002), while Roper Reports Worldwide compared social values in the United States and Saudi Arabia (Miller and Feinberg 2002).

The latest waves of the World Values Survey/European Values Survey (WVS/EVS), a global investigation of socio-cultural and political change, allow comparison of democratic values across a wide range of Western and Muslim nations, as well as in many other states.[*] The study has carried out representative national surveys of the basic values and beliefs of publics in more than 70 nations on all six inhabited continents, containing over 80% of the world's population. It builds on the European Values Surveys, first carried out in 22 countries in 1981. A second wave of surveys, in 43 nations, was completed in 1990-1991, a third wave was carried out in 50 nations in 1995-1996, and a fourth wave with more than 60 nations took place in 1999-2001.[3] This total sample includes almost a quarter-million respondents, facilitating analysis of minority sub-groups, such as the Muslim populations living in Russia, India, Bulgaria, and Macedonia. This study focuses on analyzing attitudes and values in the last two waves of the survey, from 1995-2001. To test the evidence for the 'clash of civilizations' thesis, this study compares values at *societal*-level, based on the assumption that predominant cultures exert a broad and diffuse influence upon all people living under them[4].

---

http://www.gallup.com/poll/releases/pr020305.asp. In addition Roper Reports Worldwide conducted an annual worldwide survey from October 2001-January 2002 in 30 nations, including an urban sample of 1000 residents in the metropolitan areas in Saudi Arabia. For details of the Roper results see Miller and Feinberg (2002).

[*] The following analysis draws upon a unique data base, the World Values Survey/European Values Survey (WVS/EVS). We owe a large debt of gratitude to the WVS and EVS participants for creating and sharing this invaluable dataset. Their names are listed in the WVS and EVS websites. For more information about the World Values Survey, see the WVS web sites http://wvs.isr.umich.edu/ and http://www.worldvaluessurvey.com. Most of the European surveys used here were gathered by the European Values Survey group (EVS). For detailed EVS findings, see Loek Halman, *The European Values Study: A Sourcebook Based on the 1999/2000 European Values Study Surveys*. Tilburg: EVS, Tilburg University Press, 2001. For more information, see the EVS website, http://evs.kub.nl.

[3] Full methodological details about the World Values Survey/European Values Survey (WVS/EVS), including the questionnaires, sampling procedures, fieldwork procedures, principle investigators, and organization can be found at: http://wvs.isr.umich.edu/wvs-samp.html. The four waves of this survey took place from 1981 to 2001, although it should be noted that all countries were not included in each wave.

[4] In addition a distinct 'Jewish' culture could be identified, but Israel was not included within the current release of the WVS.

Classifying cultural regions

In Huntington's account nine major contemporary civilizations can be identified, based largely on the predominant religious legacy in each society:

- Western Christianity (a European culture that subsequently spread to North America, Australia and New Zealand),
- Islamic (including the Middle East, Northern Africa, and parts of South East Asia),
- Orthodox (Russian and Greek),
- Latin American (predominately Catholic yet with a distinct corporatist, authoritarian culture),
- Sinic/Confucian (China, South Korean, Vietnam and Korea),
- Japanese,
- Hindu,
- Buddhist (Sri Lanka, Burma, Thailand, Laos, and Cambodia), and (possibly)
- Sub-Saharan Africa.[5]

Huntington treats states or societies as the core actors exemplifying these civilizations, although recognizing that populations with particular cultural and religious identities spread well beyond the border of the nation-state. Moreover some plural societies are deeply divided, so there is rarely a clean one-to-one mapping, apart from exceptional cases such as Japan and India.

To analyze the survey evidence for these propositions, societies were classified into these categories, (see Table 1) based on the predominant (plurality) religious identities within each nation. The survey includes nine societies with a Muslim majority (ranging from 71 to 96 percent), including Jordan, Pakistan, Turkey, Azerbaijan, Bangladesh and Albania, Morocco, Iran and Egypt. This allows us to compare a range of states within the Islamic world, including semi-democracies with elections and some freedoms, exemplified by Albania, Turkey and Bangladesh, as well as constitutional monarchies (Jordan), and suspended semi-democracies under military rule (Pakistan). Geographically these nations are located in Central Europe, the Middle East, and South Asia. In addition, the comparative framework includes 22 nations based on 'Western Christianity' (using Huntington's definition to include both predominately Catholic and

---

[5] Although it should be noted that despite the centrality of the concept, the definition, labeling and classification of 'civilizations' remains inconsistent in Huntington's work, for example it remains unclear whether Huntington believes that there is or is not a distinct African civilization, and the major discussion of types (pp. 45-47) excludes the Orthodox category altogether.

Table 1

Classification of societies by the historically predominant religion

Protestant	Catholic	Islamic	Orthodox	Central Europe	Latin America	Sinic/Confucian	Sub-Saharan Africa
Australia	Austria	Albania	Belarus	Croatia	Argentina	South Korea	Nigeria
Britain	Belgium	Azerbaijan?	Bosnia	Czech Republic	Brazil	Taiwan	South Africa
Canada	France	Bangladesh	Bulgaria	East Germany	Chile	Vietnam	Tanzania
Denmark	Ireland	Egypt	Georgia	Estonia	Colombia	China	Uganda
Finland	Italy	Iran	Greece	Hungary	Dominican Rep		Zimbabwe
Iceland	Malta	Jordan	Macedonia	Latvia	El Salvador		
Netherlands	Portugal	Morocco					
New Zealand	Spain	Pakistan	Moldova	Lithuania	Mexico		
Northern Ireland	Portugal	Turkey	Montenegro	Poland	Peru		
Norway			Romania	Slovakia	Uruguay		
Sweden			Russia	Slovenia	Venezuela		
Switzerland							
United States			Serbia				
West Germany			Ukraine				

Note: This study compares 72 nation states and 75 societies, dividing states with distinctive historical traditions, cultural legacies and political institutions including the UK (Northern Ireland and Great Britain), Germany (East and West), and the Federal Republic of Yugoslavia (Serbia and Montenegro). The Catholic and Protestant societies are classified as 'Western Christianity.' In addition India and Japan are each treated as separate religious cultures.

Source: The World Values Survey/European Values Survey (WVS/EVS), 1995-2001.

Protestant postindustrial societies, and countries like Australia and New Zealand which are not located regionally in the 'West' yet which inherited a democratic tradition from Protestant Britain). Other nations are classified into distinct civilizational traditions including Latin America (11), Russian or Greek Orthodox (12), Central European (10 nations sharing a common Western Christian heritage with the West yet with the distinct experience of living under Communist rule), sub-Saharan Africa (5), South-East Asian (4 societies reflecting Sinic/Confucian values), plus Japan and India. In addition, ten societies contain a significant *minority* Islamic population (ranging from 4 to 27 percent), including Bosnia, Macedonia, Nigeria and India, although these nations have Orthodox, Protestant, or Hindu majority populations. In the multivariate regression models, each type of society was coded as a dummy variable and the 'Western' societies category was used as the (omitted) reference category. The models therefore measure the impact of living in each of these types of society, with controls, compared with living in the West.

To rule out intervening variables, multivariate regression models compare the influence of predominant religious cultures in each type of society controlling for levels of human and political development. Modernization theories suggest that this process brings certain predictable shifts in cultural values, including declining belief in traditional sources of religious authority and rising demands for more participatory forms of civic engagement (Inglehart 1997; Inglehart and Baker 2000; Norris 2002). The WVS/EVS survey contains some of the most affluent market economies in the world, such as the US, Japan and Switzerland, with per capita annual incomes as high as $40,000; together with middle-level industrializing countries such as Taiwan, Brazil, and Turkey, as well as poorer agrarian societies, such as Uganda, Nigeria, and Viet Nam, with per capita annual incomes of $300 or less. It also includes many different types of states, including established and newer democracies, semi-democracies, and non-democracies. Accordingly structural differences among societies are measured by the United Nations Development Program (UNDP) Human Development Index (HDI) 2000, (combining levels of per capita income, literacy and schooling, and longevity), and levels of democratization, which are classified based on the 1999-2000 Freedom House analysis of political rights and civil liberties.[6] The structural differences among groups within societies are measured by the standard social indicators, including income

---

[6] These countries are ranked as equally 'free' according to the 2000-2001 Freedom House assessments of political rights and civil liberties Freedom House. 2000. *Freedom in the World 2000-2001*. www.freedomhouse.org.

(as the most reliable cross-cultural measure of socioeconomic status in different societies), education, gender, age, and religiosity.

The latter was included to see whether the *strength* of religious beliefs influenced values more than the *type* of religious faith or identity (which, like being baptized as a Protestant or Catholic, can be purely nominal). To develop a religiosity scale, factor analysis was used with six indicators selected from the pooled World Values Survey/European Values Survey (WVS/EVS), namely the proportion of the population in different societies: (i) who say that religion is 'very important' in their lives, (ii) who find comfort in religion, (iii) who believe in God, (iv) who identify themselves as religious, (v) who believe in life after death, and (vi) who attend a religious service regularly. All these items tap values and beliefs common throughout the world's religions and they were carried in all four waves of the WVS/EVS, to facilitate comparison over time. Factor analysis among the pooled sample (not reproduced here) showed that all the items fell into one dimension and formed a consistent and reliable 'strength of religiosity' scale (Cronbach's Alpha = 0.48). After recoding, the scale was standardized to 100-points, for ease of interpretation, where the higher score represents the strongest religiosity.

Measuring Political and Social Values
Attitudes were compared towards three dimensions of political and social values: (i) support for democratic ideals and performance, (ii) attitudes towards political leadership, and (iii) approval of gender equality and sexual liberalization. As argued elsewhere (Norris 1999), an important distinction needs to be drawn between support for the *ideals* of democracy and evaluations of the actual *performance* of democracy. Evidence from previous waves of the World Value Study (Klingemann 1999; Dalton 1999) suggests that citizens in many countries adhere strongly to the general principles of democracy, such as believing that it is the best form of government and disapproving of authoritarian alternatives, and yet at the same time many remain deeply dissatisfied with the way that democratic governments work in practice. The phenomenon of more 'critical citizens' (Norris 1999) or 'disenchanted democrats' (Putnam and Pharr 2001) has been widely observed. To examine these dimensions, attitudes towards the principles and performance of democracy are measured in this study using the items listed in Table 2, where respondents are invited to express agreement or disagreement with the statements. It should be noted that the performance items do not ask people about their experience of democracy in their own country, such as how well their government works, but rather taps their expectations of how well democratic governments generally function in taking decisions and maintaining order.

Table 2

Factor analysis of political values

	Democratic performance	Democratic ideals	Religious leadership	Strong leadership
V170	*Democracies are indecisive and have too much squabbling*	.862			
V171	*Democracies aren't good at maintaining order*	.854			
V172	*Democracy may have its problems but its better than any other form of government*		.853		
V167	*Approve of having a democratic political system*		.780		
V200	*Politicians who do not believe in God are unfit for public office*			.881	
V202	*It would be better for [this country] if more people with strong religious beliefs held public office.*			.879	
V165	*Approve having experts, not government, make decisions*				.838
V164	*Approve having a strong leaders who does not have to bother with parliament and elections*				.721
	% Of total variance	19.6	17.7	19.6	15.7

Note: Principal component factor analysis was used with varimax rotation and Kaiser normalization. The total model predicts 72.6% of cumulative variance. The democratic performance scale was reversed so that a positive response expressed greater satisfaction with democracy.
Source: The World Values Survey/European Values Survey (WVS/EVS), Waves III and IV (1995–2001).

In addition, it is commonly assumed that one of the primary contrasts between Islamic and Western cultures relates to attitudes towards the role of religious leaders, who exercise power by virtue of their spiritual authority, or secular leaders who hold authority through elective office, reflecting deeper beliefs about the separation of church and state. We therefore also monitored support for the role of religious leaders in public life with the items listed in Table 2. Neither of these items cued respondents with any explicit reference to 'democracy' and indeed, in principle, there is no inconsistency in believing both in the value of spiritual authorities and in the principles of democracy, if the religious leaders exercise power through elected office, exemplified by Christian Democrat parties or politicians from the Christian far right. We also sought to compare attitudes towards preferences for strong leadership, measured by questions tapping support for non-democratic forms of government by experts or by leaders unaccountable to parliament or elections. Factor analysis confirmed that these political items did indeed fall into four distinct dimensions. Accordingly summary scales were constructed, each standardized to 100-points for ease of interpretation and consistent comparison across measures.

Yet the alternative proposition is that the transformation of social values towards sexuality and women's equality, which has profoundly affected the younger generation in postindustrial societies, may lie at the heart of any cultural clash between modern and traditional societies in general, and between the West and Islam in particular. In this regard, Huntington may have correctly identified the importance of civilizational values, but may have misdiagnosed the most crucial aspects of cultural differences. To explore this proposition we can compare support for gender equality, using a standardized scale developed elsewhere, also based on factor analysis, monitoring attitudes towards the roles of women and men in the workforce, education, politics, and the family.[7] The Gender Equality items are similar

---

[7] The combined 100-pt gender equality scale is based on the following 5 items: MENPOL Q118: "On the whole, men make better political leaders than women do." (Agree coded low); MENJOBS Q78: "When jobs are scarce, men should have more right to a job than women." (Agree coded low); BOYEDUC Q.119: "A university education is more important for a boy than a girl." (Agree coded low); NEEDKID Q110 "Do you think that a woman has to have children in order to be fulfilled or is this not necessary?" (Agree coded low); SGLMUM Q112 "If a woman wants to have a child as a single parent but she doesn't want to have a stable relationship with a man, do you approve or disapprove?" (Disapprove coded low). Three items used statements with Lickert-style 4-point agree-disagree responses, while two used dichotomies, and these items were all recoded so that higher values consistently represent greater support for gender equality. Principal component factor analysis revealed that all five items fell into a single consistent scale (not reproduced here), with a Cronbach's Alpha of 0.54. For details of the construction, reliability, validity, and distribution of this scale see Ronald Inglehart and Pippa Norris.

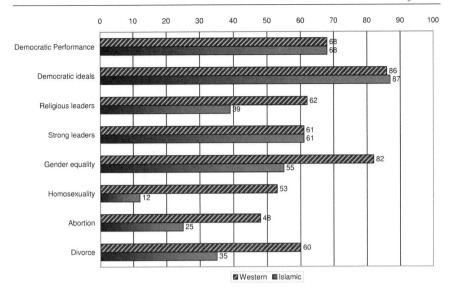

Figure 1. Approval of Political and Social Values in Western and Islamic
Societies.

Note: Mean approval. See Table 3 for details.
Source: (WVS/EVS), pooled sample 1995-2001.

to those commonly contained in the more comprehensive psychological
scales of sex roles. The gender equality scale was summed across the
component items and standardized to 100-points for ease of interpretation.
We also compared attitudes using 10-point scales monitoring approval
or disapproval of three related dimensions of changing sexual mores,
concerning homosexuality, abortion and divorce.

Part III: Analysis of the Results

Table 3 compares the mean scores on these scales for each type of society,
without any prior social or demographic controls, and the significance of
the difference between societies. Figure 3 illustrates the contrasts between
Western and Islamic societies. The results show that, contrary to the first
hypothesis, Western and Islamic societies generally *agreed* on three of the
four indicators of political values. Approval of how well democracy worked
in practice was similar for those living in the West and in Islamic societies
while, in contrast, far more critical evaluations were expressed in all other
cultures around the globe, with the single exception of Japan. Similar
patterns were evident when people were asked whether they supported

2003. *Rising Tide: Gender Equality and Cultural Change Around the World.* New York: Cambridge
University Press.

Table 3

Mean scores on the political and social value scales

Type of society	Democratic Political Values				Liberal Social Values			
	Approve of Democratic Performance	Approve of Democratic ideals	Disapproval of Religious leaders	Disapproval of strong leaders	Approve of gender equality	Approve of homosexuality	Approve of abortion	Approve of divorce
Western Christianity	**68**	**86**	**62**	**61**	**82**	**53**	**48**	**60**
Islamic	**68**	**87**	**39**	**61**	**55**	**12**	**25**	**35**
All Other	**63**	**80**	**53**	**55**	**67**	**28**	**36**	**47**
All Other								
Orthodox	61	78	54	55	64	22	46	51
Central Europe	63	81	62	56	67	36	48	56
Latin America	62	81	51	55	75	31	23	49
Sinic/Confucian	68	80	64	52	62	17	33	40
Sub-Saharan Africa	65	83	40	52	64	21	22	31
Hindu	60	84	N/a	53	61	17	25	31
Japanese	70	81	66	58	63	40	46	61
ALL	**65**	**83**	**53**	**57**	**67**	**33**	**38**	**50**
Difference between all group means	.18***	.20***	.49***	.19***	.46***	.45***	.38***	.33***
Difference between Western and Islamic group	.02***	.03***	.30***	.01	.64***	.51***	.33***	.37***
N.	116629	117855	49903	83223	84932	135846	139841	139311

Note: For the classification of societies see Table 1. All items have been scaled to 0-100. The significance of the difference between group means is measured by ANOVA (Eta) without any controls. *** Sig. P.000.
Source: The (WVS/EVS), Waves III and IV (1995-2001).

democratic ideals, for example whether democracy was better than any other form of government. As others have reported (Klingemann 1999), in recent years high support for democratic ideals is almost universally found in most nations around the globe. Both Western and Islamic societies expressed similar levels of approval, while in contrast slightly less positive attitudes were evident elsewhere, with Sinic and Orthodox societies proving the least enthusiastic. Attitudes towards leadership by experts and by unaccountable government officials were also similar in Islamic and Western societies. Therefore the major political disagreement between Western and Islamic societies was found in attitudes towards the role of religious leaders, where Islamic nations proved far more favorable. Yet at the same time it would be an exaggeration to claim that this latter difference represents a simple dichotomous 'clash of values'. Although it is true that many more Muslims than Westerners supported the idea of religious authorities, there was widespread agreement with this idea in many other parts of the world including Sub-Saharan Africa and Catholic Latin America. The West proved more secular in orientation, as did Central Europe, the Sinic/Confucian nations, and Japan.

Yet comparing the simple means in each type of religious culture could be misleadingly if other endogenous factors are influencing the results, such as the level of democratization or economic affluence typically found in Western and Islamic societies. The multivariate OLS regression models presented in Table 4 therefore compare the impact of living within each type of religious culture after including controls for the societal-level of human and political development, and individual-level measures for age, gender, education, income, and strength of religiosity. In these models, each type of society was coded as a dummy (0/1) variable. The Western category was excluded from the analysis, so that the dummy coefficients can be interpreted as the effect of living in these societies, after applying prior controls, compared with the effect of living in the West. The data was entered in blocks, including development and social controls in the first block, then the additional effects of the full model in the second block, including the type of society as well.

The results show that after controlling for all these factors, contrary to Huntington's thesis, compared with Western societies, support for democracy was marginally slightly *stronger* (not weaker) among those living in Islamic societies. This pattern was evident on three indicators: approval of the way democracy works in practice, support for democratic ideals, as well as disapproval for the idea of strong government leaders. It should be stressed that the difference on these items between Islam and the West were extremely modest in size, as shown by the strength of the standardized beta coefficient, and the statistical significance is largely the product of

Table 4

Political values by type of society, with controls

Scale	Approve of democratic Performance 0-100				Approve of democratic Ideals 0-100				Favor religious leadership 0-100				Favor strong leadership 0-100			
	B	St. Err.	Beta	Sig	B	St. Err.	Beta	Sig	B	St. Err.	Beta	Sig	B	St. Err.	Beta	Sig
Type of society																
Islamic	1.3	.34	.03	***	2.6	.27	.06	***	9.7	.41	.19	***	-2.8	.35	-.06	***
Orthodox	-8.9	.25	-.18	***	-7.9	.21	-.18	***	5.2	.33	.09	***	5.5	.27	.13	***
Central European	-5.4	.21	-.11	***	-5.3	.17	-.12	***	0.1	.27	.00	N/s	3.5	.24	.08	***
Latin American	-6.1	.24	-.11	***	-3.5	.19	-.08	***	3.8	.35	.05	***	3.3	.25	.07	***
Sinic/Confucian	1.4	.45	.01	**	-3.1	.37	-.03	***	-5.1	.79	-.03	***	16.6	.47	.16	***
Sub-Saharan African	-3.6	.43	-.05	***	-4.1	.34	-.07	***	7.6	.46	.13	***	4.3	.48	.07	***
Hindu	-8.9	.60	-.06	***	-2.5	.47	-.02	***	N/a			***	6.0	.62	.05	***
Japanese	3.3	.49	.02	***	-3.5	.39	-.03	***	-0.1	.59	.00	N/s	1.7	.54	.02	**
(Constant)	68.8				82.1				61.8				54.1			
Adjusted R² Block 1 (Control variables only)	*.01*				*.01*				*.32*				*.01*			
Adjusted R² Block 2 (Controls + type of society)	*.05*				*.06*				*.33*				*.06*			
N.	93965				95550				45209				64412			

Note: OLS regression models with blockwise entry with the political value scales as the dependent variables. The full model is illustrated in Table A1. Block 1 in all models control for the *level of human development* (Human Development Index 1998), *level of political development* (Freedom House 7-point index (reversed) of political rights and civil liberties 1999-2000), age (years), gender (male = 1), education (3 categories from low to high), income (10 categories), and religiosity. Block 2 then enters the type of society, based on the predominant religion, coded as dummy variables. Western societies represent the (omitted) reference category. The coefficients can be understood to represent the effect of living in each type of society compared with living in Western societies, net of all prior controls. *Political value* scales: For details see Table 2. *Type of society*: see Table 1. Sig. *** p.001; ** p.01; * p.05. Source: All (WVS/EVS), pooled sample 1995-2001.

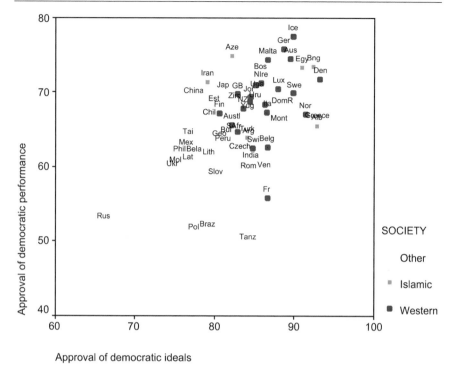

Figure 2.   Democratic Values.

Source: (WVS/EVS), pooled sample 1995-2001.

the large number of respondents in the pooled sample, but nevertheless the difference was in the contrary direction to that predicted by the Huntington thesis. Moreover, as observed earlier, even after introducing controls, lower support for democratic values was found in many other types of non-Western society, especially countries in Eastern and Central Europe, and Latin America, while the Sinin/Confucian states showed the greater approval of strong government. At the same time, after introducing all the controls, Islamic societies did display greater support for a strong societal role by religious authorities than do Western societies. This pattern persists despite controlling for the strength of religiosity and other social factors, which suggests that it is not simply reducible to the characteristics of people living in Islamic societies. Yet this preference for religious authorities is less a cultural division between the West and Islam than it is a gap between the West and many other types of less secular societies around the globe, especially in Sub Saharan Africa and, to a lesser extent, in Latin America.

To examine these results in more detail, Figures 2 and 3 compares the location of each nation on these scales. Of all countries under

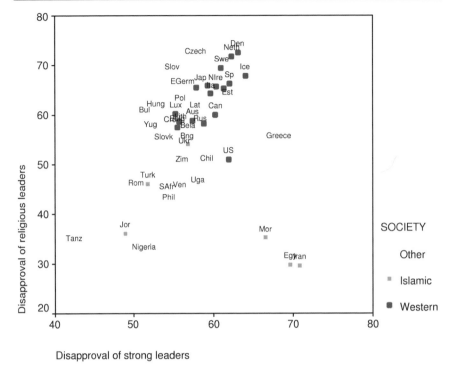

Figure 3.   Leadership attitudes.

Source: (WVS/EVS), pooled sample 1995-2001.

comparison, Russia proved a striking outlier in Figure 2, displaying widespread disillusionment with the way that democratic processes worked, as well as little enthusiasm for democratic ideas. Other Orthodox societies also showed minimal faith in democracy, including the Ukraine, Moldova, Belarus, Georgia and Macedonia. A few other developing countries from different cultures proved extremely critical of the way that democracy worked in practice, although showing greater support for democratic ideals, including Tanzania, Brazil and Poland. Many diverse cultures were located in the middle of the distribution, including Turkey and Jordan as Islamic societies, as well as the United States, Italy, and the Netherlands. Nations that gave the strongest endorsement for democratic ideals and practices included the Scandinavian societies of Denmark, Iceland, and Sweden, along with Germany and Austria, but high support was also registered in Muslim Bangladesh, Egypt and Azerbaijan. Therefore in general slightly lower levels of support for democracy were evident in some Eastern European states, notably in Russia, lending some confirmation for claims of a division between the Orthodox and Western worlds. But attitudes towards democratic principles and performance generally showed a broad distribution across many diverse cultural groups, providing minimal support for the stronger claim that the West is particularly distinctive to Islam in its faith in democracy. Indeed the difference between public opinion in Eastern and Western Europe could be explained equally satisfactorily as reflecting a residual hangover from the Cold War era, and the poor performance of electoral democracies and states in these nations, rather than being interpreted as the result of cultural legacies or the emergence of any 'new' ethno-religious cleavage.

Figure 3 compared leadership attitudes by nation. Support for religious leaders was lowest in many secular societies in Scandinavia and Western Europe, as well as in certain nations in Eastern Europe like the Czech Republic. The United States proved distinctive, showing higher than average support for religious leaders, compared with other Western nations, while Greece was another outlier. At the other extreme, support for religious leaders was relatively strong in African societies including Nigeria, Tanzania, and South Africa, as well as the Philippines, all countries with strong religiosity. Compared with Western nations, many of the Islamic nations expressed greater support for the principle of religious authorities, but they were far from alone in this regard. There is also a fascinating split over the issue of strong leadership evident within the Islamic world; more democratic countries with greater political rights and civil liberties and parliamentary traditions, exemplified by Bangladesh, and Turkey, expressed greater reservations about strong leadership. To a lesser extent, Jordan also fell into this category. In contrast the public living in Islamic countries characterized by more limited political freedoms, less democratic states, and by strong executives, expressed greater support for strong leadership, notably in Egypt, Iran, and Morocco.

Yet so far we have not compared the alternative modernization thesis that the social values of gender equality and sexual liberalization could plausibly lie at the heart of any 'clash' between Islam and the West. The mean scores on these social attitudes in Table 3 reveal the extent of the gulf between Islam and the West, generating a far stronger cultural gap on these issues than across most of the political values. Regression models, including the same prior controls used earlier, show that many structural factors consistently help to predict attitudes, since egalitarian and liberal values are stronger among the young, women, the well-educated, and the less religious, as well as in modern societies with greater human and democratic development. After these controls are introduced, Table 5 shows that there remains a strong and significant difference across all the social indicators (including approval of gender equality, homosexuality, abortion and divorce) among those living in Western v. Islamic societies. Figure 4 shows the distribution of nations on the scales for gender equality

Table 5

Social values by type of society, with controls

Scale	Approve of gender equality 0-100				Approve homosexuality 1-10				Approve of abortion 1-10				Approve of divorce 1-10			
	B	St. Err.	Beta	Sig	B	St. Err.	Beta	Sig	B	St. Err.	Beta	Sig	B	St. Err.	Beta	Sig
Type of society																
Islamic	-8.2	.35	-.18	***	-1.9	.05	-.18	***	-0.67	.05	-.07	***	-0.25	.05	-.03	***
Orthodox	-8.9	.30	-.17	***	-2.1	.04	-.26	***	0.24	.04	.03	***	-0.20	.04	-.03	***
Central European	-6.6	.30	-.09	***	-1.6	.03	-.18	***	0.24	.03	.03	***	0.01	.03	.01	N/s
Latin American	2.6	.25	.05	***	-1.0	.03	-.11	***	-1.20	.03	-.14	***	0.15	.04	.02	***
Sinic/Confucian	-0.3	.69	-.01	N/s	-2.9	.07	-.13	***	-2.10	.06	-.10	***	-2.30	.07	-.11	***
Sub-Saharan African	7.3	.42	.13	***	-0.6	.06	-.05	***	-0.08	.06	-.01	N/s	0.29	.06	.03	***
Hindu	3.4	.53	.03	***	-1.2	.08	-.05	***	-0.05	.08	-.01	N/s	-0.10	.08	-.01	N/s
Japanese	-14.4	.52	-.09	***	-1.5	.06	-.06	***	-0.45	.06	-.02	***	-0.05	.07	-.01	N/s
(Constant)	32.7				1.6				3.1				2.16			
Adjusted R^2 Block 1 (Control variables only)	.26				.20				.23				.26			
Adjusted R^2 Block 2 (Controls + type of society)	.33				.21				.26				.31			
N.	63476				99980				103290				105432			

Note: Note: OLS regression models with blockwise entry with the social value scales as the dependent variables. The full model is illustrated in Table A1. Block 1 in all models control for the *level of human development* (Human Development Index 1998), *level of political development* (Freedom House 7-point index (reversed) of political rights and civil liberties 1999-2000), age (years), gender (male = 1), education (3 categories from low to high), income (10 categories), and religiosity. Block 2 then enters the type of society, based on the predominant religion, coded as dummy variables. Western societies represent the (omitted) reference category. The coefficients can be understood to represent the effect of living in each type of society compared with living in Western societies, net of all prior controls. *Type of society:* see Table 1. *Gender equality scale:* For details see fn.7. *Sexual liberalization scales:* "Please tell me for each of the following statements whether you think it [Homosexuality/ abortion/ divorce] can always be justified, never be justified, or something in-between, using this card from 1 (never justifiable) to 10 (Always justifiable)." Sig. *** p.001; ** p.01; * p.05. N/s Not significant. Source: All (WVS/EVS), pooled sample 1995-2001.

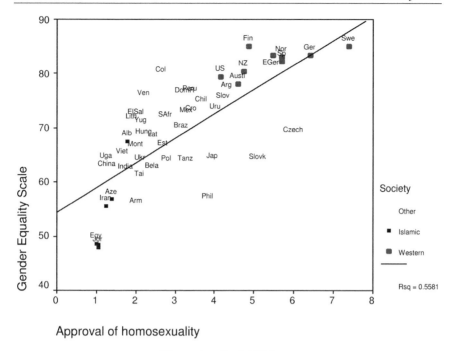

Figure 4.   Social Values.

Source: (WVS/EVS), pooled sample 1995-2001.

and homosexuality in more detail. The results confirm the consistency of the sharp differences between Islam and the West on these issues. All the Western nations, led by Sweden, Germany and Norway, strongly favor equality for women and also prove tolerant of homosexuality. Many other societies show a mixed pattern, falling into the middle of the distribution. In contrast the Islamic nations, including Egypt, Bangladesh, Jordan, Iran and Azerbaijan, all display the most traditional social attitudes, with only Albania proving slightly more liberal.

We lack time-series survey data that would allow us to trace trends in the post-war era, to see whether these cultural differences between societies have widened, as we suspect, due to the modernization process in post-industrial economies. Nevertheless, if we assume that people acquire their basic moral and social values as the result of the long-term socialization process, in the family, school and community, leading to generational rather than life-cycle effects, we can analyze these attitudes for different 10-year cohorts of birth. The results in Figure 5 confirm two striking and important patterns: first, there is a persistent gap in support for gender equality and sexual liberalization between the West (which proves most liberal), Islamic societies (which prove most traditional), and all other societies (which are in the middle). Moreover, even more importantly,

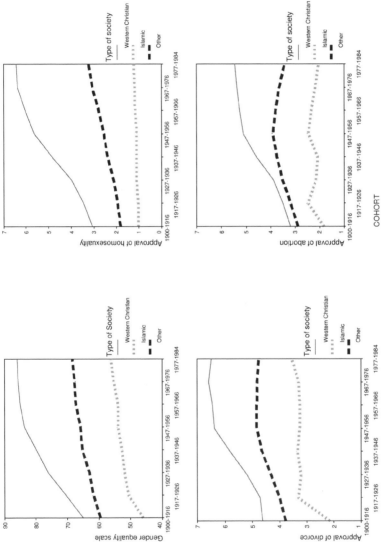

Figure 5. Support for sexual liberalization values by cohort and society.

Source: (WVS/EVS), pooled sample 1995-2001.

the figures reveal that the gap between the West and Islam is usually narrowest among the oldest generation, but that this gap has steadily widened across all the indicators as the younger generations in Western societies have become progressively more liberal and egalitarian, while the younger generations in Islamic societies remain as traditional as their parents and grandparents. The trends suggest that Islamic societies have not experienced a backlash against liberal Western sexual mores among the younger generations, but rather that young Muslims remain unchanged despite the transformation of lifestyles and beliefs experienced among their peers living in postindustrial societies.

Conclusion and Discussion

The thesis of a 'clash of civilizations' has triggered something of a 'clash of scholarship' among those seeking to understand the causes and consequences of ethnic-religious conflict. This task has long been of interest to academe but it has received fresh impetus by the dramatic events and aftermath of 9/11. Alternative interpretations of these issues are important for themselves, but also because they carry important policy implications, not least for how far differences between the United States and Middle Eastern states primarily reflect the views of political elites and governing regimes, or whether they tap into deeper currents of public opinion. To summarize the core components of the Huntington thesis, the claims are threefold: societal values in contemporary societies are rooted in religious cultures; the most important cultural division between the Western and Islamic world relates to differences over democratic values; and, in the post-Cold War era, this 'culture clash' is at the source of much international and domestic ethnic conflict.

The comparative evidence from this study, drawing upon public opinion towards democracy in more than seventy societies around the globe in 1995-2001, suggests four main findings:

(i) First, when political attitudes are compared (including evaluations of how well democracy works in practice, support for democratic ideals, and disapproval of strong leaders), far from a 'clash of values,' there is minimal difference between the Islamic world and the West.

(ii) Instead the democratic 'clash' (if it can be called a clash) divides Post-Communist states in Eastern European (exemplified by Russia, Ukraine and Moldova), which display minimal support for democracy, from many other countries that display far more positive attitudes, including both Western *and* Islamic nations. This pattern could be explained equally well as reflecting the residual legacy of the Cold War and a realistic evaluation of the actual performance of democracy in these states, rather than by the reemergence of ethnic conflict based on the values of the Orthodox church which are, after all, part of Christendom.

(iii) Support for a strong societal role by religious authorities is stronger in Islamic societies than in the West, but here it is not a simple dichotomy, as many other types of society also support an active role for religious leaders in public life, including the Sub Saharan African countries under comparison as well as many Catholic nations in Latin America.

(iv) Yet there *is* a substantial cultural cleavage, although one underestimated by Huntington, in social beliefs about gender equality and sexual liberalization. In this regard, the West is far more egalitarian and liberal than all other societies, particularly Islamic nations. Moreover cohort analysis suggests that this gap has steadily widened as the younger generation in the West has gradually become more liberal in their sexual mores while the younger generation in Islamic societies remains deeply traditional.

The results indicate that modern Western societies are indeed different, in particular concerning the transformation of attitudes and behavior associated with the 'sexual revolution' that has occurred since the 1960s, fundamental changes in the nature of modern families, and more expressive lifestyles. Equality for women has progressed much further, and transformed traditional cultural beliefs and values about the appropriate division of sex roles far more deeply, in affluent Western societies. But at the same time any claim of a 'clash of civilizations,' especially of fundamentally different *political* values held by Western and Islamic societies, represents an over-simplification of the evidence. Across many political dimensions examined here, both Islamic and Western societies are similar in their positive orientation toward democratic ideals. Where Islam societies do differ significantly from the West, in supporting religious authorities, they are far from exceptional around the world. Any black-and-white 'Islam versus the West' interpretation of a 'culture clash' as conveyed by the popular media is far too simple. We need to compare public opinion across more dimensions, and across a wider range of nations in the Middle East, Africa and Asia. Moreover it seems likely that different understandings of what "democracy" means, prevail in different societies: some people are attracted to democracy in so far as it seems linked with prosperity, while others emphasize individual liberty and freedom of expression. Nevertheless our findings indicate that one needs to be very cautious in generalizing from the type of regime to the state of public opinion in a given country. Support for democracy is surprisingly widespread among Islamic publics, even among those who live in authoritarian societies. The most basic cultural fault line between the West and Islam involves issues of gender equality and sexual liberalization. As another article in this journal indicates (see Inglehart, Norris and Welzel), these issues have important implications for democracy. But the democratic ideal is widely shared among Islamic publics. Western cultural norms may be rejected, but the goal of living under a democratic government is *not* — quite the contrary, it is endorsed by clear majorities of the public throughout Islamic society.

References

CHIROT, D.
2001   'A clash of civilizations or of paradigms? Theorizing progress and social change.' *International Sociology* 16(3): 341-360.
DALTON, RUSSELL
1999   'Political Support in Advanced Industrialized Democracies.' In *Critical Citizens: Global Support for Democratic Governance*. Ed. Pippa Norris. Oxford: Oxford University Press.
ESPOSITO, JOHN L. AND JOHN O. VOLL
1996   *Democracy and Islam*, New York: Oxford University Press.
ESPOSITO, JOHN (ED.)
1997   *Political Islam: Revolution, Radicalism or Reform?* Boulder, CO: Lynne Reinner.
FOX, J.
2001   'Two civilizations and ethnic conflict: Islam and the West.' *Journal of Peace Research* 38(4): 459-472.
FREEDOM HOUSE
2002   'Freedom in the World 2002: The Democracy Gap.' New York: Freedom House. www.freedomhouse.org
FULLER, GRAHAM E.
2002   'The Future of Political Islam.' *Foreign Affairs* 81(2): 48-60.
FUNKHOUSER, G.R.
2000   'A world ethos and the clash of civilizations: A cross-cultural comparison of attitudes.' *International Journal of Public Opinion Research* 12(1): 73-79.
GURR, TED
2000   *Peoples versus States*. Washington DC: US Institute for Peace Press.
HENDERSON, R.A. AND R. TUCKER
2001   'Clear and Present strangers: The clash of civilizations and international politics.' *International Studies Quarterly* 45(2): 317-338.
HUNTER, SHIREEN T.
1998   *The Future of Islam and the West: Clash of Civilizations or Peaceful Coexistence?* Westport, CT: Praeger.
HUNTINGTON, SAMUEL P.
1993a   'The Clash of Civilizations?' *Foreign Affairs* 72(3): 22-49.
HUNTINGTON, SAMUEL P.
1993b   'If not civilizations, what? Paradigms of the Post-Cold War World.' *Foreign Affairs* 72(5): 186-194.

HUNTINGTON, SAMUEL P.
1996   *The Clash of Civilizations and the Remaking of World Order.* New York: Simon and
            Schuster.
HUNTINGTON, SAMUEL O.
1996   'The West unique, not universal.' *Foreign Affairs* 75(6): 28-34.
HUNTINGTON, SAMUEL P.
1997   'The clash of civilizations — response.' *Millenium — Journal of International
            Studies* 26(1): 141-142.
INGLEHART, RONALD AND PIPPA NORRIS
2003   *Rising Tide: Gender Equality and Cultural Change Around the World.* New York:
            Cambridge University Press.
INGLEHART, RONALD AND WAYNE E. BAKER
2000   'Modernization, Globalization and the Persistence of Tradition: Empirical
            Evidence from 65 Societies.' *American Sociological Review* 65: 19-55.
INGLEHART, RONALD
1997   *Modernization and Postmodernization: Cultural, Economic and Political Change in 43
            Societies.* Princeton, NJ: Princeton University Press.
KABULI, NIAZ FAIZI
1994   *Democracy according to Islam.* Pittsburgh, PA: Dorrance Publications.
KLINGEMANN, HANS DIETER
1999   'Mapping political support in the 1990s: A global analysis.' In *Critical Citizens:
            Global Support for Democratic Governance.* Ed. Pippa Norris. Oxford: Oxford
            University Press.
LEWIS, BERNARD
2002   *What went wrong? Western impact and Middle Eastern response.* New York: Oxford
            University Press.
MIDLARSKY, M.I.
1998   'Democracy and Islam: Implications for civilizational conflict and the
            democratic process.' *International Studies Quarterly* 42(3): 485-511.
MILLER, THOMAS A.W. AND GEOFFREY FEINBERG
2002   'Culture Clash.' *Public Perspective* 13(2): 6-9.
NORRIS, PIPPA
2002   *Democratic Phoenix: Political Activism Worldwide.* NY/Cambridge: Cambridge
            University Press.
NORRIS, PIPPA (ED.)
1999   *Critical Citizens: Global Support for Democratic Governance.* Oxford: Oxford Univer-
            sity Press.
PUTNAM, ROBERT D. AND SUSAN PHARR (EDS.)
2001   *Disaffected Democracies: What's Troubling the Trilateral Countries?* Princeton, NJ:
            Princeton University Press.
RUSSETT B.M., J.R. O'NEAL AND M. COX
2000   'Clash of civilizations, or realism and liberalism déjà vu? Some evidence.'
            Journal of Peace Research 37(5): 583-608.
SAID, EDWARDS
2001   'A Clash of Ignorance.' *The Nation.*
SHADID, ANTHONY
2001   *Legacy of the prophet: despots, democrats, and the new politics of Islam.* Boulder, Co:
            Westview Press.

Technical Appendix

Table A1
Illustration of the full regression model used in Tables 4 and 5

	Approve of Democratic Performance			
	B	St. Err.	Beta	Sig
Developmental controls				
Level of human development (100-point scale)	−2.4	1.0	−.02	**
Level of political development	0.16	.06	.01	**
Social controls				
Age (Years)	−0.05	.01	−.05	***
Gender (Male = 1)	0.41	.12	.01	***
Education (3 categories low to hi)	1.56	.07	.08	***
Income (10 categories low to hi)	0.01	.01	.02	***
Religiosity scale (100-pt low to hi)	−0.01	.01	−.02	***
Type of society				
Islamic	*1.3*	*.34*	*.03*	***
Orthodox	−8.9	.25	−.18	***
Central European	−5.4	.21	−.11	***
Latin American	−6.1	.24	−.11	***
Sinic	1.4	.45	.01	***
Sub-Saharan African	−3.6	.43	−.05	***
Hindu	−8.9	.61	−.06	***
Japanese	3.4	.50	.02	***
(Constant)	68.8	.94		
Adjusted R^2 Block 1	*.01*			
(Control variables only)				
Adjusted R^2 Block 2	*.05*			
(Controls + type of society)				

Note: This illustrates the full OLS regression model, with blockwise entry, in this case with the approval of democratic performance 100-point scale as the dependent variable. Block 1 of the model controls for the level of development of the society and the social background of respondents. Block 2 then enters the type of society, based on the predominant religion, coded as dummy variables. Western societies represent the (omitted) reference category. The coefficients represent the effects of living in each type of society compared with living in Western societies, net of all prior controls. *Democratic performance* scale: For details see Table 2. *Level of human development:* Human Development Index (HDI) 2000, including longevity, literacy and education, and per capita GDP in $US PPP (UNDP Development Report 2000). *Levelofpoliticaldevelopment:* (Freedom House 7-point index (reversed) of political rights and civil liberties 1999-2000) (www.freedomhouse.org). *Type of society:* see Table 1. Sig.
***p.001; **p.01; *p.05. N/s Not significant.
Source: (WVS/EVS), pooled sample 1995-2001.

Is There an Islamic Civilization?

Yilmaz Esmer[*]

Regarding religion as the foundation of civilizations is certainly not a novel or recent idea. For thousands of years religion has formed (and to a large extent still does form) the basis of an individual's identity. Even today, roughly two-thirds of the population of a traditionally secular Islamic country say they are first Muslim and then Turkish rather than the other way around.[1] It was roughly a millennium ago when the Crusaders risked their lives in "infidel lands" in the name of God and Jesus.[2] After more than a thousand years, and in the same lands, Palestinian youths explode themselves almost daily without the blink of an eye, this time in name of Allah and Mohammed. *Plus ça change, plus c'est la meme chose*, as the French saying goes!

It is, therefore, no surprise that civilizations have frequently been identified by religions. Thus, we talk about an "Islamic civilization" or a "Christian civilization" implying that each religion has its civilization. The assumption here is that almost all Muslims, for example, have certain important cultural traits, values that they more or less share and that are different from those of non-Muslims. To be sure, there are those trivial differences in behavior and beliefs that are obvious even to the casual observer. Thus, cows are sacred for Hindus but are sacrificed annually to please Allah by Muslims who, in turn, do not even touch pigs let alone eat pork. Christian monasteries also functioned as wineries

---

[*] Boğaziçi University, Istanbul.

[1] Turkish World Values Survey carried out in December 2000 and January 2001. When asked whether they regarded themselves above all as Muslim or Turkish, 68 percent chose the former.

[2] Whether or not some, most or all religious wars had more material and tangible motives at the level of ruling elites is immaterial here. The Crusaders and others were innocent of such designs and could not have been persuaded to welcome martyrdom without direct reference to divine powers.

while the pleasure of sipping the smallest amount of duly fermented grapes was strictly forbidden for the Muslim believer. But these are rather superficial differences from a social science perspective[3] and they could hardly be regarded as sufficient for defining civilizations. What, then, are the criteria for defining a civilization? This seems to be the first question one needs to address — an obvious starting point. Second, we need empirical evidence showing that sets of societies that are classified into civilizations are indeed distinctive and different with respect to these criteria. Many authors, classical and contemporary, have proposed taxonomies for grouping civilizations and cultures. However, until recently, it was not possible to test these in any meaningful way because the data simply did not exist. Fortunately, this problem is being overcome to a large extent thanks to the World and European Values Surveys. We are now in a position to compare societies, including predominantly Islamic ones, with respect to a wide range of cultural values using systematic data since the last wave of the WVS includes a number of Islamic countries for the first time ever.

This paper is an attempt in that direction: In what respects and to what extent Islamic cultures are different from others? The answer to this question would always have had significant theoretical import. However, Huntington's much acclaimed and, at the same time, bitterly criticized "clash of civilizations" thesis (Huntington 1993; 1998) and then the tragic events of September 11, made it the "burning question" of the day. Therefore, "the clash of civilizations" is a natural starting point for a paper on the subject of contemporary Islamic cultures.

Huntington and the "Clash of Civilizations"

Huntington's thesis on the world's new fault line after the Cold War and the collapse of the Soviet Union has been discussed so widely both in academic publications and in the media that one need not summarize it here once again. Therefore, I shall limit myself to those points which will be helpful in deriving testable hypotheses.

It goes without saying that a definition of the concept of "civilization" is crucial to any meaningful discussion and test of the thesis. Nevertheless, and as noted by Norris and Inglehart (2002: note 5), Huntington does not give us a clear definition of civilization except in general terms and uses civilization and culture interchangeably. He writes (1998:41) that "a

---

[3] Among those who took a dissenting view on this topic, Marvin Harris was perhaps the most prominent social scientist. Harris (1974) argued that all these "riddles of culture" had sound economic and materialistic explanations. Thus he saw them as dependent variables which were only consequences of a culture's adapting itself to the environment for survival.

civilization is a cultural entity outside Germany. [...] This distinction has persisted in German thought but has not been accepted elsewhere. [...] ... efforts to distinguish culture and civilization [...] have not caught on, and, outside Germany, there is overwhelming agreement with Braudel that it is 'delusory to wish in the German way to separate culture from its foundation civilization.'" Thus, "civilization and culture both refer to the overall way of life of a people, and a civilization is a culture writ large. They both involve the 'values, norms, institutions, and modes of thinking to which successive generations in a given society have attached primary importance'" (Huntington, 1998:41).[4] Of course, this does not tell us which specific "values, norms, institutions, and modes of thinking" we are to analyze let alone how to measure them. However, Huntington (1998:42) is unequivocal on one point: "Of all the objective elements which define civilizations, however, the most important usually is religion." Thus, "religion is a central defining characteristic of civilizations" (1998:47).

If we are, then, to test Huntington's thesis, religion is our crucial independent variable. Put differently, "the values, norms, institutions, and modes of thinking" should, to a large extent, be dependent on religious affiliation and faith. Religion is also the clue for classifying civilizations and it is proposed that in the contemporary world we can delineate the following major civilizations (Huntington 1998:45-47):

> Sinic/Confucian
> Japanese
> Hindu
> Islamic
> Orthodox
> Latin American
> African (possibly)

We now derive testable hypotheses from these arguments:

H1. Societies which belong to one civilization should be significantly different from societies that belong to another civilization with respect to their values, norms, etc.

H2. Variance in values within civilizations should be smaller than variance between civilizations.

H3. Within a given society, groups affiliated with a certain religion (that forms the "central defining characteristic of civilizations") should be significantly different from groups affiliated with other major religions.

---

[4] Huntington quotes Bozeman (1975) here.

H4. Within a given society, within group variance in cultural values should be smaller than between group variance.

Of course, it is one huge step from here to require that different civilizations must clash. Nevertheless, if the theory is to hold, at a minimum we must demonstrate that differences do indeed exist and that a religion-based classification of cultures is plausible.

Commenting briefly on each one of the four hypotheses stated above, H1 predicts that if a given religion is predominant in a given society, then the cultural traits, characteristics that are typical of the corresponding civilization will be more observable among the people of that society. It follows that the higher the proportion of individuals affiliated with the given religion, the more pronounced the traits will be in that society.

H2 states that, whatever the important characteristics that define a civilization (culture) are, a civilization and a society belonging to that civilization should be more or less coherent within itself with respect to those characteristics. There is much variation among various breeds of dogs but a terrier and a golden retriever should have more in common between themselves than either one with a cat or a horse.

If religion is at the foundation of cultures, then individuals living in a given society and belonging to different faiths should display certain characteristics that are thought to be typical of their religion and thus their civilization. Therefore, H3 predicts that Muslims, for example, and Catholics living in the same society should exhibit certain differences in their values and norms. Needless to say, each group should be closer to the mean of its respective civilization. A finding to the contrary would have devastating effects on the theory.

H4 corresponds to H2 when the unit of analysis is individuals in one society. To repeat, if we are to talk about two different groups in a society, we cannot expect as much difference within the group as there is between the groups.

In this paper, I limit myself to a comparison of the Islamic culture with each of four major cultures only: Protestant, Orthodox, Catholic and Hindu. Furthermore, the analysis uses a within society approach and deals mainly with H3 although H2 and H4 are also addressed to some extent.

Before presenting the findings, the all-important question of "what is it that we are comparing" should be dealt with. Put differently, the dimensions for defining and grouping civilizations should be made specific.

Dimensions of Culture and Cultural Values

This subtitle has been the subject of a great number of volumes and the literature is replete with proposals for different value dimensions (many of them theoretical and some tested with data) from different perspectives — anthropological, sociological, social psychological and others. It is beyond the scope of this paper to even begin to summarize or discuss these various approaches here and I certainly would not be doing justice to them within these limits of space. However, Ronald Inglehart's scheme and the modifications proposed to it by Halman and Pettersson are particularly relevant to the analysis that follows and, therefore, deserve attention.

Inglehart (Inglehart 1997; Inglehart and Baker 2000) has proposed a two-dimensional scheme to position societies with respect to the myriad data collected through World Values Surveys. The two dimensions are labeled "Secular-Rational vs. Traditional" and "Survival vs. Self Expression."[5] The first dimension, with traditional values at one and secular-rational values at the opposite pole, include measures of the importance of God in one's life, importance of obedience and religious faith in child rearing rather than independence and determination, attitude towards the justifiability of abortion, degree of sense of national pride, and respect for authority. Clearly, traditional values emphasize the importance of religion, obedience, respect for authority, national pride and also are opposed to abortion. The indicators of the second dimension, survival and self-expression values, are emphasis on economic/physical security or quality-of-life, individual happiness, attitude toward signing a petition, degree of approval of homosexuality, and interpersonal trust (Inglehart and Baker 2000:24).[6]

In various publications, it has been reported that there is much empirical support for the two-factor model summarized above. "The items in each dimension are highly intercorrelated. The two dimensions explain 70 percent of the total cross national variation among these 10 variables" (Inglehart and Baker 2000:25). Is there a theoretical justification for the choice of this particular set of indicators? Halman and Pettersson (2002) question this point and suggest that, from a theoretical perspective, the inclusion of "some of the indicators are more or less 'accidental.'" For instance, they argue that individual happiness is "an emotion rather than a value" but, more importantly, it is context dependent. To give another example, they are not convinced that attitudes towards homosexuality and abortion should be used as indicators of not the same but rather

---

[5] The term "well-being" instead of "self-expression" is used in Inglehart 1997.

[6] The indicators are summarized from Table 1 of Inglehart and Baker 2000. Although the list of indicators may vary in different publications (see, for example, Inglehart 1997 where the author uses 22 indicators instead of the 10 summarized above), the thrust of the argument that this two-dimensional scheme can adequately represent a society's value system does not change.

different dimensions. One suggestion they make is to replace the survival-self expression axis by what is called "civic orientation."

At this point, I would like to explain briefly — and hopefully justify — my choice of criteria for comparing Muslim and non-Muslim populations in a number of societies.

Summarizing a wide-range of values with a limited number of dimensions has the great advantage of parsimony. Regardless of whether or not one likes the choice of indicators, Inglehart's two dimensions, for example, is extremely useful in placing a society on the world cultural map and makes intuitive sense. It even has the advantage of lending itself readily to graphic representation. Leaving theoretical considerations aside, summarization to such extent, however, inevitably risks losing much detail. With that consideration, in this paper I take a somewhat different approach and compare Islamic and non-Islamic groups with respect to four main criteria which have received attention in the literature. In other words, in deciding the important characteristics that should help us to distinguish cultures, I take a blindfolded approach to data. At this point the issue is not to see which variable or question correlates with which others but rather to shortlist broader value dimensions which have been proposed to have significant effects on economic and political structures and change. The question then is whether these are related to religious affiliation. Surely, these broad latent concepts will have to be operationalized with the help of individual variables (questions in the context of surveys). Practical data constraints aside, my choice of indicators was also motivated by theoretical factors with no regard to empirical considerations. Only then do I carry out tests to see if the indicators should form a scale. And if the answer to that question is negative, so be it. The variable is not dropped out of the analysis — just not included in a scale and is analyzed individually.

The four value orientations on which I wish to base my comparisons are:

   a. Protestant ethic
   b. Social capital
   c. Modernity
   d. Democracy

These four dimensions can provide us with a good basis for the comparison of populations with respect to their values and address the major arguments found in the relevant literature. Some are (modernity, for example), nevertheless, still too broad and are divided into subcategories before they are operationalized.

Data and Measurement

Data from the 1999-2001 wave of World Values and European Values Surveys are used to carry out the analyses. The set used includes data from 70 societies with a total sample size of 95,341. However, as explained in the next section, data only from eight countries are utilized.[7] Although the questionnaires cover the widest possible range of norms, values and attitudes, it goes without saying that no questionnaire is ideal for all purposes. Furthermore, there are always problems of missing data and some questions are not asked in some countries for various reasons. Notwithstanding these usual constraints and limitations, we are in the fortunate position of finding at least one — and usually more than one — indicator of the concepts that need to be measured.

a. Protestant Ethic

Very few theories in social sciences can claim the fame and attention that Weber's (1958) thesis on the prime cause of capitalist development has enjoyed. Weber's argument is so widely known that the reader is spared yet another summary here. Thrift, determination and hard work as ends in themselves are the core values of the Protestant Ethic.

Both WVS and EVS questionnaires contained a list of items which are thought to be important to instill in children. The respondents were asked to choose five from among this list, which included hard work, thrift and determination. These three indicators come as close to measuring the concept as one can ideally hope. A scale combining the three was not formed, however, since choosing one of the three decreases the probability of choosing one or both of the other two. All three variables are dichotomous with '0' indicating that the item was not chosen and '1' indicating that the item was mentioned as important.

b. Social Capital

Almond and Verba (1963), in their now classical five-nation study, emphasized the importance of interpersonal trust in a society as one of the forming blocks of "the civic culture" some four decades ago. Since then, and particularly in the 1990's, trust has become in vogue and received a great deal of attention. Voluminous books have been written with this title (some examples are, Fukuyama 1995; Misztal 1996; Warren 1999). It is regarded as the key component of social capital which, in turn, is argued to be a significant independent variable for sustainable economic growth and the consolidation of democracy. Putnam's (1993) seminal work

---

[7] I do not repeat here detailed descriptions of WVS and EVS projects which are readily available in a number of publications and, more conveniently, in the website www.worldvaluessurvey.org.

on the role of social capital in the development of democracy in Italy has rightfully stirred much excitement and debate as well as criticism over the role of social capital. In addition to trust, cooperation, norms of reciprocity and civic engagement comprise the core values of the concept of social capital.[8]

Three indicators of social capital are used in the analysis:

Interpersonal trust. A dichotomous variable with respondents saying most people can be trusted coded '1' and those who say one needs to be careful in dealing with others coded '0'.

Respect. Respondents choosing "respect for others" from among a list of items important in raising children are coded '1' and others '0'. This question is used to operationalize a cooperative attitude.

Signing a Petition. As a measure of civic engagement, the question about signing a petition was used. Although a very benign and easy way of displaying civicness, it still requires that such an act is not likely to bring any harm on the individual. Therefore, it can be "context contaminated" in certain authoritarian countries. Variable is coded '1' for respondents who have signed a petition and '0' for those who said they might or they never would do such a thing.

c. Modernity

Modernization theories, whose origins can be traced to Karl Marx, seem to have a cyclical life. They reach a peak in popularity only to be followed by intense criticism and then a trough. Then they undergo some sort of adaptive mutation and regain a status of respectability. The debate may continue but one thing is clear: modernization, modern, modernity are now household words and are not meaningless. Modernity is a syndrome with a number of symptoms which usually are intercorrelated. It may not be a unilineal process. It may not necessarily lead to convergence on all fronts. It may at times have been presented as a Western and ethnocentric concept. Nevertheless, modernization, almost always accompanied by economic growth, has certain common discernable consequences. As Taylor (2001:184-5) puts it "what is required by the wave of modernity is that one come up not with identical institutions but with functionally equivalent ones. The 'bottom line' is, for example, competing successfully in the international market. More than one kind of firm and business culture can enable this." According to him there is "a gamut of alternative modernities" in the contemporary world. Just like we do not expect modernization to produce identical institutions in societies, we do not

---

[8] For recent treatments of and differing viewpoints on social capital see Dasgupta and Serageldin (2000) and Rotberg (2001).

expect the process to produce individuals with identical values. We do predict, however, that the values of a "modern" individual will tend to change in a certain general direction. By arguing that the process will produce certain changes in cultural values "we do not assume that *all* elements of culture will change, leading to a uniform global culture: we see no reason to expect that the Chinese will stop using chopsticks in the foreseeable future, or that Brazilians will learn to polka. But certain cultural and political changes *do* seem to be logically linked with the dynamics of a core syndrome of Modernization" (Inglehart 1997:69; italics original).

It would be a monumental task and a heroic accomplishment to come up with a complete and agreed-upon list of cultural changes that modernization is expected to produce. Certain items, however, could serve as a common denominator. I suggest the following:

Importance of religion. Industrialization, economic growth and prosperity, advances in science and technology, and higher levels of education are all expected to result in a decrease in religiosity — both belief and practice. There are exceptions, no doubt, and the United States is a case in point. But the negative correlation between modernity and religiosity generally holds and we can make a probabilistic prediction to that effect. Our questionnaires include a number of questions on religiosity and I use the following:

   i) A 10-point scale measuring the importance of God in one's life. The coding is reversed so that (as with all variables) higher scores indicate higher levels of modernity. Thus a score of '1' means that God is extremely important and '10' indicates that God has no importance in the individual's life.

  ii) A composite scale comprising seven dichotomous variables with each one coded '0' for high and '1' for low religiosity. The variables are:

> Is the respondent a religious person?
> Does the respondent believe in:
> > God?
> > Life after death?
> > Hell?
> > Heaven?
>
> Does the respondent draw comfort and strength from religion?
> Does the respondent choose religious faith as important in raising children?

These seven variables are all positively correlated and a scale is constructed by adding them. The resulting measure has a minimum value of '0' (extremely religious) and a maximum of '7' (not religious at all). The scale has high reliability with a Cronbach's alpha of 0.83 for WVS countries and 0.88 for EVS countries.

Secularism. Modernization is expected to encourage secular values which I define here not in terms of individual faith but rather with respect to attitudes toward the separation of the church and the state. A scale is constructed with two questions in order to measure secularism:

> Politicians who do not believe in God are unfit for public office.
> It would be better if more people with strong religious beliefs held public office.

Both questions have five response categories (strongly agree, agree, neither, disagree, strongly disagree) so the resulting scale has a minimum value of '2' (extremely non-secular) and a maximum value of '10' (very secular). The scale has an alpha of 0.65 for WVS and 0.76 for EVS countries.

Efficacy. A 10-point scale is used to measure efficacy, that is, how much freedom and control individuals think they have over their lives. At the lower end are those respondents who believe "what they do has no real effect on what happens to them" and at the higher end are those who think they have complete freedom over their lives.

Marriage and family. Traditional cultures attach great importance to family and the institutional arrangement that bring it to existence. Inglehart and Baker (2000:25) write that "The importance of family is a major theme: In traditional societies a main goal in life is to make one's parents proud — one must always love and respect one's parents regardless of how they behave. Conversely parents must do their best for children even if their own well-being suffers." Seven indicators have been added to construct the "importance of family and marriage scale." They are:

> Children must love and respect parents unconditionally
> Parents are dutybound to sacrifice their well being to do the best for their children
> Child needs a home with both father and mother to grow happily
> Women have to have children in order to be fulfilled
> Marriage is an outdated institution
> Approval of woman having a child without marriage/stable relationship
> More emphasis on family life would be good/bad

All of these seven questions are coded '0' or '1' with the former indicating emphasis on traditional family values. Thus a maximum score of '7' on the scale means the respondent does not attach importance to any of the family values included. The scale has an acceptable reliability with a Cronbach's alpha of 0.48 for WVS and 0.46 for EVS countries.

Female employment. Widespread participation of women in the workforce is one of the most far-reaching consequences of industrialization that had profound impact on the whole social structure. Rates of female employment continue to increase and to affect people's (women and men) outlook on life. In their pioneering study of modernization in six countries, Inkeles and Smith (1974:18) proposed *"to classify as modern those personal qualities which are likely to be inculcated by participation in large-scale modern productive enterprises such as the factory...* [italics original]."[9] Employment changes a woman's role as a wife and a housewife and it changes her values, her general outlook on life. Work for pay is not a role assigned to women in traditional societies. Therefore, acceptance of this new role is a good indicator of one important aspect of modernity. Two variables are added to measure attitudes towards working women:

> Working mothers can establish warm and secure relationship with their children
> Both the husband and wife should contribute to household income

Both questions have four answer categories (strongly agree, agree, disagree, strongly disagree) and both are coded so that higher scores indicate approval of working women. The combined variable has the lowest reliability scores of all the scales constructed (alpha = 0.39 for WVS and 0.31 for EVS countries).

Sexual tolerance. Sexual liberation is a characteristic more of the postmodern, postindustrial rather than the modern, industrial society. More liberal, permissive sex norms tolerant of sex between unmarried couples and homosexuality have been gaining increased approval in the West. Some countries, like the Netherlands to be followed by others, have legalized homosexual marriages. Linking this development to the increase in the proportion of postmaterialists, Inglehart (1990:195) writes that "Postmaterialists are far more permissive than Materialists in their attitudes toward abortion, divorce, extramarital affairs, prostitution, and euthanasia." This correlation between sexual norms and materialism/postmaterialism is confirmed seven years later (Inglehart 1997:276-80).

The last dimension of modernity that I analyze is sexual norms. It has already been observed that Inglehart (1997), and Inglehart and Baker (2000) have treated attitudes towards homosexuality and abortion as components of two different dimensions and that Halman and Pettersson (2002) disagree. In this paper, the scores of three 10-point scales are added to construct a sexual tolerance scale:

---

[9] Inkeles and Smith (1974) studied a sample of males only in six countries, but their basic conclusion is, I believe, even more valid for women.

Justifiability of
  Homosexuality
  Abortion
  Prostitution (or casual relationships in Europe).

However, approval of prostitution question was only optional in the EVS questionnaire and was asked in a very limited number of countries. Therefore, in those countries it is replaced with "casual relationships." The two, obviously, are not the same thing but perhaps functionally equivalent for our purposes since all of these four questions are positively correlated with coefficients ranging between 0.38 and 0.65. In both cases (that is using prostitution or casual relationships as the third item of the sexual tolerance scale) reliabilities are high with alphas of 0.56 and 0.67 for WVS and EVS countries, respectively.

d. Democratic Culture

What is broadly referred to as the "democratic culture" is the last dimension of our comparisons between Muslim and non-Muslim populations. Democracy needs democrats. It is difficult, if not impossible, for any system (even at the micro level) to survive unless an appreciable proportion of its members have internalized the basic values and norms of the system. Is it possible that a family can survive for long if husband and wife believe that it is an outmoded, useless, dysfunctional institution that does not serve the interests of any member?

No one disputes that commanding high levels of legitimacy and enjoying wide support of its citizenry is helpful to the survival of a political system and that this is particularly true for democracies. However, what is important here is whether the core values of the system are shared by the citizens. Expressed support for this government or that regime can change dramatically within relatively short periods depending on perceived performance. Such support is superficial and fickle if it is not sustained by a deeper value structure that is in congruence with the political system. In this respect, Klingemann's (1999) concept of "dissatisfied democrats" is of particular importance. As he explains, dissatisfaction with how the system is functioning does not pose a threat to democracy. "Quite to the contrary they [dissatisfied democrats] may well be the hope for the future of democratic governance" (Klingemann 1999:56).

This is very important for the specific purposes of the present article because it tells us that questions about government or system performance are less than ideal to gauge public support for democracy. Similarly, general and abstract questions of the type "do you believe democracy is the best system of government?" have low validity for at least two reasons. First, being a democrat is very fashionable in the contemporary world

(Klingemann 1999) and it is very easy to be a "democrat" in the abstract. Thus the answers can be expected to be biased towards democracy because of global trends and the operation of a social desirability effect. Second, such a question will suffer from context contamination. An individual living under an authoritarian system that does not deliver to her/his satisfaction is more likely to say "democracy is best" that an individual who is very satisfied with the performance of the system regardless of its authoritarian or totalitarian nature. I propose that values related to, for instance, tolerance, freedom, or participation are better measures of democratic culture.

The following analysis utilizes a five dimensional scheme for assessing and comparing democratic values in different cultures.

Tolerance. It goes without saying that a democrat is a tolerant person — tolerant of different ideas, different lifestyles, different religions and ethnicities, etc. WVS/EVS questionnaires have an excellent and time-tested battery for measuring the level of tolerance. Respondents are presented with a list of potentially "undesirable" groups and are asked to pick the ones that they would *not* like as neighbors. The scale of tolerance used in the analysis includes the following items:

> People with a criminal record
> People belonging to a different race
> Emotionally unstable people
> Muslims (or relevant religious minority)
> Immigrants/foreign workers
> People with AIDS
> Jews (or another visible minority group)

Two groups that are included in the battery are not included in this scale: homosexuals and heavy drinkers. Homosexuals are not a scale item because, as already discussed, sexual tolerance is treated as a separate dimension and it is felt that this question should belong to that specific dimension rather than a measure of general tolerance. Heavy drinkers are excluded because Islam specifically forbids the use of alcohol. Therefore, this item does not have the same status as the others. For a Hindu, being tolerant of, say, Muslims or former criminals or immigrants and being tolerant of killing cows are not the same thing.

The seven items in the tolerance scale are all dichotomous and higher scale values (maximum is 7) indicate higher levels of tolerance. In some countries, questions about certain groups (particularly religious minorities) were not asked. In those countries, the scale is constructed using six (for example, Montenegro) or five (for example, India, Nigeria) items. [10] The scale has high reliability with an alpha of 0.74 for WVS and 0.77 for EVS countries.

Support of freedom. Support for freedom is measured with the help of a variable constructed from two questions included in the material-ism/postmaterialism battery. Respondents were asked to choose the most and the second most important aims of their countries from a list that contained:

> Maintaining order in the nation
> Giving people more say in important government decisions
> Fighting rising prices
> Protecting freedom of speech

The variable is coded '1' if the respondent chooses "protecting freedom of speech" either as the first or the second aim and '0' otherwise.

Participation. Participation is an important dimension of "civic culture." An apathetic and nonparticipating citizenry that is as little involved in politics as possible is the dream of many dictatorships. Democracy requires the opposite — a point emphasized by all students of democratic culture. A comparative analysis of democratic values should not ignore the participation dimension. Our measure of political participation includes three items:

> How much the respondent is interested in (in EVS talk about) politics?
> Would the respondent join a boycott?
> Would the respondent attend a lawful demonstration?

All three items have three response categories resulting in a scale with a maximum of 9 (very high participation). Alpha coefficients are 0.56 both for WVS and EVS countries.

Problems with democracy. Three items that are collected under this heading tap opinions on problems that are frequently associated with democratic systems. Unfortunately they, too, can be influenced by context. If an individual is living under a democratic system where stability is a serious problem and governments come and go once every few months (recall France before the 5th Republic or Italy in the not too distant past) he/she is more likely to agree that indecisiveness is a problem for democratic systems. Similarly, if internal security and terror are serious problems, one

---

[10] Needless to say, these five or six-item tolerance scales were only used for within country comparisons.

is expected to accept the evaluation that democracies have difficulties in maintaining order. With these caveats, the items that form the "problems of democratic systems" scale are:

> In democracies, the economic system runs badly
> Democracies are indecisive and have too much quibbling
> Democracies are not good in maintaining order

All three items are scored on a four-point scale (strongly agree, agree, disagree, strongly disagree). Higher scale values (maximum 12) represent pro-democracy attitudes. Alpha coefficients are 0.76 for WVS and 0.79 for EVS countries, respectively.

Alternatives to democracy. It is interesting to note that an appreciable number of people who think democracy is the best system of government, can also accept solutions that are incompatible with a democratic system: another reason for arguing against "is democracy good?" type of direct questions. Why would someone who expresses agreement with a statement like "democracy may have its problems but it is better than any other form of government" also think "it would be good to have the army rule?" And this is not a hypothetical question. Even in the sample of European countries with levels of education much higher than the world average, close to 10 percent (unweighted sample from 32 European societies) fall into that category! Thus, alternatives to democracy scale, comprising three items listed below, is another measure indicative of the support for democracy. The items are:

> Having a strong leader who does not have to bother with elections or parliament
> Having experts, not government, make decisions according to what they think is best
> Having the army rule

Respondent were asked to rate these as "very good," "good," "bad," or "very bad." Again with higher scores indicating higher degrees of support for democracy, alpha's are 0.57 for WVS and 0.52 for EVS countries.

The scheme developed for the comparison of Islamic groups with others is summarized in Table 1. The results reported in the next section are based on analyses following this scheme.

Results: Global Perspective

Having completed the discussion of our measurement model, we can now take up the hypotheses derived from Huntington's thesis. It will be recalled that the first hypothesis, H1, was:

Table 1

Dimensions for Comparing Cultural Values

1. Protestant Ethic
   a. Hard work
   b. Thrift
   c. Determination and perseverance
2. Social Capital
   a. Interpersonal trust
   b. Respect for others
   c. Petitioning
3. Modernity
   a. Religiosity
      i. Importance of God
      ii. Degee of religiosity
   b. Secularism
      i. Nonbelievers in public office
      ii. Strong believer in public office
   c. Efficacy
      Fate versus Free Choice
   d. Marriage and family
      i. Unconditional love for parents
      ii. Unconditional parental sacrifice for children
      iii. Need for both parents
      iv. Female need for children
      v. Outmodedness of marriage
      vi. Motherhood out of wedlock
      vii. Emphasis on family life
   e. Female employment
      i. Working mother and children relations
      ii. Contribution to household income
   f. Sexual tolerance
      i. Justifiability of homosexuality
      ii. Justifiability of prostitution (or casual relationships)
      iii. Justifiability of abortion
4. Democratic culture
   a. Tolerance
   b. Support of freedom
   c. Participation
      i. Interest in politics
      ii. Joining boycotts
      iii. Attending demonstrations
   d. Problems of democracy
      i. Democracy and economic performance
      ii. Democracy and indecisiveness
      iii. Democracy and the maintenance of order
   e. Alternatives to democracy
      i. Preference for a strong leader
      ii. Preference of expert rule
      iii. Preference for army rule

Societies which belong to one civilization should be significantly different from societies that belong to another civilization with respect to their values, norms, etc.

Inglehart and Norris (2002) report a test of this hypothesis. To my knowledge, this is the first published test, based on extensive comparative data, of Huntington's thesis. Briefly, the approach taken by Inglehart and Norris is to code everyone living in a society as belonging to the same civilization (determined by the religious group that has the plurality in that society) and then comparing individuals living in predominantly Islamic societies with those living in Catholic, Protestant, Orthodox, Central European, Latin American, Sinic/Confucian, Sub-Saharan African, Hindu and Japanese societies. Individuals are compared with respect to — surprisingly, not the two dimensions developed by Inglehart but rather — "democratic political values" (approval of democratic performance, democratic ideals, religious leaders, strong leaders) and "liberal social values" (approval of gender equality, homosexuality, abortion, divorce). Evaluating a series of multiple regression models with civilization as the independent variable and including a number of control variables, they conclude that "Any black-and-white 'Islam versus the West' interpretation of a 'culture clash' as conveyed by the popular media is far too simplistic" (Inglehart and Norris 2002:15). Their findings indicate that there is indeed a difference between Islam and the West but the difference concerns, in their words, "the eros and not the demos." In other words, the observable differences between the Islamic world and others pertain to values related to gender differences and sexual liberalization rather than support for democracy.

Inglehart and Norris do not test H2 about the variances within civilizations. This hypothesis is important because it will give us an idea about the consistency of civilizations with respect to cultural values. This point has been made frequently by scholars who object to the idea that there is "one Islam" and that the variances within it are insignificant. If the objection is not valid, we should expect low variances within the Islamic civilization, — certainly lower than the total variance that includes all other civilizations in addition to Islam.

A standard ANOVA test is not appropriate in this context because of the huge sample size which yields thousands of degrees of freedom for within groups estimates. Statistical significance under these circumstances is not very meaningful since it is impossible not get significant F ratios.[11]

---

[11] Technically, statistical tests are only appropriate for probability samples. Since a number of countries employed quota sampling, statistical tests should only be regarded as an approximate guide.

Table 2

Countries and Civilizations[a]

Protestant	*Catholic*	*Islamic*	*Orthodox*	*Central Europe*	*Latin America*
Canada	Austria	Albania	Bosnia	Crotia	Argentina
Denmark	Belgium	Algeria	Belarus	Czechia	Chile
Finland	France	Egypt	Bulgaria	Estonia	Peru
Germany	Ireland	Indonesia	Greece	Hungary	Puerto Rico
Iceland	Italy	Iran	Macedonia	Latvia	Venezuella
N. Ireland	Luxembourg	Jordan	Moldova	Lithuania	
Sweden	Malta	Morocco	Montenegro	Slovakia	
U.K.	Netherlands	Pakistan	Romania	Slovenia	
U.S.A.	Poland	Turkey	Russia		
	Philippines		Serbia		
	Portugal		Ukraine		
	Spain				

Sino Confucian	*SubSaharan Africa*	*Hindu*	*Judaic*	*Japanese*	
China	Nigeria	India	Israel	Japan	
S. Korea	S. Africa				
Vietnam	Tanzania				
	Uganda				
	Zimbabwe				

[a] Following the classifications of Huntington (1998) and Inglehart and Norris (2002).

Instead, we take an informal approach and simply examine the standard deviations for four civilization groups. Societies that are included in the 1999-2001 WVS/EVS surveys are classified following Huntington's scheme and Inglehart and Norris's (2002) criteria with minor modifications (the full list is given in Table 2). For purposes of brevity, results for four civilizations (Protestant, Catholic, Islamic and Orthodox) are compared in Table 3 which tells a very interesting story.

Figures in Table 3 measure only the coherence within civilizations with respect to the measures employed but certainly do not give any clues about the existence or direction of differences. Therefore, it should be interpreted with reference to the means. For example, we may find that, on the average, a given civilization has comparatively lower levels of sexual tolerance as indicated by group means. If, however, the group has a very high variance for this variable, then we know that although on the average members of Civilization X are less tolerant, there are great differences among them and one would be hard pressed to refer to them as if they all display their "civilization characteristic" — in this example, low sexual tolerance. Conversely, a low mean and a small variance would be an

Table 3

Consistency of Values within Civilizations (standard deviations[a])

	Protestant	*Catholic*	*Islamic*	*Orthodox*	*Total*
Protestant Ethics					
Hard work	0.46	0.50	0.49	0.45	0.50
Thrift	0.45	0.49	0.47	0.49	0.48
Determination	0.49	0.47	0.44	0.49	0.48
Social Capital					
Interpersonal trust	0.50	0.45	0.46	0.42	0.47
Respect for others	0.39	0.43	0.48	0.48	0.45
Signing petition	0.47	0.50	0.33	0.41	0.49
Modernization					
Religiosity					
Importance of God	3.29	3.13	1.59	3.10	3.22
Religiosity scale	2.52	2.36	1.28	2.45	2.47
Secularism					
Secularism scale	2.00	2.23	1.95	2.17	2.35
Efficacy					
Fatalism/free choice	1.86	2.15	2.73	2.51	2.37
Marriage and Family					
Family scale	1.43	1.45	0.90	1.20	1.44
Female employment					
Women and work scale	1.25	1.27	1.43	1.15	1.29
Sexual tolerance					
Sexual tolerance scale	7.69	7.34	2.67	6.00	7.34
Democratic Culture					
Tolerance					
Neighbor scale	1.49	1.78	1.64	1.79	1.81
Participation					
Participation scale	1.58	1.61	1.43	1.47	1.59
Problems with Democracy					
Problems scale	1.77	1.97	2.01	2.14	2.00
Alternatives to Democracy					
Alternatives scale	1.81	1.97	1.95	2.02	2.04

[a] The sample is weighted so that the sample size in each country is fixed at 1,000.

indication that low tolerance is a consistent characteristic of that culture. In other words, when defined in terms of the dimension in question, we could speak about the *existence* of a civilization.

The standard deviations reported in Table 3 can be summarized as follows:

 a. With respect to values related to Protestant Ethic, standard deviations for all four civilizations can be considered equal.

b. For all indicators of democratic culture, populations of Islamic societies are as likely to differ around their means as the other three groups.

c. Efficacy and social trust variables (with the possible exception of signing a petition) have roughly similar standard deviations for all four groups. Islamic civilization can be said to be somewhat more consistent about signing a petition.

d. Interestingly, Islamic culture has the largest variance in attitudes towards female employment. Apparently, the Islamic world is divided on that issue.

e. The standard deviation for Islamic cultures is somewhat low for the marriage and family scale.

f. The most striking difference in standard deviations between the Islamic culture and others is sexual tolerance. This scale has a variance of 2.67 for people living in Islamic societies. The next lowest standard deviation is 6.00 (Orthodox) and Protestants have a standard deviation of 7.69. This finding warrants a look at the scale means:

Protestant 14.5
Catholic 11.8
Orthodox 9.3
Islamic 4.3

Out of a possible high of 30, Muslims or non-Muslims living in Islamic societies score a mean of 4.3 on sexual tolerance scale. This is remarkable indeed. And coupled with a very low standard deviation, we find a telltale sign for the existence of a civilization here.

g. The next group of variables that stand out in Table 3 are related to religiosity. God is extremely important in the lives of Islamic populations which are also considerably more religious that others. Furthermore, the variance for these measures in Islamic culture is much lower than any of the other three cultures.

These conclusions are very much consistent with the findings reported by Inglehart and Norris (2002). Two factors gain prominence in defining an Islamic civilization: high religiosity and low sexual tolerance. And with respect to both of these characteristics, Islamic culture is much more coherent and consistent then Protestant, Catholic or Orthodox cultures. It seems that one cannot speak about a clear and distinct Islamic cultural zone if one is concerned with values related to Protestant Ethic, social capital or democratic culture. But it makes sense to refer to an Islamic civilization within the context of religiosity, treatment of women, and sexual tolerance (or rather the lack thereof).

Results: Country Analysis

The conclusions of the previous section were based on global level analyses where it was assumed that the predominant characteristics of a society tend to determine the value systems of individuals living in that society regardless of religious faith. To test our third hypothesis, we have to change our unit of analysis and turn our attention to comparisons of groups within countries. If we regard religion as the defining characteristic, the foundation of civilizations, then H3 should be confirmed such that the values of different religious groups living in one society should differ in the predicted direction. Referring to the previous section, Muslims in a given country should have significantly higher levels of religiosity and lower levels of sexual tolerance than, say, the Protestant citizens of that country. To test this hypothesis, we have to have data on multi religion societies with sizeable Muslim populations. At the time of this writing, we have data for eight such societies:

Bulgaria
Macedonia
Bosnia
Montenegro
Nigeria
Uganda
India

This set allows us to compare Islamic populations within a country with Protestants (Nigeria and Uganda), with Roman Catholics (Uganda), with Hindus (India) and finally with the Orthodox populations of Albania, Bosnia, Bulgaria, Macedonia and Montenegro. The Muslims in these societies are indigenous populations and not immigrants (who could still carry the traits of their home countries) and this is an advantage for our purposes. Nevertheless, it is clear that this set of countries presents severe data limitations. First, five out of eight are in the Balkans and allow comparisons only with the Orthodox culture. Second, this is an area where ethno-religious conflicts reached war proportions in the very recent past. Third, all eight are low — and mostly very very low — income countries. And finally, these countries score so much lower than average on a number of our value dimensions that it may be difficult to find differences between groups within a society.

H3 was derived from Huntington's thesis. But, among others, Coleman (1990) and Putnam (1993) would also make the same prediction since they argue that a correlation exists between religious affiliation and values (in their case values related to social capital). Halman and Pettersson (1999) analyzed the relationship between social capital and religious denomination in Germany, Spain, Sweden and the U.S. They concluded that, with the individual as the unit of analysis, one could not readily confirm the correlation. Inglehart and Baker (2000) reached a similar conclusion with regards to interpersonal trust. They found Catholics to have about the same levels of trust as Protestants within given societies. They have an explanation: "… once established, the cross-cultural differences linked with religion have become part of a national culture that is transmitted by the educational institutions and mass media of given societies to the people of that nation. Despite globalization, the nation remains a key unit of shared experience, and its educational and cultural institutions shape the values of almost everyone in that society" (Inglehart and Baker 2000:37).

In Tables 4 through 7, I present within country comparisons for all value dimensions that have been described in previous sections and summarized in Table 1. Entries in bold indicate a significance level of 0.05 or better (two-tailed difference of means test with no assumptions about equality of variances). As explained above (note 11), because of sample properties, significance levels should not be regarded as exact probabilities.

a. Protestant Ethic

With respect to the first two indicators (hard work and thrift) one does not find any consistent differences between Muslims and non-Muslims in our sample of eight countries. In fact, Muslim, Orthodox, Catholic and Hindu populations attach similar (almost equal) levels of importance to instilling values of hard work and thrift in children with two exceptions: Orthodox groups score low on hard work in Macedonia and on thrift in Montenegro. But these indeed are exceptions and overall similarity of groups prevail for these two variables. The findings for the third indicator (determination, perseverance) are more interesting: in six of the eight countries, Muslims score significantly lower than other groups and in the remaining two (Bulgaria and Uganda) the differences are in the same direction although they do not attain statistical significance.

Can this finding be generalized to the rest of the world? The answer is 'yes' when we examine the means for civilization groups. Those living in the Islamic zone attach significantly less importance to determination and perseverance in children than Protestants, Catholics or the Orthodox. Is there a determination and perseverance problem in the Islamic culture? Following Weber, could this finding give a clue as to why Islamic countries have been painfully slow on the road to capitalist development and industrialization? It is certain that more research — both theoretical and empirical — is needed on this topic.

Table 4

Protestant Ethics

		Hard Work		Thrift		Determination	
		Mean	Std.Dev.	Mean	Std.Dev.	Mean	St.Dev.
ALBANIA							
	Muslim	0.66	0.47	0.58	0.49	0.52	0.50
	Orthodox	0.63	0.48	0.54	0.50	**0.66**	0.48
BULGARIA							
	Muslim	0.90	0.30	0.37	0.49	0.49	0.50
	Orthodox	0.85	0.35	0.42	0.49	0.55	0.50
MACEDONIA							
	Muslim	0.71	0.45	0.33	0.47	0.17	0.38
	Orthodox	**0.27**	0.44	0.40	0.49	**0.51**	0.50
BOSNIA							
	Muslim	0.56	0.50	0.43	0.50	0.42	0.49
	Orthodox	0.53	0.50	**0.34**	0.47	**0.50**	0.50
MONTENEGRO							
	Muslim	0.82	0.39	0.50	0.50	0.34	0.47
	Orthodox	0.83	0.38	**0.34**	0.47	**0.48**	0.50
NIGERIA							
	Muslim	0.78	0.42	0.11	0.31	0.19	0.39
	Protestant	0.81	0.39	0.10	0.30	**0.25**	0.43
TANZANIA							
	Muslim	0.84	0.36	0.56	0.50	0.53	0.50
	Roman Catholic	0.83	0.38	0.50	0.50	**0.60**	0.49
	Protestant	0.84	0.37	0.52	0.50	0.58	0.49
UGANDA							
	Muslim	0.84	0.36	0.10	0.30	0.32	0.47
	Roman Catholic	0.87	0.33	0.09	0.29	0.35	0.48
	Protestant	0.85	0.36	0.12	0.33	0.36	0.48
INDIA							
	Muslim	0.86	0.35	0.64	0.48	0.36	0.48
	Hindu	0.87	0.34	0.64	0.48	**0.49**	0.50

b. Social Capital

An examination of the means reported in Table 5 shows that there is no consistent pattern for any of the indicators of social capital. Some differences are significant but are usually in opposite directions in different countries. By looking at the data from these eight countries, one certainly cannot say there is a correlation between religion (in our case Islam) and social capital. Thus, the conclusions reached by Halman and Pettersson (1999) for four developed Western countries are confirmed. They found no consistent differences between Catholics and Protestants and we find no consistent differences between Muslims and others.

Table 5

Social Capital

		Interpersonal Trust		Respect for Others		Signing a Petition	
		Mean	Std.Dev.	Mean	Std.Dev.	Mean	St.Dev.
ALBANIA							
	Muslim	0.24	0.43	0.76	0.43	0.21	0.41
	Orthodox	0.23	0.42	**0.86**	0.35	0.17	0.37
BULGARIA							
	Muslim	0.36	0.48	0.58	0.50	0.12	0.32
	Orthodox	**0.25**	0.44	0.58	0.49	0.12	0.33
MACEDONIA							
	Muslim	0.19	0.39	0.77	0.42	0.22	0.42
	Orthodox	**0.12**	0.32	0.74	0.44	0.28	0.45
BOSNIA							
	Muslim	0.14	0.35	0.74	0.44	0.24	0.43
	Orthodox	0.15	0.36	**0.65**	0.48	**0.13**	0.33
MONTENEGRO							
	Muslim	0.37	0.48	0.63	0.48	0.14	0.35
	Orthodox	0.33	0.47	**0.55**	0.50	**0.27**	0.45
NIGERIA							
	Muslim	0.28	0.45	0.55	0.50	0.07	0.25
	Protestant	0.24	0.43	**0.61**	0.49	0.07	0.25
TANZANIA							
	Muslim	0.09	0.29	0.85	0.36	0.13	0.33
	Roman Catholic	0.08	0.28	0.85	0.36	**0.07**	0.25
	Protestant	**0.03**	0.18	0.80	0.40	0.10	0.30
UGANDA							
	Muslim	0.07	0.25	0.46	0.50	0.20	0.40
	Roman Catholic	0.06	0.25	**0.61**	0.49	0.15	0.36
	Protestant	0.09	0.29	**0.56**	0.50	0.26	0.44
INDIA							
	Muslim	0.49	0.50	0.53	0.50	0.36	0.48
	Hindu	0.42	0.49	**0.64**	0.48	**0.28**	0.45

c. Modernity

Religiosity. It has already been observed that, at the global level with countries as the units of analysis, religiosity is one of the two important characteristics that may define Islamic civilization. By and large, this finding is confirmed at the micro level. In Albania, Bulgaria, Macedonia, Bosnia, and Nigeria non-Muslim populations attach significantly less importance to God in their lives and score significantly lower on religiosity scale than Muslims. Importance of God scale is not available for India. In the remaining countries, *t* values do not reach 5 percent significance level but the differences (for both indicators) are always in the predicted direction (the one and only exception is Protestants in Uganda whose mean religiosity is very slightly above Muslims).

In short, at this level of analysis too, it is confirmed that Muslims are more pious than others. Could this finding be related to the higher proportions of fundamentalists and dogmatics found in Islamic populations since unquestioned faith should be a prerequisite for fundamentalism? Surely, there is no evidence of such a relationship in our analyses but the question seems worthy of exploration.

Secularism. The separation of religion and the political/legal system has always been problematic in Islam. The Holy Quran is not restricted to matters of faith but is also a constitution, a legal code and a civil law for a society of believers. At least, this was the original intention although changes in economic and political conditions as well as advances in science and technology have always forced modifications and relaxations. It should also be noted that Islam is the only major religion with the Prophet serving as the commander-in-chief and the head of state as well. All these attributes have made it particularly difficult for Islamic societies "to give unto Cesar what belong to him." Is the legacy still alive? Our eight-country analysis indicates that there are significant differences between Muslims and non-Muslims living in the same society and that the former are likely to be less secular. The differences (all in the same direction) are significant at the 5 percent level or better in Albania, Bulgaria, Macedonia, Bosnia and Nigeria. In Uganda, the differences do not attain statistical significance although, there too, Muslims are, on the average, less secular than both Catholics and Protestants. In Montenegro, the Orthodox seem slightly less secular than Muslims and the same holds true for India (in both cases, the differences are not significant). Of course, secularism has a very different meaning in the context of Hinduism as compared to the major monotheistic religions.

Efficacy. Fate is an important concept in all monotheist religions but perhaps even more so in Islam. The slave in Diderot's *Jacques le Fatalist* keeps reminding to his master that "it is written yonder." A good Muslim is required to believe that all are "written yonder." The individual is, then, powerless against fate. In our set of eight countries, Muslims in Macedonia, Nigeria and India are significantly more fatalistic than non-Muslims. The difference is nearly significant (significant if equal variances are assumed) in Bulgaria. In short, although certainly not as pronounced as some other dimensions, there is a tendency for Muslims to believe they have less control over their lives.

Table 6

Modernity

	Importance of God		Religiosity Scale		Secularism Scale		Fatalism vs Free Choice		Family Scale		Women and Work		Sex. Tolerance Scale	
	Mean	Std.Dev.	Mean	Std.Dev.	Mean	St.Dev.	Mean	St.Dev.	Mean	St.Dev.	Mean	St.Dev.	Mean	St.Dev.
ALBANIA														
Muslim	3.38	2.66	2.53	2.49	5.41	1.99	5.87	2.14	0.72	0.87	6.60	1.03	6.73	3.34
Orthodox	**3.98**	2.75	**3.47**	2.33	**6.07**	2.05	5.99	2.44	0.78	0.98	6.72	0.95	7.14	3.29
BULGARIA														
Muslim	3.59	2.83	1.88	2.18	5.06	2.16	5.64	2.76	0.54	0.75	6.32	1.17	8.71	5.48
Orthodox	**5.03**	2.80	**3.68**	2.45	**6.27**	2.05	6.21	2.57	**1.44**	1.21	6.50	1.33	**10.41**	6.07
MACEDONIA														
Muslim	1.43	1.19	0.60	0.97	4.96	2.02	5.29	3.06	1.77	1.09	6.45	1.28	4.95	2.94
Orthodox	**3.83**	2.87	**3.47**	1.94	**6.92**	2.19	**5.83**	2.69	**1.40**	1.19	6.48	1.16	**7.94**	5.42
BOSNIA														
Muslim	2.48	2.26	1.41	1.77	6.45	1.94	6.23	2.15	1.05	1.07	6.45	1.06	6.63	4.05
Orthodox	**3.68**	2.56	**3.34**	2.11	**6.86**	1.91	6.17	2.35	**1.48**	1.09	6.50	1.03	**7.60**	4.74
MONTENEGRO														
Muslim	4.34	3.53	3.45	2.51	6.66	2.12	5.75	2.34	1.14	0.99	6.21	1.14	6.85	4.22
Orthodox	4.61	2.86	3.78	2.13	6.48	2.10	5.91	2.36	1.10	1.19	6.36	1.03	6.80	4.60
NIGERIA														
Muslim	1.28	1.07	0.47	0.68	3.04	1.35	6.84	2.53	0.49	0.76	6.39	1.29	4.37	3.41
Protestant	**1.42**	1.26	**0.60**	0.73	**3.42**	1.65	**7.17**	2.35	**0.61**	0.83	**6.64**	1.16	**4.95**	4.12

Table 6
(Continued)

	Importance of God		Religiosity Scale		Secularism Scale		Fatalism vs Free Choice		Family Scale		Women and Work		Sex. Tolerance Scale	
	Mean	Std.Dev.	Mean	Std.Dev.	Mean	St.Dev.	Mean	St.Dev.	Mean	St.Dev.	Mean	St.Dev.	Mean	St.Dev.
TANZANIA														
Muslim	1.38	1.50	0.54	0.89	4.32	2.29	5.86	3.50	0.70	1.06	6.39	1.29	3.71	2.69
Roman Catholic	1.41	1.62	0.59	0.98	4.60	2.39	5.54	3.58	0.85	1.09	**6.66**	1.23	3.52	1.99
Protestant	1.22	0.96	0.47	0.75	4.54	2.39	6.15	3.63	0.63	0.79	6.56	1.22	3.75	2.42
UGANDA														
Muslim	1.50	1.33	0.76	1.06	4.28	1.71	6.80	2.43	1.24	1.12	5.89	0.95	5.02	3.25
Roman Catholic	1.50	1.32	0.80	1.02	4.54	1.90	6.70	2.38	**1.49**	1.26	6.01	1.16	5.21	3.82
Protestant	1.72	1.58	0.72	0.99	**4.81**	1.82	6.85	2.64	1.42	1.17	6.02	1.12	4.66	3.37
INDIA														
Muslim	na	na	1.52	1.59	6.75	2.45	4.77	2.69	0.94	1.25	5.64	1.20	5.78	5.36
Hindu	na	na	1.68	1.80	6.37	2.16	**5.66**	2.89	0.96	1.08	**5.93**	1.32	**9.81**	9.31

Marriage and family. Unlike some other variables, there is no reason to believe that Islam emphasizes family values more than other religions. Divorce has been possible and relatively easy in Islam from the very beginning. Adultery, especially for women, was punishable by death but it is one of the Ten Commandments after all. Islam's emphasis on having children is certainly not greater than that of the Catholic Church and Muslims have some more flexibility in birth control and abortion. Nevertheless, Muslims score significantly more conservatively (i.e. more emphasis on marriage and family) on family values scale in Bulgaria, Bosnia, and Nigeria. It is interesting to note that the difference between Muslims and Catholics in Uganda is also significant (for Protestants it is nearly significant). However, in Macedonia, the Orthodox population is found to possess more conservative family values compared to Muslims and the difference is significant. The findings about family and marriage values are not conclusive.

Female employment. The differences with respect to working women are significant only in Nigeria and India. In both cases, Muslims are less favorable to female employment. In the remaining six cases, without exception, Muslims have more conservative views on the subject but these do not attain statistical significance.

Sexual tolerance. As we already know, for distinguishing Islamic civilization from others, sexual tolerance is the criterion to watch for. The last column of comparisons in Table 6 in general conforms to our expectations. In five of our eight countries (Bulgaria, Macedonia, Bosnia, Nigeria and India) Muslims are significantly less tolerant then others (Orthodox, Protestant, and Hindu). In Albania, we observe the same difference but the significance level does not reach 5 percent. In Montenegro, the means for the sexual tolerance scale is roughly equal in the two groups (Islamic and Orthodox). In Uganda, Catholics are more and Protestants less tolerant than Muslims but neither difference is significant. We conclude that, even within the same society, Muslims are less tolerant in general on matters pertaining to "the eros."

d. Democratic Culture

Of the 45 comparisons reported in Table 7 on democratic values, only 15 are statistically significant. But more importantly, the direction of the differences are not predictable and display a somewhat erratic pattern. From these findings, it is certainly not possible — even in very general terms — to say that the Islamic culture is either less or more supportive of a democratic system of government. Thus, we find strong support for the conclusion that "the basic cultural fault line between the West and Islam does not concern democracy" (Inglehart and Norris 2002).

Our fourth and the last hypothesis predicted that in each country variance within a civilization should be smaller than total variance and also variance between civilizations. Once again ANOVA proves inappropriate to test this hypothesis because of highly inflated significance levels resulting from large sample sizes. Due to space limitations, it is not possible to examine the variances for all of our eight countries. Table 8 reports the within groups (Protestant and Muslim) and total standard deviations for Nigeria. Clearly, within a single country we cannot expect to find the dramatic differences observed at the global level. Nevertheless, the results in Table 8 are interesting. For the following variables, within Muslim standard deviations are smaller than total (including all religious groups in the country) and within Protestant standard deviations:

> Determination, perseverance in children
> Importance of God
> Religiosity scale
> Secularism scale
> Marriage and family scale
> Sexual tolerance scale
> Neighbor tolerance scale

Every single variable on this list, with the sole exception of the neighbor tolerance scale, conforms to expectations. I do not contend that results from a single country can be generalized but it is highly unlikely that the Nigerian results are just a coincidence. Islamic populations do have certain cultural characteristics.

Conclusion

After the events of September 11, Huntington's thesis on the clash of civilizations gained exceptional prominence. It has been lauded and attacked with equal fervor but almost always without empirical evidence. A complete formalization and testing of the theory is still to come but a recent article by Inglehart and Norris (2002) is the first time Huntington's theory is subjected to the test of data. Their conclusion is that the real difference between the Islamic world and the West has nothing to do with political values but rather with attitudes towards women and sex.

This paper starts out with four testable hypotheses derived from Huntington's thesis. It is noted that the first hypothesis is tested by Inglehart and Norris. A theoretical and comprehensive scheme is developed to obtain a framework with which cultures can be compared. The scheme has four basic dimensions: Protestant Ethic, Social Capital, Modernity and Democratic Culture. Huntington argued that, above all, it would be the last dimension on which Islamic societies would score miserably.

Table 7

Democratic Culture

	Tolerance Neighbor Tol. Scale		Support for Freedoms Choosing Free Speech		Political Participation Participation Scale		Problems of Democracy Tolerating Prob. Scale		Alternatives to Democracy Pref. for Alternatives Scale	
	Mean	Std.Dev.	Mean	Std.Dev.	Mean	St.Dev.	Mean	St.Dev.	Mean	St.Dev.
ALBANIA										
Muslim	3.73	1.65	0.25	0.43	4.96	1.50	8.95	2.03	8.63	1.49
Orthodox	3.83	1.59	0.27	0.45	4.86	1.33	9.09	2.05	8.82	1.46
BULGARIA										
Muslim	4.20	1.86	0.29	0.46	4.68	1.54	8.08	2.22	7.85	1.90
Orthodox	4.36	1.93	0.24	0.43	4.91	1.43	7.92	2.18	8.07	1.73
MACEDONIA										
Muslim	4.67	0.93	0.41	0.49	4.97	1.56	8.35	2.13	6.46	1.77
Orthodox	**4.41**	1.90	**0.21**	0.41	5.07	1.55	**7.41**	2.27	**6.99**	2.14
BOSNIA										
Muslim	4.22	1.42	0.22	0.42	4.60	1.31	8.61	1.96	8.18	1.77
Orthodox	**3.87**	2.11	0.28	0.45	4.71	1.41	**8.07**	1.93	8.31	1.49
MONTENEGRO										
Muslim	3.66	1.21	0.21	0.41	5.09	1.43	9.06	1.71	9.43	1.17
Orthodox	3.59	1.35	0.25	0.43	**5.46**	1.69	8.85	2.19	**8.61**	1.55
NIGERIA										
Muslim	2.37	1.06	0.31	0.46	4.97	1.57	6.98	2.17	7.45	2.26
Protestant	2.46	0.96	0.33	0.47	**4.82**	1.54	**7.92**	2.09	**8.01**	2.02

Table 7
(Continued)

	Tolerance Neighbor Tol. Scale		Support for Freedoms Choosing Free Speech		Political Participation Participation Scale		Problems of Democracy Tolerating Prob. Scale		Alternatives to Democracy Pref. for Alternatives Scale	
	Mean	Std.Dev.	Mean	Std.Dev.	Mean	St.Dev.	Mean	St.Dev.	Mean	St.Dev.
TANZANIA										
Muslim	4.23	1.08	0.17	0.38	5.54	1.15	8.31	2.64	9.98	1.81
Roman Catholic	4.27	1.19	0.15	0.36	5.47	1.14	8.49	2.24	10.22	1.68
Protestant	4.37	1.00	0.13	0.34	**5.27**	1.07	**8.97**	2.28	**10.39**	1.47
UGANDA										
Muslim	4.62	1.30	0.50	0.50	5.01	1.58	8.35	1.94	9.03	2.46
Roman Catholic	**4.93**	1.25	**0.41**	0.49	4.88	1.66	8.74	1.88	9.28	2.34
Protestant	4.82	1.27	0.46	0.50	5.16	1.66	8.61	1.94	8.95	2.31
INDIA										
Muslim	2.91	1.05	0.16	0.37	5.03	1.87	8.15	2.05	8.21	1.93
Hindu	2.91	1.32	0.18	0.38	4.83	1.77	**7.49**	1.85	**7.44**	1.95

Table 8

Consistency of Values: Results for Nigeria (Standard Deviations)

	Protestant	Muslim	Total
Protestant Ethic			
Hard work	0.39	0.42	0.40
Thrift	0.30	0.31	0.30
Determination	0.43	0.39	0.42
Social Capital			
Interpersonal trust	0.43	0.45	0.44
Respect for others	0.49	0.50	0.49
Signing petition	0.25	0.25	0.25
Modernization			
Religiosity			
Importance of God	1.26	1.07	1.20
Religiosity scale	0.73	0.68	0.75
Secularism			
Secularism scale	1.65	1.35	1.59
Efficacy			
Fatalism/free choice	2.35	2.53	2.41
Marriage and Family			
Family scale	0.83	0.76	0.81
Female employment			
Women and work scale	1.16	1.28	1.21
Sexual tolerance			
Sexual tolerance scale	4.12	3.41	3.90
Democratic Culture			
Tolerance			
Neighbor scale	0.96	1.06	1.52
Freedom			
Freedom scale	0.47	0.47	0.47
Participation			
Participation scale	1.54	1.57	1.56
Problems with Democracy			
Problems scale	2.09	2.17	2.16
Alternatives to Democracy			
Alternatives scale	2.02	2.26	2.12

An analysis of the variances within civilizations at the global level confirms Inglehart and Norris's thesis: if we try to classify civilizations according to political values we are not going to make much progress: the data tell us to look elsewhere.

With these clues in mind, we compared Islamic and non-Islamic populations in eight countries for which data are available. Global level correlations cannot be expected to be repeated at the national level. These are multi-religion societies and the nation-state is a powerful socializing agent. It is natural that some of the cultural differences that have their foundations in religion are ironed out to a great extent through schooling, mass media, etc. Nevertheless, by and large, our expectations were confirmed even at the level of the nation. Some cultural differences do continue to exist between Islamic populations and others within the boundaries of the same state.

The list of characteristics that would define the Islamic culture is very consistent. First and foremost, for Muslims their faith is important — more so, it seems, than those who belong to other religions. Our analyses provided strong evidence of this.

Another very significant characteristic of the Islamic culture is its outlook on women and sex. Islamic values are less supportive of gender equality and less tolerant of sexual liberalization. This finding was repeated enough times that we would be justified to regard it as more than tentative.

Of the three indicators of Protestant Ethic that were employed, two (hard work and thrift) turned out to be insignificant. However, determination and perseverance consistently appeared as values to which Muslims do not attach much importance.

Political culture and more specifically democratic culture variables failed to distinguish the Islamic from the Protestant, Catholic, Orthodox or Hindu worlds. These cultures are not related in any significant way to political tolerance, support of freedom, participation or the search for alternatives to the democratic system.

To sum up in one sentence: if one wishes to define Islamic civilization in the contemporary world, religiosity, sexual tolerance, perseverance and determination, and support of gender equality are the key concepts to look for. If these make up the yardstick, the answer to the title of this article then is: "yes, there is an Islamic civilization." But why is it inevitable that this should lead to a clash? That question will have to be tackled elsewhere.

References

ALMOND, G. AND VERBA, S.
1963   *The Civic Culture*. Princeton: Princeton University Press.
BOZEMAN, A.B.
1975   "Civilizations under Stress." *Virginia Quarterly Review* 51(winter): 1-18.
COLEMAN, J.S.
1990   *Foundations of Social Theory*. Cambridge: Harvard University Press.
DASGUPTA, P. AND SERAGELDIN, I., EDS.
2000   Social Capital: A Multifaceted Perspective. Washington, D.C.: The World
            Bank.
FUKUYAMA, F.
1995   *Trust: The Social Virtues and the Creation of Prosperity*. New York: Free Press.

HALMAN, L. AND PETTERSSON, T.
2002   "A Modified Model for the Cross-Cultural Measurement of Two Basic Value
        Orientations." Paper presented at the ISA Conference. Brisbane, Australia.
        July 8, 2002.
HALMAN, L. AND RIIS, O., EDS.
2002   *Religion in Secularizing Society: The European's Religion at the End of the 20th Century.*
        Leiden: Brill Academic Publishers.
HARRIS, M.
1974   *Cows, Pigs, Wars and Witches: The Riddles of Culture.* New York: Vintage Books.
HUNTINGTON, S.P.
1993   "The Clash of Civilizations?" *Foreign Affairs* 75(6): 28-34.
1998   *The Clash of Civilizations and the Remaking of the World Order.* London: Touchstone
        Books.
INGLEHART, R.
1990   *Culture Shift in Advanced Industrial Society.* Princeton: Princeton University Press.
1997   *Modernization and Postmodernization: Cultural, Economic and Political Change in 43
        Societies.* Princeton: Princeton University Press.
INGLEHART, R. AND BAKER, W.E.
2000   "Modernization, Cultural Change and the Persistence of Traditional Values."
        American Sociological Review 65(February): 19-51.
INKELES, A. AND SMITH, D.H.
1974   *Becoming Modern: Individual Change in Six Developing Countries.* Cambridge:
        Harvard University Press.
KLINGEMANN, H.D.
1999   "Mapping Political Support in the 1990's: A Global Analysis" in Norris, P.
        (ed.), *Critical Citizens: Global Support for Democratic Governance.* Oxford: Oxford
        University Press.
MISZTAL, B.A.
1996   *Trust in Modern Societies.* Cambridge: The Polity Press.
NORRIS, P. AND INGLEHART, R.
2002   "Islamic Culture and Democracy: Testing the Clash of Civilizations Thesis."
        Comparative Sociology 1.3: 235-263.
PUTNAM, R.D.
1993   *Making Democracy Work: Civic Traditions in Modern Italy.* Princeton: Princeton
        University Press.
ROTBERG, R.I., ED.
2001   *Patterns of Social Capital: Stability and Change in Historical Perspective.* Cambridge:
        Cambridge University Press.
TAYLOR, C.
2001   "Two Theories of Modernity" in Gaonkar, P.D. (ed.), *Alternative Modernities.*
        Durham and London: Duke University Press.
WARREN, M.E., ED.
1999   *Democracy and Trust.* Cambridge: Cambridge University Press.
WEBER, M.
1958   *The Protestant Ethic and the Spirit of Capitalism.* Trans. Talcott Parsons. New
        York: Charles Scribner's Sons.

The Worldviews of Islamic Publics: The Cases of Egypt, Iran, and Jordan

MANSOOR MOADDEL[*] AND TAQHI AZADARMAKI[**]

ABSTRACT

This paper analyzes the religious beliefs, religiosity, national identity, and attitudes toward Western culture, family, and gender relations of the publics of three Islamic countries. It is based on national representative surveys of 3000 Egyptians, 2532 Iranians, and 1222 Jordanians that were carried out in 2000-2001, as part of the World Values Surveys. We first discuss the views of the respondents concerning key indicators of religious beliefs, religiosity, identity, and attitudes toward Western culture. Then, we describe variations in such values as the ideal number of children, attitudes toward marriage and women, family ties, and trusts in major social institutions in these three countries. Next, we present age and educational differences in religious beliefs, trust in mosque, identity, trust in government, attitude toward women and gender relations. We conclude by pointing to the variation in the nature of the regime as an important determinant of the variations in the worldviews among the public in these three Islamic countries.

National surveys carried out for the first time in Egypt, Iran, and Jordan in 2000-2001 yield informative data about the worldviews and value

[*] Eastern Michigan University.

[**] University of Tehran.

[***] This study is supported by grants from the National Science Foundation (SES-0097282), the Ford Foundation and Bank of Sweden Tercentenary Foundation.

orientations of the public on a wide variety of issues related to family life, gender relations, religion, education, government, economy, cultural and national identity. Since the samples are based on random sampling procedures of 3000 Egyptians, 1222 Jordanians, and 2532 Iranians, the findings can be generalized to the adult population of these countries with a high level of validity. A preliminary analysis of the data suggests interesting answers to some of the basic questions on religiosity, national identity, nationalism, gender relation, democracy, and Muslim attitudes toward the West.

In this essay, we discuss some of the key findings of these surveys about the religious beliefs, religiosity, national identity, and attitudes toward Western culture, family, and gender relations of the Egyptian, the Jordanian, and the Iranian respondents. We first present and discuss the views of the respondents in terms of some of the key indicators of religious beliefs, religiosity, identity, and attitudes toward Western culture in Egypt, Jordan, and Iran. Then, we describe the variations in such values as the ideal number of children, attitudes toward marriage and women, family ties, and trusts in major social institutions in these three countries. Next, we present age and educational differences in religious beliefs, trust in mosque, identity, trust in government, attitude toward women and gender relations. Finally, we conclude by pointing to the variations in the nature of the regime as an important determinant of the variations in the worldviews among the public in these three Islamic countries.

Religiosity in Egypt, Jordan, and Iran

Religion plays a crucial role in the lives of the great majority of respondents in all three countries. Across the three societies, virtually everyone said that they belong to some religion: Among the Egyptians 94 percent said they were Muslims and 5.6 percent said they were Christians. These figures for Jordan were 95 percent and 5 percent, and for Iran 97 percent and 1 percent, respectively. In most Western countries, by contrast, a substantial share of the population professes no religious denomination. In all three Middle Eastern societies, at least 94 percent of all respondents said they believed in all of the following: God; life after death; the existence of a soul, heaven and hell.

Fully 97 percent of the Egyptians said that religion was very important in their lives — as did 96 percent of the Jordanians and 79 percent of the Iranians. This high level of importance accorded to religion does not correspond to a high level of spiritual needs. If we operationalize spiritual needs in terms of concerns about the meaning and purpose of life, which in sociology of religion is considered the most fundamental factor giving rise to religious beliefs, we find that there is a considerable gap between

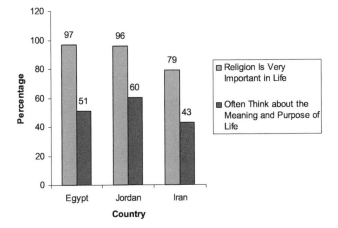

Figure 1. Religiosity versus Spirituality.

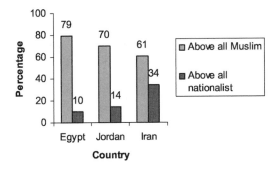

Figure 2. Identity: Religion versus Nationalism.

religiosity and spiritual needs in these three countries. The percentage of the respondents who reported that they **often** (as opposed to sometimes, rarely, or never) thought about the meaning and purpose of life is 51 for Egypt, 60 for Jordan, and 43 for Iran. However, the data from these three countries indicates that lower levels of spiritual needs correlate with lower levels of religiosity (Fig. 1).

One of the most impressive indications of the strength of religion in these three countries is that it appears to be a more important basis of identity than nationality — usually a very powerful factor. In all the three countries, people were more likely to describe themselves as Muslims, above all, than as Egyptians, Jordanians or Iranians. In Egypt, 79 percent of the respondents said that they were Muslims above all, while 10 percent said they were Egyptians above all. The comparable figure were 70 percent versus 14 percent in Jordan and 61 percent versus 34 percent in Iran (Fig. 2).

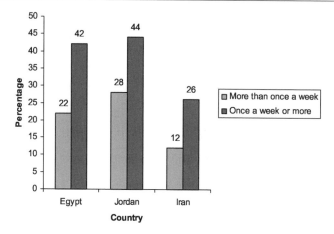

Figure 3.   Participation in Religious Services.

The significance of religion in life does not translate into a high participation in religious services, however. Only 22 percent of the Egyptians, 28 percent of the Jordanians, and 12 percent of the Iranians indicated that they attend religious services more than once a week (for those attending once a week or more, these figures were 42 percent for the Egyptians, 44 percent for the Jordanians, 26 percent for the Iranians) (Fig. 3).

The State's Cultural Orientation and the Religiosity of the Public
In conformity with the findings of comparative historical study of cultural movements in Islamic countries on how the state's cultural orientation tended to shape oppositional discourses, our comparative national surveys find an interesting correlation between the variations in people's religiosity and the variations in the nature of the regime. This finding also supports recent views in the sociology of religion regarding the connection between religiosity and religious pluralism.

In Iran, a theocracy dominates sociopolitical order. In Jordan, religious institutions, including the Muslim Brothers, have close ties to the state. In Egypt, on the other hand, the orthodox religious establishment is controlled by the state, while the popular Islamic fundamentalist movements have been in opposition to the ruling regime. Among the three countries, Egypt is the most and Iran is the least secular state. Since the ruling regimes are in varying degrees authoritarian, the cultural expressions of the opposition groups in these societies are often formulated in reaction to the cultural orientation of their regimes.

Thus, the Iranians, despite living under a theocratic regime, placed *less* emphasis on religion *more* emphasis on *nationalism* than did the Egyptians and Jordanians, as shown by the above indicators. Likewise, in terms of

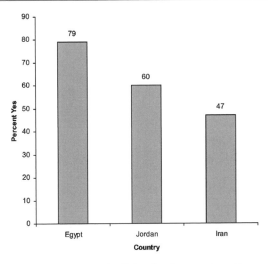

Figure 4.   Religious Authorities Sufficiently Respond to Country's Problems.

the significance of religion in life, spiritual needs, participation in religious services, the Iranians appeared to be less religious than the Egyptians or Jordanians.

Two other indicators also reflect this pattern. One is the respondents' attitudes toward the role of the religious institutions in responding to the country's problems, which appeared to be inversely related to the degree of secularism of the regime. In Egypt, where the regime appeared to be more secular than Jordan or Iran, 70 percent of the public indicated that religious authorities adequately responded to the country's social problems. This figure for Jordan is 60 percent, but for Iran is dropped to only 47 percent (Fig. 4).

The other indicator is the variations in attitudes toward Western culture: 64 percent of the Egyptians, 85 percent of the Jordanians, and 55 percent of the Iranians considered cultural invasion by the West among very important problems facing their country. It appears that the extent to which the public considered Western cultural invasion to be a very important problem is inversely related to the extent of the connection between the regime and Western countries. In Jordan, where the regime has been a close ally of the West, the US in particular, the highest percentage of the public expressed concerned about Western cultural invasion, while in Iran, where the regime is avowedly anti-West, the lowest percentage of the public expressed a similar concern (Fig. 5).

We conclude that the experience of having lived for more than two decades under an Islamic fundamentalist regime has had a counter-productive effect, making Iranians *less* religious and less concerned about Western cultural invasion instead of more so. We have also indications of

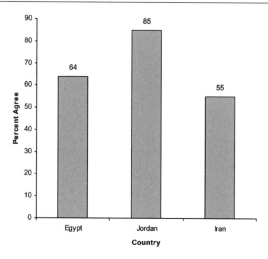

Figure 5. Western Cultural Invasion Is a Very Important Problem.

an intergenerational shift away from fundamentalist beliefs in contemporary Iran.

Nevertheless, it is clear that the publics of all three societies continue to attach great importance to religion. Across the three societies, a high percentage of the respondents (87 percent for the Egyptians, 84 percent for the Jordanians, and 71 percent for the Iranians) indicated that religious faith was an important trait for children to learn — ranking it higher than such other traits as independence, hard work, responsibility, imagination, tolerance, frugality, determination and perseverance, non-selfishness, and obedience. The only trait that surpassed religious faith (for Iran and Jordan) among important traits for children to learn was good manners (78 percent of the Egyptians, 95 percent of the Jordanians, 89 percent of the Iranians).

Egypt, Jordan, and Iran in a Broader Comparative Context
One would probably conclude, on the basis of this evidence, that the people of all three societies are very religious. But such a statement requires some yardstick of comparison: they are "very religious" compared with what? The World Values Surveys enable us to put this statement into cross-cultural perspective. One item here was replicated from the WVS, which had shown it to be a good indicator of the strength of religiosity. Our respondents were asked, independently of whether you attend religious services or not, would you say you are (1) a religious person, (2) not a religious person or (3) a convinced atheist. The responses in these three countries and in some representative societies surveyed in the WVS follow:

Percentage describing self as "A Religious Person"	
Egypt	**98**
Nigeria	94
Jordan	**85**
Iran	**82**
U.S.	82
India	80
Turkey	75
Spain	75
Mexico	65
Russia	64
Germany	50
Sweden	33
Japan	24

Egypt, Iran and Jordan all rank near the top of the scale, together with Nigeria where about half of the public is Islamic. In societies like Japan and Sweden, only a small minority of the public consider themselves religious. Nevertheless, we do not find a black and white difference between the three Islamic countries studied here and the rest of the world. By this measure, the U.S. public seems to be as religious as the Iranians. But the Americans are exceptional among industrialized societies; across the 65 societies included in the World Values Surveys, the Egyptians, Nigerians, Iranians, and Jordanians rank at the very top.

Although the American public is about as likely to describe themselves as religious as are Iranians, religion takes a more intense form and makes much more pervasive demands on society than it does in Western societies, where religious institutions are clearly differentiated from political, economic and other social institutions.

It should, however, be noted that religion does not uniformly affect all aspects of life in the three countries. For example, although between 68 percent and 70 percent of the respondents across the three countries considered it very important for a woman to wear a veil in public places, there is little support for such oppressive institution as polygamy, as between 71 percent and 82 percent of the respondents expressed their disagreement with a man having more than one wife. Thus despite the fact that both veiling and polygamy were supported in the Quran, the publics in all the three countries expressed opposing views about these two practices and rejected the aspect of their religious faith that appeared oppressive.

Value Variations in Egypt, Jordan, and Iran

Although Egypt, Jordan, and Iran cover only a small portion of the worlds total Muslim population, they display enough variations on some of basic values to dispel the suggestion that Muslims carry uniform religious and cultural outlooks. For example, the Egyptians, Jordanians, and Iranians expressed varied views on the ideal family size, gender role, and parent-child relationship.

The Ideal number of children
The number of children considered ideal in the family varies among the three countries. In Egypt, the highest percentage of the respondents preferred to have three children (44 percent), and 82 percent considered two or three children to be the ideal number. In Jordan, the highest percentage of the respondents preferred four children (44 percent), and 71 percent considered four or more to be the ideal number. In Iran, in contrast, the highest percentage preferred to have two children (58 percent), and 76 percent felt that two or less was the ideal number of children in the family (Fig. 6).

Attitudes toward Marriage
Like in other countries, a considerable value is attached to the institution of marriage in Egypt, Jordan, and Iran. There are, however, variations among the three Islamic countries on the importance of marriage. While there is a strong support for marriage among the Egyptians (95 percent),

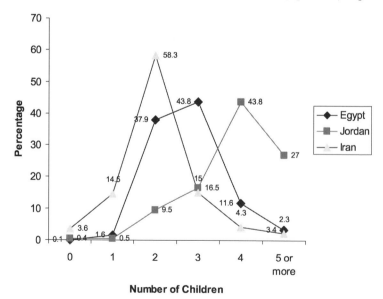

Figure 6.   Ideal Number of Children.

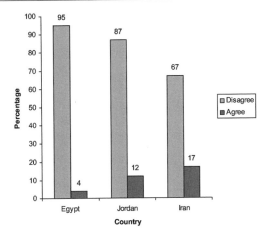

Figure 7.   Marriage Has Become an Outdated Institution.

Jordanians (87 percent), and Iranians (67 percent), a considerably higher percentage of the Iranians (17 percent) agreed with the statement that marriage has become an outdated institution. The corresponding figures for Egypt and Jordan are 4 percent and 12 percent respectively (Fig. 7).

The fact that 17 percent the Iranian respondents hold a view about marriage that is diametrically opposed to the official view of the Islamic Republic about the sanctity of marriage may indicate the existence of a small yet significant cultural trend in the country. We may speculate that this trend is either (1) a counter cultural and rebellious movement against the cultural policy of the ruling regime, (2) broadly reflects the changes in structure and function of the family in post revolutionary Iran, or (3) simply indicates dissatisfactions with the existing costly forms and practice of marriage in the country.

Children as a Source of Satisfaction for a Woman
Does a woman need to have children in order to feel satisfied? The Egyptians and Jordanians predominantly agreed, but the Iranians were not so sure. While in Egypt and Jordan 89 percent percent of the respondents agreed with the statement, in Iran this percentage is dropped to 45 percent. On the other hand, only 12 percent of the Egyptians and 9 percent of the Jordanians disagreed with the statement, while those who disagreed in Iran jumped up to 47 percent (Fig. 8). It should be noted that this finding corresponds to the variations in the ideal number of children among the respondents in the three countries, as was noted in figure 6. Since for more than 70 percent of the Iranians the ideal number of children was two or less, naturally a much higher percentage of the Iranians than of the Egyptians or Jordanians would be expected to disagree with the notion that children are the source of women's satisfaction.

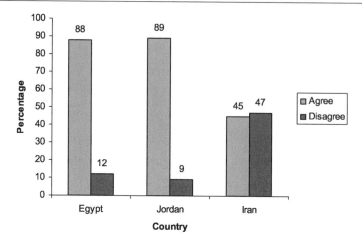

Figure 8.   Woman Needs to Have Children in order to Feel Satisfied.

Working Mother versus Mother-Child Intimacy
Are there perceived conflict between a woman's role as an employee outside the home and her role as a mother? Cross-national variations in this perception may explain the differences among nations in the persistence of the cultural biases against women's participation in the labor market. Naturally, where such a perception predominates and where larger families are strongly valued, people tend to be less sympathetic to women's work outside the home. If we take our cue from figures 6 and 8 about the variations in the ideal number of children and in attitudes toward marriage, then naturally a larger percentage of the Iranians (40 percent) than of the Egyptians (19 percent) or Jordanians (23 percent) would strongly agree with the statement that a working mother can develop intimate relationship with her children just like a non-working mother (Fig. 9).

Religiosity as an Ideal Trait for a Woman and Obedience for a Wife
The majority of the respondents across the three countries agreed that being religious was a very important trait for a woman. There were, however, variations among the Egyptians (94 percent), Jordanians (86 percent) and Iranians (69 percent). Nevertheless, emphasis on women's religiosity does not translate into public support for other religiously sanctioned traits for women that appeared oppressive. We have already noted that an overwhelming majority of the respondents disagreed with the institution of polygamy. Likewise, on the issue of wife obedience, only 47 percent of the Egyptians, 42 percent of the Jordanians, and 24 percent of the Iranians strongly agreed with the statement that a wife must always obey her husband (Fig. 10).

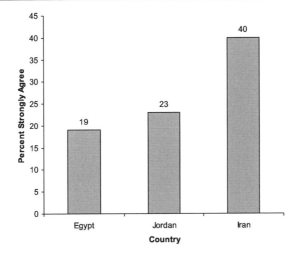

Figure 9. A Working Mother Can Develop Intimate Relationships With Her Children Just Like a Non-working Mother.

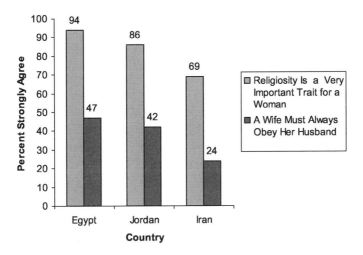

Figure 10. Woman's Religiousity and Wife Obedience.

The Significance of Family Ties

Family ties are very important in Egypt, Jordan, and Iran as 78 percent of the Egyptians, 86 percent of the Jordanians, and 53 percent of the Iranians strongly agreed with the statement that "making my parents proud of me is one of my main goals in life." Iran's contrast with Egypt and Jordan is consistent with its position on attitudes toward marriage in figure 7 and attitudes toward children as a source of woman's satisfaction in figure 8. This may reflect the reformist and anti-authoritarian movement that is currently unfolding in the country. If the youth value orientations on key

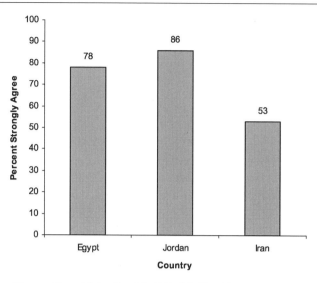

Figure 11.   Main Goal in Life Making Parents Proud.

issues are different from parents, then they tend to stress less on their parents' desires and more on their own (see the following section). A more detailed analysis of the data may, however, yield a more effective explanation of this contrast.

Attitude toward major institutions

How strong are supports for the regime and such other major social institutions as the mosque, the press, the TV in the three countries? One of the strongest indicators of system support is the level of trust in these institutions. The existence of a great trust in these institutions may be indicative of political and cultural stability, while low trust pointing to a potential for political instability and cultural change.

According to our data, people do not have a very great trust in their government in Egypt and Iran as expressed by only 16 percent of the Egyptians and 22 percent of the Iranians. This figure for Jordan is much higher as 50 percent of the Jordanians indicated having a very great trust in their government. By this standard, the Jordanian government enjoys the highest support, while the Egyptian government has the lowest (it should be noted that this question for Egypt was phrased in terms of trust in local government). The percentage of the public who expressed a very great trust in the press and TV is not high. Between 20 percent and 23 percent of the Egyptians and Jordanians said that they had a very great trust in the press and the TV. The figures for Iran were much lower as only 10 percent and 16 percent of the respondents expressed having a very great trust in the press and the TV, respectively, perhaps reflecting current Iranian

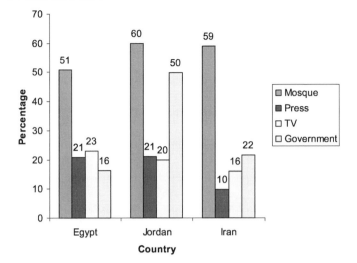

Figure 12.   Percentage Expressing Very Great Trust.

attitudes toward the official news. Across the three countries, however, the respondents appeared to place a much greater trust in the religious institution as indicated by between 51 percent and 60 percent of the respondents expressing that they had a high trust in mosque (Fig. 12).

Social Change and Variations in Attitudes in Terms of Age and Education

Are there differences in the public attitudes toward religion, politics and government, gender, and national identity in terms of age and education? What do these differences signify? Do they point to a move toward traditionalism or modernity? Do they reflect an intergenerational change or an aging effect?

Age-Education Differences in the importance of religion
Age and education have different effects on the importance the respondents have attached to religion in the three countries. In Egypt and Jordan, education and age did not appear to have any significant effect on the percentage of the people who expressed religion to be very important in their lives. In Iran, on the other hand, a higher percentage of older generation, and more so, people with lower level of education tended to express religion as being very important in their lives than younger and more educated respondents (Figs 13-14).

Age-Education Differences in Trust in Mosque
There are variations in age- and education differences in trust in mosque among the three countries. In Iran, there is a positive relationship between

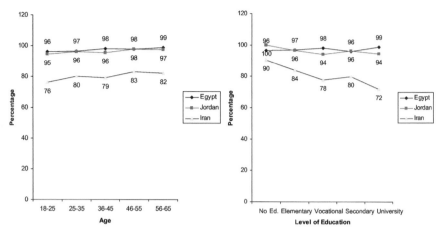

Figures 13, 14. Percentage Expressing Religion Is Very Important in Their Lives.

age and the percentage of those who expressed very great trust in mosque — a smaller percentage of the younger age groups expressed very great trust in mosque. In Egypt and Jordan, there is no distinctive pattern (Fig. 15).

In terms of education differences in trust in Mosque, there is an inverse relationship between the percentage of the people who expressed a very great trust in mosque and level of education. The contrast in trust in mosque between people with no education and those with university education is quite noticeable among the Jordanian and Iranian respondents (Fig. 16).

Age-Education Differences in National Identity
Does the inverse relationship between trust in Mosque and level of education across all the three countries mean that the more educated respondents tended to be less religious than the less educated? We may answer this question by analyzing age-education differences in religious versus national identity. In Egypt, the difference between the youngest and oldest age groups in the percentage of those who identified themselves as above all Muslim is not large (82 percent versus 79 percent in Fig. 17), and such a difference for those who identified themselves as Egyptians above all was nil (8 percent versus 8 percent in Fig. 18). For the Egyptians, however, religion is constituted a basis for identity much more extensively than for the Jordanians or Iranians. In Jordan, on the other hand, this difference is more paramount as the younger age group tended to be more religious (71 percent versus 60 percent) and less nationalistic (10 percent versus 22 percent). The findings on Egypt and Jordan, however, reflect the current tendency among the young toward Islamic activism. In Iran, in contrast,

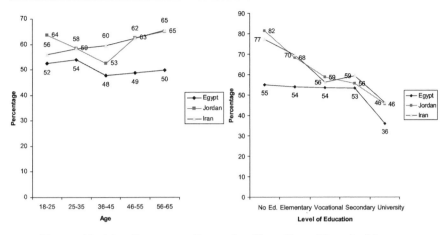

Figures 15, 16.   Percentage Expressing Very Great Trust in Mosque.

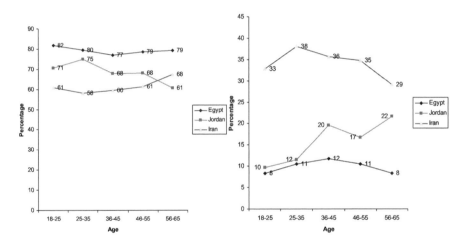

Figure 17. Percentage Expressing
Above All Muslim.

Figure 18. Percentage Expressing
Above All Nationalist.

the youngest age group tended to be less religious (61 percent versus 68 percent) and more nationalist (33 percent versus 29 percent) than the oldest age group (Figs 17-18).

A more dramatic contrast between Egypt and Jordan, on the one hand, and Iran, on the other, is in the effect of the level of education on individual identity. In Egypt, the level of education appeared to have a small inverse effect on both the percentage of the people who reported as being Muslim above all (from 80 percent among those with no education, to 82 percent among those with a university education: see Fig. 19) and of those who reported as being Egyptians above all (from 11 percent to 8 percent: see

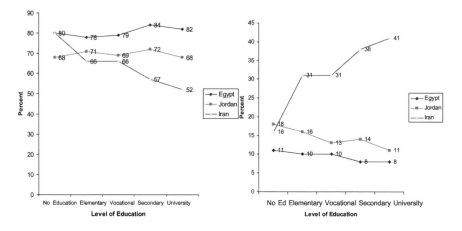

Figure 19. Percentage Expressing Above All Muslim.

Figure 20. Percentage Expressing Above All Nationalist.

Fig. 20). In Jordan, education appeared to have no significant effect on the percentage of the people who identified themselves as Muslim above all (see Fig. 19) and an inverse effect on those identified themselves as Jordanian above all (see Fig. 20). If, based on these figures, we try to extrapolate cultural trend in Egypt and Jordan, it would be a tendency toward Islamic activism on the part of more educated individuals. While these individuals may be critical of the mosque, as indicated by the decline in trust in mosques with the increase in education (see Fig. 16), these data do not provide any indication of a move toward secularism.

Iran shows a strikingly different pattern. The percentage who said that they were Muslim above all, was dramatically higher among people with the *lowest* level of education (see Fig. 19), and the percentage who said they were Iranian above all, was dramatically lower among those with the lowest level of education (see Fig. 20). This trend among the Iranians is very much in keeping with current student activism against the conservative religious establishment and toward a form of secularism.

Age-Education Differences in Trust in Government
The age differences in trust in government do not follow a pattern of either consistently increasing or declining in the three countries (Fig. 21). Educational differences in trust in government, however, display a distinct pattern. In all the three countries, the percentages of the people who expressed very great trust in government declined with the increase in the level of education. The rate of the decline from those with no education to those with university education is about the same in all the three countries

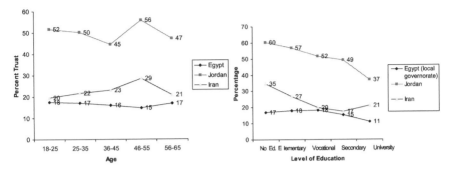

Figures 21, 22. Percentage Expressing Very Great Trust in Government.

(37/60 = .62 for Jordan, 21/35 = .60 for Iran, and 11/17 = .65 for Egypt) (Fig. 22).

Based on these findings, we would conclude that the more educated public in the three countries are critical of the government, but the form of their cultural expression is formulated in opposition to the state ideology. Since Egypt and Jordan are perceived as secular and pro-Western government, the opposition groups tended to use Islam as a language for their political protest. In Iran, on the other hand, since an anti-secular and fundamentalist regime is in power, secular and (Islamic) reformism has shaped the discourse of the opposition groups, particularly on the nation's campuses.

Age-Education Differences in Attitudes toward Women's Political Leadership
In the three countries, the percentage of the respondents who strongly agreed with the statement that men are better political leaders than women increases from the younger to older age groups. Age differences on this question are greatest among the Iranians, followed by the Egyptians, and then by the Jordanians (Fig. 23). Education has a negative effect on the percentage of the people who believed that men are better political leaders than women across all three countries (Fig. 24).

The Right of Women versus Men in the Job Market
Although a considerable majority of the Egyptian, Jordanian, and Iranian respondents favored men over women in a tight job market, the younger age groups displayed less gender bias than older age groups (Fig. 25). Likewise, a higher percentage of people with a lower level of education tended to agree with giving priority to men over women than those with a higher level of education (Fig. 26).

Relation of Authority between Husband and Wife
Compared to the issues of political leadership and job outside the home, age and education differences in the question of the wife's obedience to

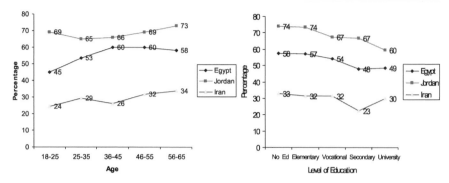

Figures 23, 24. Percentage Strongly Adreed that Men Are Better Political Leader than Women.

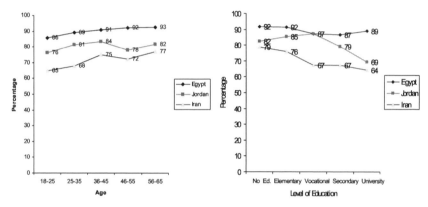

Figures 25, 26. The Percentage Who Agreed With When Job Is Scarce Priority Should Be Given to Men Over Women.

her husband are considerable. The differences in the percentage of those who strongly agreed with the statement that a wife must always obey her husband between the youngest and oldest age groups are 15 percent for Egypt, 18 percent for Jordan, and 24 percent for Iran (Fig. 27). Educational differences among the lowest and the highest education groups are even more sizeable and are 17 percent for Egypt, 35 percent for Jordan, and 31 percent for Iran (Fig. 28).

Age-Education Differences in Wearing the Veil
Both age and education have effects on the respondents attitudes toward the veil — younger and more educated individuals tended to stress less on the veil than older and less educated individuals in the three countries. These effects are, however, varied in different countries. In Egypt, the age and educational differences in the percentage of those who considered it very important for a woman to wear the veil in public between the highest and lowest groups are small. But in Jordan and Iran these differences are

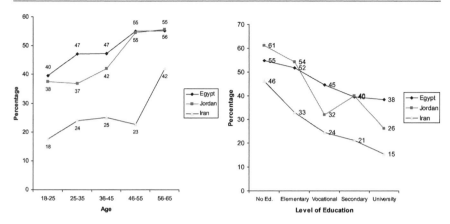

Figures 27, 28.   Percentage Who Strongly Agreed That Wife Must Always Obey Her Husband.

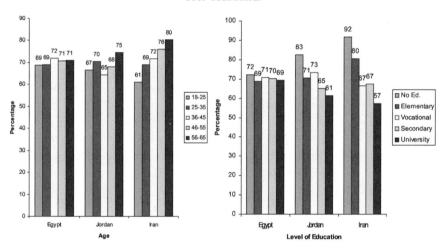

Figures 29, 30.   Percentage Who Considered It Very Important for a Woman to Wear the Veil in Public.

more marked (Figs 29 and 30). Education appeared to have a stronger effect than age on people's attitudes toward the veil. The differences in the percentage of those who considered it very important for a woman to wear the veil between the lowest and highest education groups are 22 percent for Jordan and 35 percent for Iran (Fig. 30).

Conclusions

We find several distinctive characteristics in the worldviews and value orientations of the publics of Egypt, Jordan, and Iran. We focused on such values as religious beliefs, religiosity, national identity, and attitude toward Western culture, gender relationship, marriage, ideal number of children, politics, and some of the major social institutions. Aspects of these views appeared to be by and large invariant across the three countries. These included basic religious beliefs such as belief in God, Heaven, Hell, life after death, and the existence of the soul. High percentages of the respondents in all three countries considered religion to be very important in their life.

But in other aspects of their worldviews, we find interesting cross-national variations. Egyptians and Jordanians appeared to be considerably more religious than Iranians in terms of such measures as participation in religious services and religion versus nationalism forming individual identity. Furthermore, the Jordanians appeared to be most concerned, followed by the Egyptians, and then the Iranians about Western cultural invasion. There were also variations in terms of the ideal number of children, and in terms of attitudes toward marriage, women and children, women and work, and women's religiosity, and the wife's obeying her husband. Although an in depth analysis of the data is necessary to make a more definitive conclusion, based on these measures we may tentative conclude that Iranians appeared to be less traditional (and more modern based on Western standards) than either Egyptians or Jordanians.

There are two dimensions of variations across these three countries. One is variation between and the other is variation within. The state's religiosity is an important dimension of variation between Egypt, Jordan, and Iran. Historical research has demonstrated that the state's cultural orientation and policies had determinate effects on the cultural trends in civil society. For example, the changes in the structure and cultural orientation of the state from parliamentary politics to Arab nationalism and socialism in Egypt and Syria (Kepel 1993, Moaddel 2002), from cultural conservatism to *revolution culturelle* and *revolution socialiste* in Algeria in the sixties through the seventies (Robert 1988), and from parliamentary politics of the forties and early fifties to bureaucratic intrusive state in the sixties and seventies in Iran (Akhavi 1980, Moaddel 1993) had considerable impact on the rise of Islamic fundamentalism in these countries. In all these cases, the cultural intervention of different forms of intrusive secular ideological state contributed to the politicization of religion and the rise of Islamic fundamentalism (Moaddel 2002, Esposito 2000). Our comparable survey data appeared to further corroborate these findings. In Iran, where the society has been dominated by a religious fundamentalist regime, the public appeared to be less religious, less anti-West, more secular, and more pro-modernist values than the public in either Egypt or Jordan, were the state is secular and decidedly pro-West.

The variations in worldviews within each of the three countries may be determined by a wide variety of the social attributes of the respondents such as their socioeconomic status, gender, age and education. Age and education may provide good indications of the direction of cultural change in society. Our analysis showed that while both of these variables had some effects on individual worldviews, education appeared to have a more noticeable effect than age. The effects of both of these variables were different across the three countries. In Iran, the younger and more educated respondents appeared to be more nationalistic, more secular, and less religious. In Egypt and Jordan such effects were not as pronounced and in some cases they were not noticeable. Furthermore, while the level of education was inversely related to trust in mosque and trust in government across the three countries, this pattern of relationships appeared to have different consequences in these countries. In Iran, it meant more secularism and less religiosity. In Egypt and Jordan, we may cautiously conclude that it meant more religious activism. This is because in these two countries, the level of education appeared to have a slight positive effect on religion rather than nationalism constituting individual identity. Across all the three countries, however, higher levels of education were linked with relatively favorable attitudes toward women.

References

AKHAVI, S.
1980   *Religion and Politics in Contemporary Iran.* Albany: State University of New York Press.

ESPOSITO, J.L.
2000   "Islam and Secularism in the Twenty-First Century," pp. 1-12 in *Islam and Secularism in the Middle East*, edited by Azzam Tamimi and John L. Esposito. New York: New York University Press.

KEPEL, G.
1965   *Muslim Extremism in Egypt: The Prophet and Pharaoh.* Los Angeles: University of California Press.

MOADDEL, M.
1993   *Class, Politics, and Ideology in the Iranian Revolution.* Columbia: Columbia University Press.

2002   *Jordanian Exceptionalism: An Analysis of State-Religion Relationship in Egypt, Iran, Jordan, and Syria.* New York: Palgrave.

ROBERTS, H.
1988   "Radical Islamism and the Dilemma of Algerian Nationalism: The Embattled Arians of Algiers'." *Third World Quarterly* 10, 2 (April): 556-589.

Gender Equality and Democracy

Ronald Inglehart, Pippa Norris and Christian Welzel

Abstract

Although democratic institutions existed long before gender equality, at this point in history, growing emphasis on gender equality is a central component of the process of democratization. Support for gender equality is not just a *consequence* of democratization. It is part of a broad cultural change that is transforming industrialized societies and bringing growing mass demands for increasingly democratic institutions. This article analyzes the role of changing mass attitudes in the spread of democratic institutions, using survey evidence from 70 societies containing 80 percent of the world's population. The evidence supports the conclusion that the process of modernization drives cultural change that encourage both the rise of women in public life, and the development of democratic institutions.

Introduction

Growing mass emphasis on gender equality is intimately linked with a broader process of cultural change that today is closely linked with democratization. In a sense the link between women's representation and democracy should be self-evident, since women account for over half the population of most societies: if this majority doesn't have full political rights, the society is not democratic. But for much of history, this proposition did not seem at all self-evident; until well into the 20th century, women did not even have the right to vote. Winning the vote meant overcoming traditional norms that varied from culture to culture but nearly always excluded women from politics. Thus, women attained suffrage by 1920 in most historically Protestant countries but not until after World War II in most Catholic ones, and still later in other cultural zones (IPU 1999). Even after being admitted to the electorate, women continued to be excluded from most political leadership roles until the last few decades, and they are still heavily underrepresented in parliaments and cabinets (UN 2000).

Democratic institutions existed long before gender equality, but today, this article argues, growing emphasis on gender equality is an important factor in the process of democratization. Furthermore, as we will demonstrate, support for gender equality is not just a *consequence* of democratization. It is part of a broad cultural change that is transforming many aspects of industrialized societies and supporting the spread of democratic institutions.

Part I of this article briefly reviews the relationship between culture and women's representation, and demonstrates the linkage between democratization and the proportion of women in parliaments in 65 societies worldwide. Part II examines the reasons for this relationship, including the role of changing values towards gender equality, the process of modernization and economic development, cultural legacies represented by religious values, and democratic political institutions. Part III demonstrates that growing support for gender equality in public life represents part of a broader shift towards expressive values, linked with the rise of postindustrial society. Part IV considers the implications of these findings, arguing that the process of modernization drives cultural change, which in turn leads to the rise of women in public life and the development of democratic institutions.

Cultural Barriers to Women's Representation

Many factors help shape the structure of opportunities for women's representation in elected office, including the institutional context and the resources that women and men bring to the pursuit of legislative careers (Rule 1987; Norris 1997; Karam 1998; Kenworthy and Malami 1999; Caul 1999; Reynolds 1999). In addition to these factors, traditional cultural attitudes have long been thought to present major barriers to women's representation in elected office, but previous studies have not present conclusive empirical evidence supporting this proposition. Theories of socialization have long emphasized the importance of the division of sex roles within a country — especially egalitarian attitudes towards women as political leaders (Sapiro 1983; Carroll 1994). Cultural explanations hypothesize that in traditional societies, women will be reluctant to run and, if they seek the office, will fail to attract sufficient support to win. Cultural attitudes may have a direct influence on whether women are prepared come forward as candidates for office (the supply-side of the equation), and the criteria used by gate-keepers when evaluating suitable candidates (the demand-side), as well as having an indirect influence upon the overall institutional context, such as the adoption of gender quotas in party recruitment processes (Lovenduski and Norris 1993; Norris 1997).

The cultural hypothesis provides a plausible explanation of why women in elected office have advanced much further in some democracies than others. For example, women attained leadership roles much earlier and much more extensively within the Nordic region than in such countries as France or Belgium, despite the fact that all of these countries are affluent European post-industrial welfare states, and established parliamentary democracies with similar proportional representation electoral systems (Karvonen and Selle 1995). Cultural differences also help explain why countries with a strict Islamic background — even the more affluent ones — consistently tend to fall toward the bottom of worldwide rankings of the percentage of women in parliament (Abu-Zayd 1998). Studies of post-industrial societies have found that the proportion of women in parliament is negatively associated with the historical prevalence of Catholicism, which seems to encourage more traditional attitudes towards women and the family than does a Protestant heritage (Rule 1987; Kenworthy and Malami 1999). But a broader comparison of 180 nation states by Reynolds (1999) found that on a worldwide scale, the greatest contrasts were between traditionally Christian countries (whether Protestant or Catholic) and all other religions including the Islamic, Buddhist, Confucian and Hindu faiths, all of which had lower proportions of women in legislative and Cabinet office. Consequently, cultural factors have been suspected to be an important determinant of women's entry into elected office, but previous studies have been unable to test this proposition against comparable survey evidence of attitudes towards women across a wide range of nations.

This article hypothesizes that the process of modernization leads to both democratization and a rise in the proportion of women in public life. It is well known that industrialization leads to occupational specialization, rising educational levels, and increasing levels of income. But economic development also brings unforeseen cultural changes that transform gender roles and make the emergence of democratic institutions increasingly likely. Determined elites can resist these changes, and a society's institutions and cultural traditions can facilitate or retard them, but in the long run, the underlying trend toward both gender equality and democratization becomes increasingly costly to resist. Evidence from more than 60 societies suggests that economic development propels societies in a roughly predictable direction, changing prevailing gender roles in virtually any society that industrializes.

One indication that gender equality goes with democracy is the fact that democratic societies usually have more women in parliament than undemocratic societies. Figure 1 shows the relationship between a society's

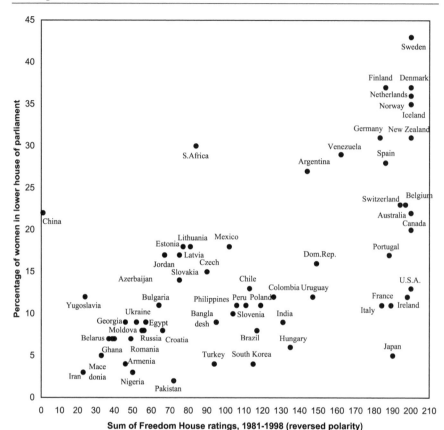

Figure 1. Percentage of women in lower house of parliament by Freedom House democracy ratings; r = .65, N = 66, p < .00.

level of civil rights and political liberties, and the percentage of women in the lower house of parliament.[1] This figure includes 65 societies containing 80 percent of the world's population.[2] Countries that rank high on civil rights and political liberties, have much higher proportions of women in

---

[1] The estimate of the percentage of women in the lower house of parliament in the latest election available is derived from the International Parliamentary Union, www.ipu.org/wmn-e/classif.htm.

[2] In order to be consistent with the survey-based analyses in this paper, the countries examined here are the ones included in the World Values Surveys. The World Values Surveys (WVS) measure people's basic values concerning politics, religion, economic life, gender roles, sexual norms and child-rearing. They have been carried out in 66 societies containing almost 80 percent of the world's population. In order to analyze social changes, they have conducted multiple waves, with a first wave in 1981-1982, a second one in 1990-1991, a third one in 1995-1997 and a fourth one being conducted in 1999-2001. For detailed information about these surveys, see the WVS web site at http://wvs.isr.umich.edu.

parliament than countries with low levels of freedom. A few authoritarian societies, such as China, have large numbers of women in parliament; while Japan, Ireland, France and the U.S. have high levels of democracy and relatively few women in parliament. But despite these exceptions, the overall relationship is strong, showing a .65 correlation. In democratic societies, women tend to be relatively well represented in parliament.

Explaining the Relationship between Gender Equality and Democratization

Why does gender equality in elected office tend to go with democracy? A key cultural change involves the belief that men make better political leaders than women. This view is still held by a majority of the world's population, but it seems to be fading rapidly in advanced industrial societies. Evidence from the World Values Surveys demonstrates that in less-prosperous countries such as India, China, Brazil, Pakistan, Nigeria or Egypt, from 50 to 90 percent of the public still believes that men make better political leaders than women (see Figure 2). But in advanced industrial societies, an overwhelming majority of the public rejects this idea. Furthermore, we find large generational differences in advanced industrial societies, where older citizens are relatively likely to believe that men make better political leaders than women, but younger citizens (especially younger women) overwhelmingly disagree. The long-standing belief that "men make better political leaders than women" is changing, as younger generations replace older ones.

This belief is not just a matter of lip service. It has important political consequences. As Figure 2 demonstrates, in countries where the public rejects the idea that men make better political leaders, relatively high proportions of women get elected to parliament. This relationship is substantially stronger than the one shown in Figure 1 (the correlation rises from .65 to .77). This suggests that cultural norms may have even more impact than democratic institutions, on the percentage of women in parliament. Moreover, although richer countries have higher proportions of women in parliament than poorer ones, this may be true mainly because economic development leads to cultural changes. Table 1 tests these claims, examining the relative impact of cultural factors, economic modernization and democratic institutions on the percentage of women in parliament.

Modernization seems to be an important factor. Rich countries generally have higher percentages of women in parliament than low-income countries. And since economic development is closely linked with erosion of the belief in male superiority, *and* with democratization, it might be argued that the findings in Figures 1 and 2 simply reflect the effects of economic growth: it transforms gender norms and brings democratization

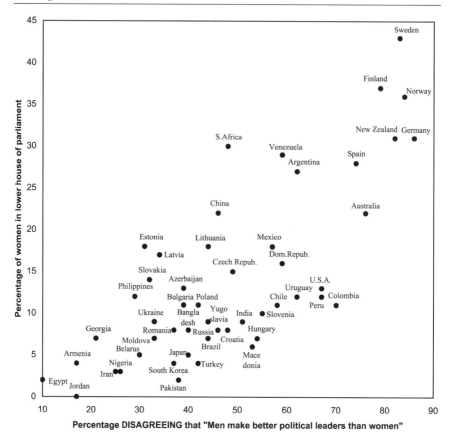

Figure 2. Percentage of women in lower house of parliament by percentage DISAGREEING that "men make better political leaders than women"; r = .77, N = 55, p < .00.

and rising numbers of women in parliament. Model 1 (see Table 1) confirms that richer countries (those with high per capita GDP) do, indeed, have higher percentages of women in parliament than poorer ones. But this factor explains only 30 percent of the variance, and when we add occupational structure and educational level to the equation (model 2), neither of them explains any additional variance.

A society's cultural heritage explains considerably more of the variance in the percentage of women in parliament than does economic development. Religion has been found to be one of the key factors predicting levels of female representation (Rule 1987; Reynolds 1999). We constructed a dummy variable that taps whether or not the society was historically dominated by Protestantism (regardless of how many practicing Protestants it has today); this variable alone explains 46 percent of the variance in the proportion of women in parliament — substantially more than all

Table 1

The impact of socioeconomic modernization factors, cultural factors and democratization on the percentage of women in the lower house of parliament (OLS regression)

	(Model 1)	(Model 2)	(Model 3)	(Model 4)	(Model 5)	(Model 6)
Modernization factors:						
Real GDP/capita, 1995	.862***	.445	–	–.403	–.386	–
($1,000s)	(.189)	(.302)		(.204)	(.244)	
% in service sector, 1990	–	.157	–	–	–	–
		(.154)				
% Educational enrollment	–	.125	–	–	–	–
		(.173)				
Cultural factors:						
Historically Protestant	–	–	16.91***	11.51***	11.49***	9.45***
(1 = Protestant, 0 = not)			(2.69)	(3.39)	(2.62)	(2.45)
Believe that men do NOT	–	–	–	18.48***	18.73***	14.56***
make better political leaders				(3.19)	(3.81)	(2.57)
Level of democracy:						
Freedom House scores,	–	–	–	–	.0037	–
(sum from 1981 to 1999)					(.030)	
Adjusted R2	.30	.29	.46	.70	.72	.70
N	46	43	46	46	46	46

Note: Table entries are unstandardized regression coefficients with standard errors in parentheses.

*p < .05; **p < .01; ***p < .001 (two-tailed tests).

Source: Attitudes toward gender equality are bassed on latest available survey from 1990-91 or 1995-97 World Values.

Surveys. Belief that men do NOT make better political leaders than women is scored: 1 = strongly agree that men make better leaders, 2 = agree, 3 = disagree, 4 = strongly disagree that men make better political leaders than women. Freedom House democracy scores are from successive editions of *Freedom in the World*.

Percentage of women in lower house of parliament is taken from International Parliamentary Union web site, www.ipu.org/wmn-e/classif.htm. Real GDP/capita purchasing power parity estimates in 1995 are from World Bank.

three modernization factors combined (model 3). Although most historically Protestant societies have higher proportions of women in parliament than historically Roman Catholic ones, Catholic societies generally rank above societies with Orthodox or Confucian or Islamic cultural traditions. Among the societies included in this study, in the median-ranking Protestant society 30 per cent of the members of the lower house were women; in the median Catholic society the figure was 13 percent; in the median Orthodox society it was 7 percent, in the median Confucian society it was 5 percent, and in the median Islamic society, only 3 percent of the members of the lower house were women. Even today, a society's cultural heritage has a surprisingly strong impact on gender equality. Societies with a Protestant heritage have about ten times as many women in parliament as do societies with an Islamic heritage.

Now let us examine the impact of another type of cultural variable: the extent to which the public believes that "men make better political leaders than women." While the religious traditions were established centuries ago, the norm of gender equality has become widespread only within recent decades. As Figure 2 demonstrates, this belief is strongly linked with the proportion of women in parliament. But does it have an impact of its own, or is it simply one more consequence of economic modernization, along with rising female representation in parliament? Model 4 analyzes the impact of belief in gender equality, while controlling for levels of economic development and religious heritage. The proportion of explained variance rises steeply when we add this variable, rising from .46 in model 3, to .70 in model 4. The extent to which the public endorses the norm of gender equality seems to have a major impact on the percentage of women in parliament. The society's religious tradition also has a powerful effect. Both a society's religion and the degree to which people believe that men make better political leaders, show statistically significant effects on the percentage of women in parliament — but GDP/capita does *not* show a significant relationship when we control for them. Economic development seems to be important mainly in so far as it is helps change prevailing gender norms: by itself, it has little direct effect.

Finally, let us examine the impact of democratic institutions on the percentage of women in parliament. Figure 1 showed that the two are closely linked — but why do they go together? Is it (1) because democratic institutions *themselves* tend to produce higher proportions of women in parliament, or (2) because of underlying cultural changes that bring rising female participation in parliament, and also favor democracy? Model 5 adds a measure of democracy to the analysis, the Freedom House ratings of political rights and civil liberties.[2] The results indicate that cultural factors drive the process. A society's level of democracy does not have a statistically significant effect on the percentage of women in parliament, when we control for them, and the proportion of explained variance rises only slightly (from .70 to .72) when we take democratic institutions into account. Cultural changes seem to bring rising female representation in parliament regardless of whether or not democratization occurs. Accordingly, when we drop the Freedom House democracy ratings and GDP/capita from the analysis (model 6), the two cultural variables by themselves explain fully 70 percent of the variance in the percentage

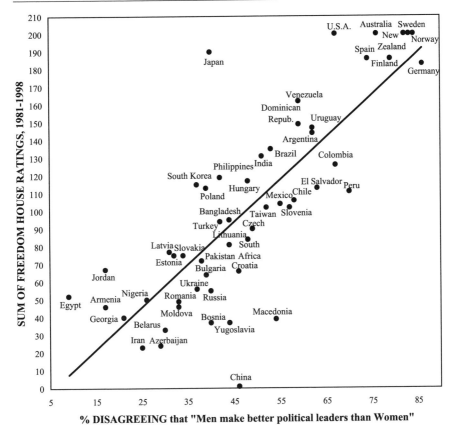

Figure 3.   Gender Equality and Democracy; r = .82, N = 55, p < .000.

of women in parliament. Democracies have relatively large numbers of women in parliament, but democracy itself does not seem to cause this phenomenon. Instead, both the trend toward democracy and the shift toward gender equality in parliament, seem to reflect underlying cultural changes that are transforming society.

Democratic institutions, by themselves, do not guarantee gender equality. But does it work the other way around: does rising emphasis on gender equality improve the chances that democratic institutions will emerge and flourish? The answer seems to be yes. Figure 3 shows the relationship between support for gender equality in politics, and the society's level of political rights and civil liberties. The relationship is remarkably strong. Although the linkage between the percentage of women in parliament and democracy (shown in Figure 1) was a substantial .65, the linkage between support for gender equality and democracy is much stronger (r = .82). In virtually every authoritarian society, a majority of the public believes that men make better political leaders than women; in virtually every stable democracy, a clear majority of the public rejects this belief (Japan be-ing the sole exception). This correlation could be taken to mean that 67 percent of the variance in levels of democracy reflects emphasis on gender equality. The reality is not that simple, of course. Growing support for gen-der equality is only one aspect of a broader process of cultural change that is transforming advanced industrial societies and contributing to democra-tization, as the multivariate analyses presented below will demonstrate. But attitudes toward gender equality are a central element — arguably, even, *the* most central element — of this cultural change. Let us examine this broader syndrome of cultural change, using data from the World Values Surveys.

Gender Equality and Cultural Change

In a factor analysis of national-level data from the 43 societies included in the 1990 World Values Survey, Inglehart (1997) found that two main dimensions accounted for over half of the cross-national variance in more than a score of variables tapping basic values in a wide range of domains ranging from politics to economic life and sexual behavior. Each of the two dimensions taps a major axis of cross-cultural variation involving many different basic values; the first dimension taps a dimension referred to as "Traditional vs. Secular-rational values," while the second one taps "Survival vs. Self-expression values."

These two dimensions of cross-cultural variation seem robust. When the 1990-1991 factor analysis was replicated with the data from the 1995-1998 surveys, the same two dimensions of cross-cultural variation emerged from as from the earlier surveys — even though the new analysis was based on surveys that covered 23 additional countries that were not included in the earlier surveys (Inglehart and Baker 2000). Inglehart and Baker (2000) provide full details on how these dimensions were measured, together with factor analyses at both the individual level and the national level, demonstrating that the same dimensional structure emerges at both levels.

The Traditional/Secular-rational values dimension reflects the contrast between societies in which religion is very important and those in which it is not. A wide range of other orientations are closely linked with this dimension. Societies near the traditional pole emphasize the importance of parent-child ties and deference to authority, along with absolute standards and traditional family values, and reject divorce, abortion, euthanasia, and suicide. These societies have high levels of national pride, and a nationalistic outlook. Societies with secular-rational values have the opposite preferences on all of these topics.

Figure 4 shows where each of 70 societies, containing most of the world's population, is located on these two dimensions, providing a cultural

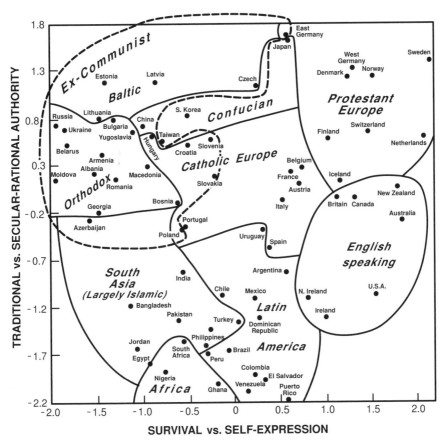

Figure 4. Locations of 70 Societies on two dimensions of cross-cultural variation. The scales on each axis indicate the country's factor scores on the given dimension.

Source: The data for the following 59 societies are from the 1995-1998 World values Survey: US, Australia, New Zealand, China, Japan, Taiwan, South Korea, Turkey, Bangladesh, India, Pakistan, Iran, Jordan, Egypt, the Philippines, Albania, Armenia, Azerbaijan, Belarus, Bosnia, Bulgaria, Croatia, Czech Republic, Estonia, Finland, Georgia, Great Britain, East Germany, West Germany, Hungary, Latvia, Lithuania, Macedonia, Moldova, Norway, Poland, Romania, Russia, Slovakia, Slovenia, Spain, Sweden, Switzerland, Ukraine, Yugoslavia, Ghana, Nigeria, South Africa, Argentina, Brazil, Chile, Colombia, Dominican Republic, El Salvador, Mexico, Peru, Puerto Roco, Uruguay and Venezuela. Canadian data are from the 1990 World Values Survey; data for Austria, Belgium, Denmark, France, Iceland, Ireland, Northern Ireland, Italy, Netherlands, and Portugal are from the 1990 European Values Survey. Data for Ghana, Egypt, Jordan and Iran are from small pilot surveys; position of Pakistan is estimated from incomplete data.

map of the world.[3] We find large and pervasive differences between the worldviews of people in rich and poor societies; their basic values and beliefs differ on scores of key variables, in a coherent pattern. Richer societies tend to be high on both of these two dimensions, while low-income societies tend to rank low on both dimensions. Does this mean that economic development brings predictable changes in prevailing values? The evidence suggests that it does: time series evidence shows that with economic development, societies tend to move from the lower left of Figure 4, toward the upper right — from the values prevailing in low-income societies, toward the values prevailing in high-income societies (Inglehart and Baker 2000). Subsequent analyses revealed that the first dimension is linked with the transition from agrarian society to industrial society: societies with secular-rational values tend to have a low percentage of their work force in the agricultural sector ($r = -.49$) and a high percentage of industrial workers ($r = .65$). The survival/self-expression dimension, on the other hand, is linked with the transition from industrial society to a service society or knowledge society, showing a .72 correlation with the percentage of the labor force in the *service* sector.

But economic differences are not the whole story. Specific religious traditions seem to have an enduring impact on the contemporary value systems of seventy societies, as Weber, Huntington and others have argued. The historically Protestant countries of Northern Europe form a distinctive cluster, reflecting the fact that their publics have relatively similar values on political, religious and economic questions, and also concerning gender roles, child-rearing and sexual behavior. The historically Roman Catholic European countries also have relatively similar values, forming another cluster — as do the publics of all eleven Latin American societies. The English-speaking countries constitute still another cluster of culturally-similar societies, as do the three African societies. Similarly, the publics

---

[3] The indicator of democracy used in this figure is based on the sum of the Freedom House scores from 1981 to 1998, in order to reflect *stable* democracy, and not just the momentary surge or decline that may occur from one year to the next. These scores are given reversed polarity, so that high scores indicate high levels of democracy. The data in this figure are based on the latest available survey for each society. It should be noted that female representation is one of the many criteria used by Freedom House when establishing their measures of political rights and civil liberties. To avoid dropping an entire society from our analysis when one of these variables is not available, the nation-level aggregate dataset sometimes uses results from another survey in the same country. Data for Egypt, Ghana, Iran and Jordan are from small pilot surveys, and these estimates cannot be considered reliable. Because African and Islamic societies are of great theoretical interest here, but these societies are seriously underrepresented in the World Values Survey, we examine these data nevertheless; we suspect that these results are at least in the right ball park. The data from these surveys are available from the ICPSR survey data archive.

of the four Confucian-influenced societies show relatively similar basic values and beliefs, despite large differences in their levels of economic development. And the ex-communist societies also form a cluster (with the historically Orthodox ones falling nearer the "Survival" pole of the horizontal dimension, and the historically Catholic ones falling closer to the center).

Societies that experience economic development tend to move from the lower left toward the upper right of the map. But cultural change is path dependent. The fact that a society was historically Protestant or Orthodox or Islamic or Confucian gives rise to cultural zones with distinctive value systems that persist when one controls for the effects of economic development (Inglehart and Baker 2000). A society's culture reflects its entire historical heritage, including religious traditions, colonial ties, the experience of communist rule and its level of economic development.

For this article, we replicated Inglehart and Baker's factor analysis, and then identified the attitudes that are closely correlated with the survival/self-expression dimension. The results demonstrate the central role that gender equality plays in the syndrome of beliefs and values tapped by the survival/self-expression dimension. Table 2 shows the wide range of beliefs and values that are strongly correlated with the survival/self-expression dimension. A central component involves the polarization between Materialist and Postmaterialist values. These values reflect an intergenerational shift from emphasis on economic and physical security, toward increasing emphasis on self-expression, subjective well-being and quality of life concerns (Inglehart 1990, 1997). Postmaterialist values emerge among birth cohorts that grew up under conditions that enable one to take survival for granted. During the past 25 years, these values have become increasingly widespread throughout advanced industrial societies, but they are only one component of a much broader dimension of cultural change.

Societies that rank high on survival values tend to emphasize Materialist values, show relatively low levels of subjective well-being and report relatively poor health, are relatively intolerant toward outgroups, low on interpersonal trust, and they emphasize hard work, rather than imagination or tolerance, as important things to teach a child. Societies high on self-expression values tend to have the opposite preferences on all of these topics. Environmental protection issues are also closely linked with this dimension. Those who emphasize survival values have not engaged in recycling, have not attended environmentalist meetings or supported environmental protection in other ways; but they favor more emphasis on developing technology and are confident that scientific discoveries will

Table 2

Orientations linked with Survival vs. Self-expression Values

Item	Correlation
SURVIVAL VALUES emphasize the following:	
R. gives priority to economic and physical security over self expression and quality of life [Materialist/Postmaterialist Values]	.87
Men make better political leaders than women	*.86*
R. is not highly satisfied with life	.84
A woman has to have children to be fulfilled	*.83*
R. rejects foreigners, homosexuals and people with AIDS as neighbors	.81
R. has not and would not sign a petition	.80
R. is not very happy	.79
R. favors more emphasis on the development of technology	.78
Homosexuality is never justifiable	.78
R. has not recycled something to protect the environment	.76
R. has not attended a meeting or signed a petition to protect the environment	.75
A good income and safe job are more important than a feeling of accomplishment and working with people you like	.74
R. does not rate own health as very good	.73
A child needs a home with both a father and a mother in order to grow up happily	*.73*
When jobs are scarce, a man has more right to a job than a women	*.69*
A university education is more important for a boy than for a girl	*.67*
Government should ensure that everyone is provided for	.69
Hard work is one of the most important things to teach a child	.65
Imagination is not of the most important things to teach a child	.62
Tolerance is not of the most important things to teach a child	.62
Leisure is not very important in life	.61
Scientific discoveries will help, rather than harm, humanity	.60
Friends are not very important in life	.56
You have to be very careful about trusting people	.56
R. has not and would not join a boycott	.56
R. is relatively favorable to state ownership of business and industry	.54
SELF-EXPRESSION VALUES take opposite position on all of above	

The original polarities vary; the above statements show how each item relates to this values index.

Source: 1990 and 1996 World Values Surveys.

help, rather than hurt, humanity. Those with self-expression values tend to have the opposite characteristics.

These are important issues. But arguably, the most important social change of the past few decades has been the revolution in gender roles that has transformed the lives of a majority of the population throughout advanced industrial society. Since the dawn of recorded history, women have been narrowly restricted to the roles of wife and mother, with few other options. In recent decades, this has changed dramatically. Several of the items in Table 2 (shown in bold face type) involve the role of women: the survival/self-expression dimension reflects mass polarization over such questions as whether "A woman has to have children to be fulfilled;" or whether "When jobs are scarce, men have more right to a job than women;" or whether "A university education is more important for a boy than a girl." But one item taps this dimension particularly well: the question whether "Men make better political leaders than women."

Responses to this question are very strongly correlated with the survival/self-expression dimension — indeed, they are almost as strongly correlated with it as is the Materialist/Postmaterialist values battery. This is remarkable, because Materialist/Postmaterialist values are measured by a multi-item battery that was explicitly designed to tap intergenerational value change and is one of the items used in the factor analyses that define this dimension. The question about whether men make better political leaders than women, on the other hand, is a single item that was not included in the first two waves of the World Values Surveys, and consequently was not used in the analyses that define this dimension. It nevertheless taps the survival/self-expression almost as well as does the Materialist/Postmaterialist values battery, and better than any of the other variables included in the World Values Survey. To put gender equality of the same footing as the other values, we reran Inglehart and Baker's (2000) societal-level factor analysis, replicating it in every detail but one: we added the question, "Do men make better political leaders than women?" The resulting analysis produced essentially the same factor structure as that reported in their article, with one difference: the question about gender roles now shows the highest loading on the Survival/self-expression dimension (a loading of .91, slightly *higher* than that of the Materialist/Postmaterialist index).

Inglehart et al. seem to have underestimated the importance of changing gender roles when they set out to measure the cultural changes linked with the emergence of post-industrial society. During the past few decades, these changes have transformed the entire way of life for over half the world's population. Throughout history, women virtually everywhere have had narrowly limited options in life. Today, increasingly, almost any career and almost any life style is opening up to them. These cultural changes have been important for men, but the transformation in the lives of women is far more dramatic, moving them from narrow subordination toward full equality. A revolutionary change is taking place in women's education, career opportunities, fertility rates, sexual behavior and worldviews. With this in mind, it is not surprising to find that that gender issues constitute such a central component — arguably, *the* most central component — of value change in post-industrial societies.

Gender Equality and Democracy

These same cultural changes seem to be closely linked with the rapid spread of democratic institutions that has occurred in the last two decades. The syndrome of survival/self-expression values shown in Table 2 reflects a set of coherent changes away from absolute social norms, toward increasing tolerance, trust, participatory orientations and self-expressive values. The shift from Materialist toward Postmaterialist values is a move from emphasizing economic and physical security as one's top priorities, toward increasing emphasis on freedom of expression and a more participatory role in society and politics. The syndrome reflects an increasingly activist role: societies that rank high on self-expression values also show much higher rates of participation in petitions, environmental activities, boycotts. Although relatively passive forms of political participation such as voting have stagnated, time series data show that these newer forms of behavior (which used to be called "unconventional political participation" [Barnes, Kaase et al. 1979]) have become increasingly widespread — so much so, that they are now a part of the standard political repertoire in advanced industrial societies. Emphasis on gender equality is linked with a broader shift toward increasing tolerance of outgroups, including foreigners, gays and lesbians. The shift from survival values to self-expression values also includes a shift in child-rearing values: from emphasis on hard work toward increasing emphasis on imagination and tolerance as important values to teach a child. And it goes with a rising sense of subjective well-being that is conducive to an atmosphere of tolerance, trust and political moderation. Finally, societies that rank high on self-expression values also tend to rank high on interpersonal trust. This produces a culture of trust and tolerance, in which people place a relatively high value on individual freedom and self-expression, and have activist political orientations. These are precisely the attributes that the political culture literature defines as crucial to democracy.

Is this cultural syndrome of self-expression values actually linked with the presence of high levels of democracy? As Figure 5 indicates, the answer is yes — and the relationship is astonishingly strong. A society's position on the survival/self-expression index is very strongly correlated with its level of democracy, as indicated by its scores on the Freedom House ratings of political rights and civil liberties, from 1981 through 1998. This relationship is remarkably powerful and it is clearly not a methodological artifact or an intra-cranial correlation, since the two variables are measured at different levels and come from different sources.

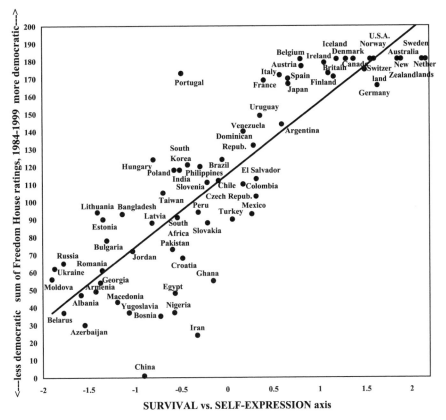

Figure 5.   Self-expression values and democratic institutions; r = .88, N = 67, p < .000.

Virtually all of the societies that rank high on survival/self-expression values are stable democracies. Virtually all of the societies that rank low on this dimension have authoritarian governments. The correlation of .88 between survival/self-expression values and democracy is higher than any of the correlations we have seen so far — higher even than the .82 linkage between support for gender equality and democracy shown in Figure 3. Gender issues constitute a central component of the cultural changes underlying this dimension, but the broader cultural dimension as a whole, involving emphasis on self-expression, tolerance of outgroups, participatory orientations, subjective well-being, health and interpersonal trust, as well as gender equality, is even more powerfully linked with democratization. The .88 correlation underlying Figure 5 is significant at a very high level, and probably reflects a causal linkage. But what is causing what?

One interpretation would be that democratic institutions give rise to the self-expression values that are so closely linked with them. In other words, democracy makes people healthy, happy, non-sexist, tolerant and trusting, and instills Postmaterialist values. This interpretation is appealing and if it were true, it would provide a powerful argument for democracy, implying that we have a quick fix for most of the world's problems: adopt democratic institutions and live happily ever after.

Unfortunately, the experience of the Soviet Union's successor states doesn't support this interpretation. Since their dramatic move toward democracy in 1991, they have not become healthier, happier, more trusting, more tolerant or more Postmaterialist: most of them have moved in exactly the opposite direction. The fact that their people are living in economic and physical insecurity, seems to have more impact than the fact that their leaders are chosen by free elections.

Democratic institutions do not automatically produce a culture that emphasizes self-expression values. Instead, it seems that economic development gradually leads to social and cultural changes that make democratic institutions more likely to survive and flourish. That would help explain why mass democracy did not emerge until a relatively recent point in history, and why, even now, it is most likely to be found in economically more developed countries — in particular, those that emphasize self-expression values over survival values.

Table 3 examines the factors linked with the emergence and survival of democracy. We hypothesize that economic development tends to bring a gradual shift from survival to self-expression values, and these values in turn are conducive to democracy. An extensive literature argues that economic development is conducive to democracy, and empirical research has demonstrated repeatedly that richer societies and "post industrial" societies (those with a relatively large percentage of the work force in the service sector) are likelier to have democratic institutions than poorer, largely agrarian or industrial, societies (Lipset 1959, etc.). Moreover, there is strong evidence that the causal connection works primarily from economics to politics: although economic development leads to democracy, democracy is *not* necessarily conducive to economic development (Burkhardt and Lewis-Beck 1994; Przeworski and Limogi 1993). Model 1 is consistent with this interpretation: relatively high levels of real per capita GDP have a positive and statistically significant impact on a society's level of democracy, as indicated by the Freedom House scores on civil liberties and political rights. But cultural factors also seem to play significant roles, even controlling for the effects of modernization. Societies that rank high on self-expression values are significantly more likely to show high levels of political rights and civil liberties than societies that emphasize survival values. An Orthodox religious tradition shows a significant (negative) impact on the level of democracy, controlling for the other variables. But the proportion of

Table 3

The impact of socioeconomic modernization factors, cultural factors and the percentage of women in parliament on level of democracy, as indicated by sum of Freedom House scores, 1981-1999 (OLS regression)

	(Model 1)	(Model 2)	(Model 3)	(Model 4)	(Model 5)
Modernization factors:					
Real GDP/capita, 1980	7.26***	7.65***	4.90*	6.64***	–
($1,000s)	(2.03)	(2.01)	(2.06)	(1.58)	
% in service sector, 1980	.819	.715	.846	–	–
	(.589)	(.584)	(.651)		
Cultural factors:					
Historically Protestant	−29.061	−26.03	–	–	–
(1 = Protestant, 0 = not)	(15.77)	(14.98)			
Historically Orthodox	−40.99*	−47.95**	–	–	–
(1 = Orthodox, 0 = not)	(18.25)	(16.80)			
Survival/self-expression	21.36*	22.07*	28.57***	38.97***	60.02***
Values	(10.17)	(9.98)	(8.05)	(4.98)	(5.41)
Women in Parliament:					
% women in lower house	.202	–	–	–	–
	(.608)				
Adjusted R2	.77	.78	.72	.69	.64
N	46	49	49	52	52

Note: Table entries are unstandardized regression coefficients with standard errors in parentheses.
*p < .05; **p < .01; ***p < .001 (two-tailed tests).
Source: Values from earliest available survey from World Values Surveys (mean year = 1988).
Percentage of women in lower house of parliament is taken from International Parliamentary Union web site, www.ipu.org/wmn-e/classif.htm.
Real GDP/capita purchasing power parity estimates in 1980 are from Penn World tables.

women in parliament does not show a significant impact on the level of freedom. Although democracies tend to have relatively high percentages of women in parliament, both democracy and gender equality are linked with the broad underlying cultural changes tapped by the survival/self-expression dimension: the proportion of women in parliament is not a direct cause of democracy. Accordingly, when we drop this variable (Model 2), the remaining factors still explain fully 78 percent of the variance in levels of democracy.

A society's traditional religious heritage seems to influence its level of democracy, but these religious traditions were established long ago. We believe their influence today largely reflects the extent to which they help shape a society's position on the survival/self-expression dimension.

Accordingly, Model 3, which drops the Protestant and Orthodox dummy variables, still explains fully 72 percent of the variance in levels of democracy. Moreover, in keeping with our interpretation, the significance level of survival/self-expression values rises sharply. This result suggests that a society's religious tradition has some impact on its level of democracy even today, but that the direct effect is relatively modest. The percentage of the work force in the service sector does not show a statistically significant effect, and Model 4 drops it from the regression. The percentage of explained variance drops slightly, indicating that this variable does play a role, although a relatively modest one. The society's level of real per capita GDP and it position on the survival/self-expression dimension both show strongly significant effects in Model 4, accounting for 69 percent of the variance in levels of freedom.

Theoretically, economic development is the key driving force behind democratization, but its impact is felt mainly in so far as it leads to a shift from survival to self-expression values. Accordingly, Model 5 drops GDP/capita from the regression equation — and a society's position on the survival/self-expression continuum by itself still explains fully 64 percent of the variance in levels of democracy. Democratization seems to be a multi-stage process in which the shift from survival to self-expression values plays the central role, but a society's religious heritage, the structure of its work force and its level of economic development all have some direct impact.

Survival/self-expression values are strongly correlated with a society's level of development, as Figure 5 demonstrates. And the multivariate analysis just performed suggests that the shift from survival to self-expression values has a significant causal impact on democracy, one that persists when we control for economic modernization and cultural heritage. But we still need to consider the question, is culture causing democracy, or does democracy transform culture? The relationship could, conceivably, work in both directions, but according to our theory the main effect is one that moves from (1) economic development to (2) culture, to (3) political institutions, with economic development bringing cultural changes that are conducive to democracy. In order to test this hypothesis, we carried out another set of regression analyses — this time, using survival/self-expression values as the dependent variable. The results in Table 3 indicate that self-expression values are conducive to democracy. The analyses in Table 4 address the question: to what extent does it work the other way around? To what degree are democratic institutions conducive to self-expression values?

Model 1 analyzes the impact of economic development and cultural heritage on the society's level of self-expression values — but it also includes the society's level of democracy as a predictor. The five independent

Table 4

The impact of socioeconomic modernization factors, cultural factors and level of democracy on Survival/Self-expression values (OLS regression)

	(Model 1)	(Model 2)	(Model 3)
Modernization factors:			
Real GDP/capita, 1980	.052	.135**	.076***
($1,000s)	(.032)	(.020)	(.027)
% in service sector, 1980	.004	–	–
	(.008)		
Cultural factors:			
Historically Protestant	.653**	.575**	.537**
(1 = Protestant, 0 = not)	(.180)	(.178)	(.187)
Historically Orthodox	−1.07***	−1.09***	−1.50***
(1 = Orthodox, 0 = not)	(.236)	(.228)	(.188)
Level of democracy:			
Sum of Freedom House	.006**	.005**	–
Scores, 1981-1999	(.002)	(.002)	
Adjusted R2	.86	.86	.83
N	49	52	53

Note: Table entries are unstandardized regression coefficients with standard errors in parentheses.
* $p < .05$; ** $p < .01$; *** $p < .001$ (two-tailed tests).
Source: Dependent variable is based on the latest available survey from 1990-91 or 1995-97 World Values Surveys.
Real GDP/capita purchasing power parity estimates are from Penn-World tables.

variables included in this model explain fully 86 percent of the cross-national variation in survival/self-expression values, and all but one of them show effects that are statistically significant, or nearly so. The percentage of the work force in the service sector shows weak effects, so it is dropped from Model 2, which still accounts for 86 percent of the variance — with all four predictors now showing statistically significant effects.

There is no question that the two religious indicators are historically and causally prior to democracy: it would be absurd to argue that a given society became Protestant or Orthodox several hundred years ago because it became democratic in the 20th century. So any overlapping causal variance that religion and democratic institutions share in this analysis can much more plausibly be attributed to the religious heritage than to the level of democracy. Similarly, convincing evidence already cited (Burkhardt and Lewis-Beck 1994; Przeworski and Limogi 1993) points to the conclusion that economic democracy is conducive to democratization, but that it doesn't necessarily work the other way around: economic development also

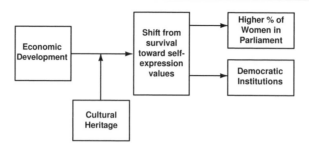

Figure 6.   Factors conducive to women's representation in parliament and democratic institutions.

seems to have a prior causal status, in relation to democracy. Accordingly, when we drop the level of democracy from the regression, in Model 3, we find that our indicators of economic development and religious heritage account for almost as much of the variance in self-expression values, as is explained in Model 2: the explained variance drops from 86 percent to 83 percent. Although democracy is very strongly correlated with self-expression values, in itself, it seems to account for only 3 percent of the variance in these values. In short, we find indications of a modest reciprocal effect in which democratic institutions help reshape culture, but the main causal sequence seems to be one that starts from the society's traditional cultural heritage, which is then transformed by economic development into relatively high or low levels of emphasis on self-expression values — which, in turn, helps shape the emergence and survival of democracy.

Conclusions: Changing Values and Changing Gender Roles

We have examined the impact of economic and cultural variables on the proportion of women in parliament, and on a society's level of democracy. Although gender equality in parliament is closely linked with democracy ($r = .65$), neither variable seems to be a direct cause of the other. Instead, both women's representation in parliament and a society's level of democracy seem to reflect an underlying cultural shift linked with economic development. Although a given society's traditional cultural heritage continues to have significant impacts on both the percentage of women in its parliament, and its level of political rights and civil liberties, rising levels of GDP and the shift toward a knowledge economy tend to transform societies in a predictable direction. They do so largely by producing a cultural shift from survival values toward increasing emphasis on self-expression values. Multivariate analyses indicate that this cultural shift is the main direct cause of both rising proportions of women in parliament, and of higher levels of democracy. A society's traditional cultural heritage and its level of economic development also influence its levels of gender equality and democracy, but their main effect seems depend on the extent to which they contribute to, or resist, the shift toward self-expression values. In regard to democratic institutions, for example, 65 percent of the variance can be attributed to the shift toward self-expression values; economic development and cultural heritage also show some direct effects, but they explain relatively modest amounts of variance (5 percent and 6 percent, respectively). Figure 6 depicts these relationships.

Although the percentage of women in parliament shows no direct impact on a society's level of democracy, the norm of gender equality is intimately involved in the process of democratization. For emphasis on gender equality constitutes one of the central themes of self-expression values — arguably, the most central component of all. This aspect of cultural change has been underemphasized in previous research, and seems to merit more attention.

In advanced industrial society, authority patterns seem to be shifting from the traditional hierarchical style toward a more collegial style that parallels the differences between stereotypically "male" and "female" styles of social interaction. While men are relatively likely to emphasize competition, women tend to emphasize cooperation; and while men tend to stress domination, women tend to have a more supportive leadership style. For reasons that are deeply rooted in the nature of advanced industrial society, the "female" leadership style tends to be more effective in these societies than the hierarchical, bureaucratic (and masculine) style that prevailed in agrarian and industrial society. And as we have seen, the cultural changes associated with changing gender roles and the "feminization" of leadership styles are closely linked with the spread of democratic institutions

For the past several decades, we have been witnessing a global trend toward gender equality that is intimately linked with a broader process of cultural change and democratization. Empirical evidence from 70 societies points to the conclusion that the process of modernization drives cultural change that encourage both the rise of women in public life, and the development of democratic institutions. Support for gender equality is not just a *consequence* of democratization. It is part of a broad cultural change that is transforming industrialized societies and bringing growing mass demands for increasingly democratic institutions.

References

ABU-ZAYD, GEHAN
1998   'In Search of Political Power: Women in Parliament in Egypt, Jordan and

Lebanon.' In *Women in Parliament: Beyond Numbers* edited by Azza Karam. IDEA: Stockholm.

BARNES, SAMUEL AND MAX KAASE

1979 *Political Action: Mass Participation in Five Western Democracies.* Beverley Hills, CA: Sage.

BURKHART, ROSS E. AND MICHAEL S. LEWIS-BECK

1994 "Comparative Democracy: The Economic development Thesis." *American Political Science Review* 88 (December): 903-910.

CARROLL, SUSAN

1994 *Women as Candidates in American Politics.* 2nd ed. Bloomington: University of Illinois Press.

CAUL, MIKI

1999 'Women's Representation in Parliament.' *Party Politics* 5(1): 79-98.

FREEDOM HOUSE

1973-1999 *Freedom in the World.* New York: Freedom House.

HUNTINGTON, SAMUEL P.

1996 *The Clash of Civilizations and the Remaking of World Order.* New York: Simon and Schuster.

INGLEHART, RONALD AND WAYNE BAKER

2000 'Modernization, Cultural Change and the Persistence of Traditional Values.' *American Sociological Review* (February):19-51.

INGLEHART, RONALD

1997 *Modernization and Postmodernization: Cultural, Economic and Political Change in 43 Societies.* Princeton: Princeton University Press.

1990 *Culture Shift in Advanced Industrial Society.* Princeton: Princeton University Press.

INTER-PARLIAMENTARY UNION

1999 *Participation of Women in Political Life.* IPU Reports and Documents No 35. Geneva: IPU.

KARAM, AZZA (ED.)

1998 *Women in Politics Beyond Numbers.* IDEA: Stockholm. http://www.int-idea.se/women/

KARVONEN, LAURI AND PER SELLE (EDS.)

1995 *Women in Nordic Politics.* Aldershot: Dartmouth.

KENWORTHY, LANE AND MELISSA MALAMI

1999 'Gender Inequality in Political Representation: A Worldwide Comparative Analysis.' *Social Forces* 78(1): 235-269.

LIPSET, SEYMOUR M.

1959 "Some Social Requisites of Democracy: Economic Development and Political Legitimacy." *American Political Science Review* 53(March): 69-105.

LOVENDUSKI, JONI AND PIPPA NORRIS (EDS.)

1993 *Women and Party Politics.* London: Sage.

NORRIS, PIPPA (ED.)

1997 *Passages to Power.* Cambridge: Cambridge University Press.

PRZEWORSKI, ADAM AND FERNANDO LIMOGI

1993 "Political Regimes and Economic Growth." *Journal of Economic Perspectives* 7(3): 51-69.

REYNOLDS, ANDREW

1999 'Women in the Legislatures and Executives of the World: Knocking at the Highest Glass Ceiling.' *World Politics* 51(4): 547-572.

RULE, WILMA
1987   'Electoral systems, contextual factors and women's opportunities for parliament in 23 democracies.' *Western Political Quarterly* 40: 477-98.
SAPIRO, VIRGINIA
1983   *The Political Integration of Women: Roles, Socialization and Politics.* Urbana: University of Illinois Press.
UN
2000   *The World's Women 2000: Trends and Statistics.* New York: United Nations.
WEBER, MAX
1904   *The Protestant Ethic and the Spirit of Capitalism* [original, 1904-1905; English translation, 1958]. New York: Charles Scribner's Sons.

Value Priorities in Israeli Society: An Examination of Inglehart's Theory of Modernization and Cultural Variation

EPHRAIM YUCHTMAN-YA'AR[*]

Introduction

This paper examines Inglehart's theory of modernization (Inglehart 1997; Inglehart and Baker (2000), using evidence from Israeli society. It addresses two related questions: First, at the aggregate level, to what extent is Israel's location on the two-dimensional cross-cultural map (based on traditional vs. secular-rational values, and survival vs. self-expression values) compatible with this theory's premises and propositions? Second, at the individual level of analysis, to what extent do Israeli value orientations on these two dimensions conform to this theory's predictions?

Influenced by the spectacular success of Western societies in terms of economic growth and material affluence in the post World War II era, proponents of the logic of industrialism wrote extensively during the 1960's and 1970's about the historical inevitability and ultimate triumph of Industrial society. Accordingly, "The world is entering a new age — the age of total industrialization. Some countries are far along the road; many are just beginning the journey. But everywhere, at a faster or slower pace, the people of the world are on the march towards industrialization" (Kerr et al. 1962:29). However, some prominent observers of modern society have argued that industrialization is not necessarily a linear process. Instead, it was suggested that it involves distinct stages of development. In

[*] Tel Aviv University.

accordance with this view, the more advanced stage of industrialization was captured by the concept of "post-industrial society" (Bell 1973, 1976). Notwithstanding the general agreement on the structural changes and the economic and material benefits associated with post-industrial society, the scholarly community has been involved in an extensive debate on the impact of industrialization on societal culture and its value system. In the context of this debate, Inglehart's theory of modernization represents an attempt to integrate two schools of thought regarding the evolution of relationships between economic progress and cultural change.

One school, originating with the Karl Marx, and further elaborated, for example, in the works of Daniel Lerner (1958), Dahrendorf (1959), (Daniel Bell (1973; 1976), Aron (1967) and Ronald Inglehart (1977; 1990), postulates that economic progress typically generates systematic changes in patterns of culture. For example, Inglehart (1977, 1990) argues that the transitions from pre-industrial to industrial society, and from industrial to post-industrial society have been accompanied by systematic shifts in the value priority of society. Preoccupation with survival needs due to the almost total dependence on the forces of nature and the dominance of religious beliefs characterized the pre-industrial era. Industrialization increased the human ability to control the environment and enhanced its productive capacity. This stage of development has been associated with a shift from an emphasis on basic survival needs to the pursuit of economic growth and material well being, along with a decline in religious and related traditional beliefs. Finally, the new phase of post-industrial society, characterized by unprecedented levels of affluence and safeguards provided by the welfare state, generates new priorities of human goals and social values that are essentially post-materialist, notably self-expression, subjective well-being and quality of life. Along with the shift towards these post-modern values, post-industrial society is moving further away from religious doctrines and traditional beliefs, becoming more rational and secular.

The other school of thought that was incorporated into Inglehart's theory of modernization acknowledges the role of cultural institutions and traditions in the process of industrialization. From Weber (1904) through the works of Dimaggio (1994) and Huntington (1993, 1996), it appears that cultural heritage, particularly its religious elements, tends to persist in the industrial era and exert its own influence on the process of modernization. Furthermore, as noted by Inglehart (2000:21), there are some salient instances when society may resort to traditional values and activate them in order to facilitate the transition to the industrial stage. Accordingly, in order to understand the evolution of a societal hierarchy of values over time, both factors of level of industrial advancement and cultural traditions must be taken into consideration.

However, in addition to cultural heritage, other situation-specific factors also may shape the value priorities of society. A striking example of the influence of such factors emerges from the body of research on environmentalism, as discussed, for example, by Inglehart (1995) Guha and Martinez-Alier (1997) and Brechin (1999). Thus, in order to explain the well-documented phenomenon of global environmental concern, these works in fact suggest a two-way theory of environmentalism. One way, typical of the affluent countries in the north, is compatible with the post-materialist thesis. Accordingly, even though the citizens of these countries are relatively less vulnerable to environmental hazards, such as air and water pollution, they tend to be highly supportive of environmental protection as an expression of the post-materialist syndrome. The other way, leading to environmental concern is more typical of citizens of countries in the south, where the degradation of the environment is relatively severe. Thus, the perception and experience of the risks associated with objective environmental problems may suffice to motivate the people in these countries to protect the environment.

Interestingly, in his more recent elaboration of modernization theory Inglehart (2000) has not acknowledged the role of situation-specific factors, other than those associated with cultural tradition. Nevertheless, we suggest that such factors — whether in the realm of environmental hazards or in other spheres of life — might have a profound influence on the value orientations of members of society. We explore this proposition through an examination of Inglehart's theory of modernization against evidence from Israeli society.

Some Features of Israeli Society

The size of the Jewish population in Israel — a little over 5 millions — makes it is one of the two largest Jewish communities in the world, [1] and the only country where Jews constitute the large majority (81%) out of a total population of about 6.5 million people. The rest of Israel's citizens consist mainly of Palestinian-Arabs (16%), most of who are Moslems, and non-Arab Christian citizens (4%). [2] This demographic reality invites the question of where does the Jewish State fit within the global modernization map, as depicted by Inglehart's (2000) research. In addressing this question, some observations about Israeli society seem in order.

---

[1] The other Jewish community of approximately the same size is located in the United States.

[2] Statistical Abstracts of Israel (CBS), 2001, # 52, table 2.1.

Firstly, Israel is a young immigrant society, where the bulk of the Jewish population is made of first (38%) and second (34%) generation immigrants.[3] Originating from many parts of the globe, most of these immigrants fall into groups that represent some of the major "cultural zones" in terms of Huntington's (1993, 1996) classification. Thus, nearly one half migrated from Moslem countries in the Middle East (for example: Iraq, Yemen and Iran) and North Africa (Morocco, Algeria and Tunisia). The rest came largely from Eastern and Central Europe, including many ex-communist countries that belong to the Orthodox (e.g. Russia, Ukraine, Belarus and Romania) or the Catholic (e.g. Poland, and Hungary) zones. Others arrived from Protestant (e.g. Germany and Holland), southern Catholic (e.g., France and Italy) or English-speaking countries such as the USA and Britain.[4] While sharing a common religious and ethnic identity, the historical background and the cultural heterogeneity of these immigrant groups, coupled with the recency of their arrival, suggest that Israeli society is multi-cultural, and cannot be assigned to any specific cultural zone. This reality is manifested in the persistence of distinct traditions of countries of origin at both levels of "high" and "low" cultures among many of the immigrant groups and their descendants (Halper, Seroussi and Squires-Kidron 1989; Regev 1996, 2000; Zrubavel 1995; Herzog and Ben-Raphael 2001). Consequently the "melting pot" and "Israelization" processes, as envisioned by the founding fathers of Israeli society, have encountered many difficulties.[5] In fact, Israeli culture has seemingly been molded by the interaction of at least three major sources of influence: The common Jewish heritage,[6] the cultural baggage of countries of origin, and the Israeli experience in itself.

Secondly, notwithstanding the pervasive impact of the Immigrants' cultural traditions, Israeli society has developed some major cultural features of its own. Perhaps the most important expression of "being an Israeli" is the revival of the Hebrew language and its functioning as a critical integrative force and major means of communication in all spheres of life (Alter 1994; Harshav 1999; Katriel 1986; Shavit 2002).[7] Of greater

---

[3] CBS, 2002, # 52, table 2.1.

[4] CBS, 2001, # 52, table 2.23.

[5] On these Issues, see, for example: Eisenstadt 1954, 1967, 1985; Smooha 1978; Ben-Raphael 1982; Ben-Raphael and Sharot 1991; Horowitz and Lissak 1989; Leshem and Shuval 1998; Lissak 1999.

[6] On the historical significance of the Jewish heritage see, for example, Eisenstadt 1992.

[7] The renaissance of Hebrew and its acceptance as the dominant language has been a major subject of cultural and political struggles, particularly at the early stages of building the new society. For example, when the "Technion" — Israel's Institute of Technology — was established in 1912 (it was actually opened in 1924), the board of trustees was

relevance to the issue under discussion is the crystallization within Israeli society of the "culture of security." Influenced by the ongoing, sanguineous conflict with its Arab neighbors, particularly the Palestinians, life in Israel has been shaped by frequent wars and constant fears faced with a hostile environment. The pervasive sense of existential threat was manifested, among other things, in the centrality of the IDF (Israel Defense Forces) in Israeli politics and the unsurpassed esteem bestowed on it by the Israeli public. (Yuchtman-Yaar and Peres 2000). In fact, Israeli democracy, both at the level of collective institutions and of individual attitudes has, in fact, been heavily influenced by the priority accorded to considerations of national and personal security (Arian, Talmud and Herman 1988; Bartal et al. 1998; Barzilay 1996; Carmi and Rosenfeld 1989; Peres and Yuchtman-Yaar 1992; Shamir and Shamir 1993; Sprinzak and Diamond 1993).

Thirdly, Israeli Jews, like Jews everywhere, share a collective historical memory that stresses the common experience of anti-Semitism, discrimination and persecution. In particular, the Jewish Holocaust that took place during World War II has played a major role in the national narrative, and the establishment of Israel as a Jewish State has been celebrated as a triumph of the Jewish people over those intending to exterminate it. At the same time, from early childhood through adulthood, Israelis are reminded through their adult lives that the danger of anti-Semitism has not passed and that the State of Israel is the only country where Jews can seek refuge in times of persecution.[8] This collective memory, captured by such slogans as "Never Again," combined with the harsh reality of the Israeli-Arab conflict, has profoundly affected Israeli culture and identity (Elon 1971; Handelman and Katz 1990; Wistrich and Ohana 1995; Zrubavel 1995). Given its preoccupation with the problem of national security and survival, it seems reasonable to expect the members of Israeli society to lag behind, regarding the development of at least some of the values associated with modernization, particularly those captured by the post-materialist syndrome.

Fourthly, along with its emphasis on the theme of national survival, Israeli society has made a considerable effort to become a modern, post-industrial society. This effort has been at least moderately successful, as manifested by a series of criteria that are commonly regarded as major

---

involved in a fierce debate about whether the institute should adopt Hebrew or German as its teaching language.

[8] In the spirit of this attitude, one of the first pieces of legislation passed by the Israeli Parliament (Knesset) is "The Law of Return" according to which every Jew is entitled to immigrate to Israel and become its citizen.

indicators of a post-industrialism. Its GDP per capita of $18,600 in 1999 [9] places Israel within the small group of advanced economies, albeit closer to the lower edge of this group. By this criterion, Israel ranks somewhat higher than Spain and Italy but considerably lower than most West European countries, and far lower than the USA. Similarly, the structure of Israel's labor force in terms of economic sectors closely follows the post-industrial pattern, with about 73% employed in the service sector, 28% in industry, and 2% in agriculture. [10] In the domain of science and technology, the Israeli government investment in research and development as a percentage of GNP — 2.3% — is one of the highest rates in the world. By comparison, it is 2.1% in the USA, 2.0%, in France 1.7% in the UK and stands at 1.6% in Canada and Norway (Aharoni and Aharoni 2000, p. 84). Correspondingly, the national expenditure on research and development in 1999, measured as an index of final expenditure per capita (US = 100), was 86.8. This figure was considerably higher than that of most OECD member countries for that year. [11] In the sphere of higher education, Israeli universities generate relatively large numbers of science and engineering doctorates. According to figures provided by the National Science Board (1996), [12] the rate of science & engineering doctorates granted per 100,000 participants in the labor force in 1992 was 14.6 in Norway, 19.6 in the USA, 21.7 in the UK, 24.2 in Israel and 26.1 in Germany. The emphasis on advanced industries is reflected in the share of information and communication technologies (ICT) in the Israeli economy. Thus, the percent of ICT from total export in 1998 was 20.1% — considerably higher than the 12.5% average for members of the OECD in that year (CBS, 2001, table 28.11). As for the participation rate of women in the labor force — still another major indicator of level of modernization — Israel's rate of 55.0% in 1999 puts it below the average of the OECD countries, which, in that year stood at 59.5% (OECD, 2000). According to figures provided by the World Bank (1999), [13] the participation of Israeli women in the civilian labor force as a percentage of men in 1997 stood at 0.7 — the same percentage as in Germany and Holland and just below Britain, France and the USA. However, the figure for Israel is somewhat inflated since the rate of participation of men in the civilian labor force is lowers than the average for the OECD. Finally,

---

[9] CBS, 2001, table 28.6.

[10] CBS, 2001, table 12.11.

[11] CBS, 2001, table 28.10.

[12] National Science Board, Science and Engineering indicators 1996, The figures for Israel are based on data provided by the Central Bureau of Statistics.

[13] World Bank, 1999. World Development Indicators 1999, table 13.

Israel's national expenditure on health services as a percentage of the GDP in 1999 was 8.3 — just above the average of the OECD at that year.[14]

For reasons of space we will just mention that Israel's modernity is also manifested in other diverse spheres such as level of schooling, life expectancy, and social services. All these indicators, taken together, indicate that Israel can be regarded as a modest member of the small group of post-industrial nations. Following Inglehart's argument concerning the relationship between economic development and value priorities, and given its post-industrial characteristics, we would expect Israeli society to be oriented towards rational/secular and self-expression values.

Fifthly, Israeli society constitutes the heritage of the over 100 years old history of the Zionist movement. Influenced by the Western model of the nation-state, along with the ideas of democracy and economic progress, the Zionist movement was essentially secular in ideology and practice. In fact, many of its leaders, particularly those on the left, were anti-religious, blaming the traditional orthodox leadership for the stagnation and misery of the Jewish people in the European Diaspora. As for the latter, the prevailing view was that the redemption of the Jews and the return to the "Land of Israel" could be accomplished only through a divine act, namely the coming of the Messiah. The radical wing of Jewish orthodoxy — the ultra-orthodox — was therefore vehemently anti-Zionist, and has remained so until the present time. Other, more moderate rabbis, have come to terms with the Zionist movement and joined its ranks in the belief that it signified the first stage towards redemption. Nevertheless, Jewish orthodoxy played a relatively marginal role in the history of the Zionist movement during the pre-State era and in the early years following statehood.

However, following the mass immigration of Jews from Moslem countries during the 1950's and early 1960's, and since most of them were at least moderately religious, Israeli society has become more balanced in terms of the secular/religious division of its citizens. Given this demographic change, along with political considerations aimed at preserving national unity, the largely secular political leadership had to reach a compromise on certain fundamental issues with the religious community. One manifestation of such a compromise is the fact that Israel is one of the few democracies that makes no separation between state and religion. Similarly, various religious norms, such as observing Kashrut in all public-owned institutions and, with a few exceptions (e.g., restaurants, prohibiting any form of work and business on the Sabbath, are enforced by law. Furthermore, even certain privately owned enterprises, such as hotels, observe Kashrut in order to be able to do business with religious

---

[14] CBS, 2001, table 28.9.

and traditional clientele. In fact, as indicated by recent survey conducted in 1998 (Levi, Levinson and Katz 2002), Israeli society represents a mixture of religious, traditional and secular influences — a reality that coincides with the varying degrees of religiousness of its Jewish citizens. [15]

Taken as a whole, this brief depiction of some of the major attributes of Israeli society suggests that this society has been under the influence of countervailing forces regarding the evolution of its value hierarchy. On the one hand, its relatively high level of socio-economic development, coupled with a viable democratic regime and a sizeable secular population, predisposes this society towards to embrace values of rational/secular nature, as well as self-expression values. On the other hand, the pervasive emphasis on national security and the constant concern with the problem of national existence, coupled with the persistence of religious heritage within notable segments of its population, pulls Israel in the direction of traditional and survival values. Since it is difficult to ascertain a-priori the resultant of these conflicting forces, we need to wait for the empirical results in order to see where Israel is located on the two dimensions of cultural variation, relatively to other societies.

Aside from its implications for inter-societal differences in value priorities, Inglehart's theory of modernization ventures to explain and predict individual variation in this domain within society, on the basis of a series of variables, such as birth cohort (coming of age in affluent times), schooling, and income (Inglehart 1977, 1990). The validity of the theory's hypotheses has been tested against empirical evidence taken from a fairly large number of societies, including evidence on changes over time. No systematic study of this kind has, however, been conducted in Israel, particularly in recent years. [16] Inglehart's recent conceptualization of the two dimensions of cultural variation provides an opportunity to examine the extent to which the theory may account for location on these

---

[15] Survey research based on national probability samples of the adult Jewish population in Israel typically shows that about 18% define themselves either as "ultra-orthodox" (7%) or "orthodox" (11%), 27% as "traditional," and 54% as "secular." In the questionnaire used for the purpose of the present study, we used two options for secular, one of which was "Secular, following some of the religious customs." This option was picked up by 25%, while the other — "secular" was chosen by 30% of the respondents. However, we believe that the seculars who keep some of the religious customs refer mostly to ceremonial events, such as Passover, that are celebrated by many Jews because of their significance in Jewish national history or as social and cultural events, rather than because of their religious significance.

[16] Some aspects of the post-materialist argument in the context of Israeli society were examined in the 1980's (Gottlieb and Yuchtman-Yaar 1983; Yuchtman-Yaar and Gottlieb 1985; Yuchtman-Yaar 1987).

dimensions across individual members of Israeli society. This task will be undertaken in the second part of the empirical analysis.

Method

The data we use is based on a representative national survey of the adult Israeli population (N = 1199).[17] Face-to-face interviews were conducted during August-September, 2001. The questionnaire included a large number of items taken from the World Values Surveys project. For the purpose of this study we chose the 10 items pertaining to the characterization of the two dimensions of value orientation, as listed in Inglehart (2000, table 1, p. 24). A factor analysis of these items, based on the World Values Survey data for 65 nations (aggregated), yielded two orthogonal factors, one representing a traditional vs. secular/rational dimension and the other a survival vs. self-expression dimension.[18] The first dimension mainly reflects cross-cultural differentiation in the importance attached to God, socialization to obedience and religious faith, and to authority. It also taps attitudes on abortion as well as sense of national pride. The variables characterizing the second dimension consist of items measuring the materialist/post-materialist syndrome, individual happiness, civil participation (signing petitions), attitudes on homosexuality, and trustfulness.[19] The countries' location on each of the two dimensions is represented in the form of standardized factor scores, obtained by the summation of the country standard score for each variable multiplied by its factor coefficient.

For the purpose of the second phase of this study, which involves individual-level analysis, namely the effects of individual attributes on value orientation as measured by the two factors, we have used the following as independent variables:

---

[17] We have excluded Arab respondents from the present analysis, since the national identity of most members of this minority is Palestinian. Therefore, some of the items comprising the two dimensions have quite different meanings for Arabs and Jews. For example, when asked "to what extent are you proud to be an Israeli?" many Arabs would answer "to a small extent" or "not at all." However, such an answer would typically reflect their strong sense of pride in being Palestinians, as well as hostility to Israel, a Jewish state in which their status is that of a discriminated against minority, rather than because of universalistic or cosmopolitan preferences. In any event, Arabs represent only about 12% of the adult Israeli population so that their exclusion from the analysis has little effect on the overall results.

[18] In this study, we used a larger sample, which includes 81 societies. However, the factorial structure obtained for this sample is essentially the same as that of the smaller sample.

[19] For a detailed discussion of the meaning of these items see pp. 25-28 in Inglehart (2000).

Age — natural scale.

Country of origin — a nominal scale, distinguishing between European-American origin (Ashekenazi Jews), Middle-Eastern and North-African origin (Sephardi Jews), and 2nd generation Israeli Jews. [20]

Income — a 9 level scale representing gross household income.

Education — a 10 level scale ranging from elementary schooling or less through academic degree.

Political orientation — a 10 level scale ranging from 1 (right) to 10 (left).

Degree of religiousness — a 5 level scale ranging from ultra-orthodox through orthodox, traditional, secular who follows some religious norms, and secular. [21]

Discussion and Findings

A. *Aggregate Analysis*

As a first step in the analysis, for the Israeli sample we computed z-scores for each of the 10 variables comprising the two scales, on the basis of the respective mean scores of the 81 nations, with the results reported in Table 1. [22]

We next computed for this sample the two total factor scores, weighting the 10 variables by their factor coefficients. The obtained scores were 0.33 and 0.68 for the Traditional/Secular-Rational and Survival/Self-Expression scales, respectively. These scores locate Israel just moderately high on the first scale and fairly high on the second one. In order to put these scores in a more detailed comparative perspective, Figures 1 and 2 depict its location on two of Inglehart's two-dimensional maps, the first of which divides the resulting space according to cultural zones and the second according to economic zones (Inglehart 2000, pp. 29 and 30).

Before dwelling on the general meaning of Israel's position on the two world maps, a discussion of the specific z-scores from which its factor scores were derived seems in order. Beginning with the variables characterizing the traditional-secular/rational dimension (Inglehart 2000, table 1), it will be noticed that three of the z-scores are positive and two are negative. These results are consistent with the argument that the value orientations of Israelis are susceptible to the effects of a variety of countervailing forces. Thus, on the one hand, they tend to be relatively open-minded on

---

[20] Largely because of their origin in Moslem countries, Sephardi Jews tend to be more traditional than Ashkenazi Jews.

[21] For a discussion of the meaning of this categorization and its scaling properties, see Yuchtaman-Ya'ar and Peres (2000), pp. 107-129.

[22] The addition of Israel increased the size of the international sample from 80 to 81.

Table 1

Means of 10 Variables Characterizing Two Dimensions of Cross-Cultural Variation for 81 Societies and Corresponding Z-scores for Israeli Society

	means	Z-scores
Importance of God	7.19	0.16
Importance of teaching obedience and religious faith vs. independence and determination	0.12	0.91
Attitude toward abortion	3.81	0.21
Sense of national pride	1.61	−0.31
Respect of authority	1.57	−0.05
Priority of economic and physical security over self-expression and quality of life	1.81	0.81
Self-happiness	1.97	−0.06
Signing a petition	2.01	−0.40
Attitude toward homosexuality	3.38	1.09
Trusting people	1.71	0.17

*Higher scores indicate preference for secular-rational or self-expression values.

the justification of abortion (z-score = 1.21), to prefer teaching children independence and determination rather than obedience and religious faith (z-score = 0.91), and somewhat less inclined to acknowledge the importance of God (z-score = 0.16). On the other hand, they tend to have a strong sense of national pride (z-score = −0.31) and to favor respect for authority (z-score = −0.05). We believe that the positive z-scores reflect the influence of Israel's experience of democracy and its commitment to post-industrialism, whereas the negative sores represent its deep concern with the threat to its national existence.

Turning to the survival/self-expression dimension, we again notice a mixture of positive and negative z-scores, though the former tends to be more salient than the latter. Thus, consistent with their attitudes towards abortion, Israelis appear to be relatively tolerant towards homosexuality (z-score = 1.09) and, albeit to a lesser extent, to prefer values of self-expression and quality of life (z-score = 0.81). The latter finding is somewhat surprising since we expected the Israeli public to be quite strongly oriented towards the materialistic, namely, the survival pole, given its pervasive concern with the problem of national existence. However, it is possible that this result derives from the composition of a battery of items used to measure the materialist/post materialist values in Inglehart's recent study (Inglehart 2000). Specifically, although one of the materialist items included in this battery refers to the goal of keeping order in the country, it does not include the item referring to the goal of ensuring that the country will have strong military forces. We believe that the inclusion of this item in the construction

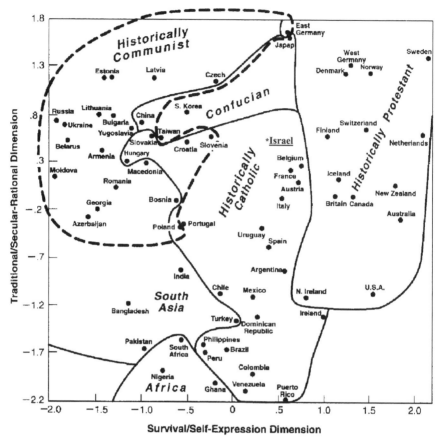

Figure 1.   Istael's Value Position/Cultural Zones.

of the materialist/post-materialist index might have considerably reduced Israel's score on this scale. This possibility is suggested by the observation that 45.0% of Israeli Jewish respondents chose this item as first priority and 30.4% as second priority. These percentages are somewhat higher than the priority given to economic growth, and considerably higher than the priorities given to the two post-materialist items included in this battery.[23] As to the negative z-score pertaining to the issue of signing a petition (–0.40), it, too, seems to fall in line with Israel's absorption with the question of national security. Like the item on national pride, it reflects the tendency to stand behind the government, particularly in times of

---

[23] This set of items, which is part of Inglehart's original scale of the materialist/post-materialist syndrome, was included in the questionnaire used in this study.

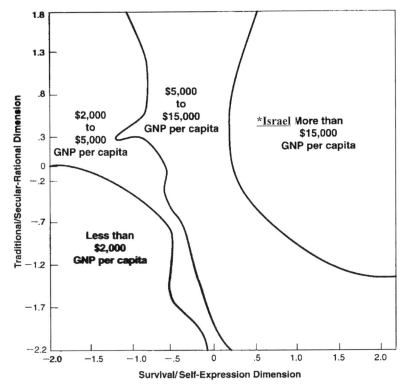

Figure 2.   Istael's Value Position/Economic Zones.

crisis, which prevailed when the fieldwork for this study took place. [24] For this reason it should come as no surprise that Israelis were not inclined to describe themselves as very happy (z-score = −0.06).

The overall position of Israel on the two dimensions of cultural variation can most clearly be seen from the maps given in figures 1 and 2. Starting with the map containing the cultural zones, it appears that Israel is located somewhat right to the mid-point of the horizontal axis (the survival/self-expression dimension) and just above the mid-point of the vertical axis (the traditional/secular-rational dimension). This puts Israel in the vicinity of such countries as Belgium, France and Austria with regard to the Survival/Self-Expression dimension and to Netherlands, Switzerland and Finland in terms of the Traditional/Secular-Rational dimension. Relatively to some other Western societies, Israel is considerably less secular/rational than, for example, West Germany, Denmark and Norway, but more so than Britain, Canada, and USA As to the Survival/Self-Expression

---

[24] It was conducted in the midst of the Palestinian intifadah, which has seriously undermined the Israelis' sense of national and personal security.

dimension, it is positioned, lower than most West-European countries, as well as the USA but somewhat higher than, say Italy and Spain. Generally speaking, Israel can clearly be regarded as part of the Western Democratic zone, at least in terms of the cultural characteristics captured by the two dimensions. From this viewpoint, it probably represents an oddity in the geopolitical zone to it belongs, namely the Middle East — a fact that might have affected its relationships with the surrounding Moslem countries. This suggestion gains support from the observation that Israel is located close to most Western societies according to the map of economic zones, as can be seen from Figure 2. By this criterion, it ranks much above its neighbors, where the GNP per capita falls in the range of $1000 to $2000. Interestingly, Israel's location in terms of the two dimensions of cultural space seems quite consistent with its position on the map of economic zones. In both respects it appears to be a modest member of the group of post-industrial and post materialist societies.

B. Individual-Level Analysis

We now turn to examine Inglehart's theory of modernization with respect to cultural variation among individual members of society. Essentially, the question under discussion is the extent to which individuals' value priorities are systematically related to various demographic and socio-economic characteristics, such as age and levels of income and education. Accordingly, we performed two regression analyses, in which the Traditional/Secular-Rational and the Survival/Self-Expression measures were used as dependent variables and the 6 individual characteristics listed above were entered as independent variables.

Beginning with the Traditional/Secular-Rational dimension, it may be noticed from the regression coefficients presented in Table 2 that all the 6 independent variables exert significant effects on this measure, though to varying degrees. Furthermore, all these effects are in the "right" direction, in terms of the considerations of modernization theory. Thus, the tendency to embrace secular-rational values is more varies positively with higher levels of education and income and negatively with age. Such values are also associated with Ashkenazi (European/American) origin, with political inclination towards the left and, in particular, with secular self-identity. Since the effects of the first four independent variables seem self-explanatory, given the premises of modernization theory, we comment briefly on the other two independent variables. The finding with regard to the effect of the right-left scale is probably consistent with the results of prior research according to which the right tends to be more patriotic and nationalist politically, as well as more conservative and traditional socially. It should be born in mind that the items characterizing the factor underlying this dimension pertain to issues such as national pride,

Table 2

Unstandardized and Standardized Coefficients from the Regression of Traditional/Secular-Rational Values on Selected Individual Characteristics (N = 726)

Independent Variable	Unstandardized Coefficients	Standardized Coefficients
(Constant)	−1.29	
	(.09)	
Sepharadi[1]	−.12*	−.09
	(.04)	
Religious-secular	.25**	.46
	(.02)	
Right-Left	.04**	.15
	(.01)	
Age	−.003	−.08
	(.001)	
Education	.04**	.20
	(.01)	
Income	.04**	.14
	(.01)	

[1] Omitted categories are Ashkenazi and 2nd generation Israeli.
Adjusted R^2 = .50.
Numbers in parentheses are standard errors.
*P < .05; ** p < .001.

respect for authority, and attitudes towards abortion. The observation that that religious-secular scale appears to have the strongest influence on this measure is apparently not surprising, given that one of its characterizing items refers to the importance of God in one's life. In order to test this explanation we ran a regression in which the item on God was deleted from the Traditional-Secular/Rational measure. However, the results of this analysis indicate that the reduction in the effect of the religious-secular variable was relatively small — from a coefficient (unstandardized) of .25 in the original regression — to a coefficient of .21 in the special regression. These results point to the central role played by religiousness in the formation of traditional versus secular-rational values, at least in Israeli society. The importance of the religious factor is further indicated by the observation that when this variable was excluded from the equation predicting the measure of the Traditional-Secular/Rational dimension, the amount of explained variance was reduced from 50% to 31%. Although the size of the total variance explained by the remaining independent variables is quite respectable, taking into account that the regression involves individual-level analysis, the explanatory power of the religious-secular scale cannot be exaggerated.

Table 3

Unstandardized and Standardized Coefficients from the Regression of Survival/Self-Expression Values on Selected Individual Characteristics (N = 780)

Independent Variable	Unstandardized Coefficients	Standardized Coefficients
(Constant)	−.22	
	(.09)	
Sepharadi[1]	−.09*	−.08
	(.04)	
Religious-secular	.004	.01
	(.02)	
Right-Left	.03**	.13
	(.01)	
Age	−.008**	−.26
	(.001)	
Education	.04**	.21
	(.01)	
Income	.06**	.26
	(.01)	

[1] Omitted categories are Ashkenazi and 2nd generation Israeli.
Adjusted R^2 = .33.
Numbers in parentheses are standard errors.
*P < .05; ** p < .001.

Turning now to the second regression equation (Table 3), it appears that the "classical" independent variables in Inglehart's modernization, namely age, education and income, exert significant effects, and in the right direction, on the measure of the Survival-Self/Expression, similarly to the previous equation. Accordingly the preference for Self-Expression values increases with younger age and with higher income and education levels. The effect of the political variable is also significant, and according priority to Self-Expression values is therefore more typical of left than right-oriented Israeli citizens. Ethnic origin also seems to play a role in this domain, with Ashkenazi and 2nd generation Israelis more likely to adopt such values, albeit to a small degree. However, the religious-secular variable, seemingly such an influential factor in the choice between traditional versus secular/rational values, is apparently an insignificant agent of socialization where the dimension of Survival-Self Expression is concerned. This finding is somewhat perplexing, since attitude on homosexuality is included among the items comprising this measure. However, an examination of the relationships between the religious-secular scale and the other variables comprising the Survival/Self-Expression measure indicates that religious people tend to be somewhat happier and more trusting of other people.

These tendencies apparently neutralize the counter-effects of the negative attitudes toward homosexuality, so that the overall influence of the religious factor is practically zero. It should also be noted that the total explained variance of this equation (33%) is approximately the same as the amount of explained variance in the previous equation (31%) — when the latter did not include the religious factor as one of its independent variables.

Conclusions

With regard to the aggregate level of analysis, the case of Israel may appear "boring" in the sense that its location vis-à-vis other contemporary societies on the global cultural map fits quite well with the hypotheses derived from Inglehart's theory of modernization. This conclusion is seemingly relevant both to the economic development thesis of this theory and to its argument regarding the importance of specific situational factors, such as cultural tradition. At the same time, the Israeli case draws attention to some aspects of the theory that may require further elaboration. In particular, we need to better understand the meaning of the materialist/post-materialist syndrome, which constitutes a central ingredient in the measure of the Survival/Self-Expression dimension. Thus, Israel's relatively advanced level of industrial and economic development has apparently been conducive to the inculcation of post-materialist values to its citizens. On the other hand, the perpetuation of the political and military threat to its existence, and the security culture that has evolved as a result of this threat, pulls Israel's citizens towards the survival pole of this dimension. What is needed, therefore, is to study more cases, such as Israeli society, where different aspects of modern values are not mutually consistent. This may lead us to a better understanding of the conditions under which such values are more likely to develop.

As for the level of individual analysis, we again notice that the results are generally in line with the basic arguments of modernization theory. However, in view of the prominence of the religious factor in regard to the Traditional-Secular/Rational dimension, and its disappearance as a relevant factor in relation to the Survival/Self-Expression dimension, it seems worthwhile to make greater efforts towards understanding the role of religiousness in these domains.

Finally, and unrelated to Israel's case, the wealth of empirical data accumulated by the World Value Project calls for a systematic hierarchical analysis that would make it possible to differentiate between individual and societal, or perhaps broader contextual effects, on the evolution of value orientations.

References

AHARONI, SARA AND MEIR AHARONI (EDS.)
2000   *Israel 2000.* Miksam, Kfar-Sava.
ALMOG, OZ
2000   *The Sabra: The Creation of a New Jew.* University of California Press, Berkeley.
ALTER, ROBERT
1994   *Hebrew and Modernity.* Indiana University Press, Bloomington.
ARAN, GIDEON
1986   "From Religious Zionism to Zionist Religion: The Roots of Gush Emunim."
            Studies in Contemporary Jewry, 2, pp. 116-143.
ARON, RAMOND
1976   *The Industrial Society.* Weidenfeld and Nicholson, London.
ARIAN, ASHER, ILAN TALMUD AND TAMAR HERMAN
1988   *National Security and Public Opinion in Israel.* Westview Press, Boulder.
BAR-TAL, DANIEL, DAN JACOBSON AND AHARON KLIENMAN (EDS.)
1998   *Security Concerns: Insights from the Israeli Experience.* JAI Press, Stanford.
BARZILAY, GAD
1996   *Wars, Internal Conflicts and Political Order: A Jewish Democracy in the Middle East.*
            State University of New York Press, Albany.
BELL, DANIEL
1973   *The Coming of Post-Industrial Society.* Basic Books, New York.
1976   *The Cultural Contradictions of Capitalism.* Basic Books, New York.
BEN-ARI, EYAL AND YORAM BILU
1987   "Saints' sanctuaries in Israeli Development Towns." *Urban Anthropology* 16, pp.
            243-272.
BEN-RAPHAEL, ELIEZER
1982   *The Emergence of Ethnicity: Cultural Groups and Social Conflict in Israel.* State
            University of New York Press, Albany.
BEN-RAPHAEL, ELIEZER AND STEPHEN SHAROT
1991   *Ethnicity, Religion, and Class in Israeli Society.* Cambridge University Press,
            Cambridge.
BRECHIN, STEVEN
1999   "Objective Problems, Subjective values, and Global Environmentalism: Eval-
            uating the Postmaterialist Argument and Challenging a New Explanation."
            Social Science Quarterly 90(4), pp. 793-809.
CARMI, SHULAMIT AND HERY ROSENFELD
1989   "The Emergence of Militaristic Nationalism in Israel." *International Journal of
            Politics, Culture and Society* 3(1), pp. 5-49.
DAHRENDORF, RALF
1959   *Class and Class Conflict in Industrial Society.* Stanford University Press, Stanford.
DiMAGGIO, PAUL
1994   "Culture and Economy." In N.J. Smelser and R. Swedberg (eds.), *The
            Handbook of Economic Sociology.* Princeton University Press, Princeton, pp. 27-57.
ELON, AMOS
1971   *The Israelis: Fathers and Sons.* Weidenfeld and Nicholson, London.
EISENSTADT, SHMUEL N.
1954   *The Absorption of Immigrants.* Routledge & Kegan, London.
1967   *Israeli Society.* Basic Books, New York.

1985   *The Transformation of Israeli Society*. Weidenfeld & Nicholson, London.

1992   *Jewish Civilization: The Jewish Experience in a Comparative Perspective*. State University of New York Press, Albany.

ELON, AMOS

1971   *The Israelis: Fathers and Sons*. Weidenfeld and Nicholson, London.

GOTTLIEB, AVI AND EPHRAIM YUCHTMAN-YAAR

1983   "Materialism, Post-Materialism, and Public Views on Socio-Economic Policy: The Case of Israel." *Comparative Political Studies*, Vl. 16(3), pp. 307-335.

GUHA, RAMACHANDRA AND JUAN MARTINEZ-ALIER

1997   *Varieties of Environmentalism: Essays North and South*. Earthscan, London.

HALPER, JEFF, EDWIN SEROUSSI AND PAMELA SQUIRES-KIDRON

1989   "Musica Mizrahit: Ethnicity and Class Culture in Israel." *Popular Music* 8, pp. 131-142.

HANDELMAN, DON AND ELIHU KATZ

1990   "State Ceremonies in Israel: Remembrance Day and Independence Day," in Handelman, Don (ed.), *Models and Mirrors: Towards an Anthropology of Public Events*. Cambridge University Press, Cambridge, pp. 191-201.

HARSHAV, BENJAMIN

1999   *Language in Time of Revolution*. Stanford University Press, Stanford.

HEZOG, HANNA AND BEN-RAPHAEL, ELIEZER (EDS.)

2001   *Language and Communication in Israel*. Transaction, New Brunswick.

HOROWITZ, DAN AND MOSHE, LISSAK

1989   *Trouble in Utopia*. State University of New York Press, Albany.

HUNTINGTON, SAMUEL

1993   "The Clash of Civilizations?" *Foreign Affairs* 72(3), pp. 22-49.

1996   *The Clash of Civilizations and the Remaking of World Order*. Simon and Schuster, New York.

INGLEHART, RONALD

1977   *Modernization and Postmodernization: Cultural, Economic, and Political Change in 43 Societies*. Princeton University Press, Princeton.

INGLEHART, RONALD AND WAYNE E. BAKER

2000   "Modernization, Cultural Change, and the Persistence of Traditional Values." *American Sociological Review*, Volume 65, # 1, pp. 19-51.

1977   *The Silent Revolution: Changing Values and Political Styles in Advanced Industrial Society*. Princeton University Press, Princeton.

1995   "Public Support for Environmental Protection: Objective Problems and Subjective Values in 43 Societies." *PS: Political Science & Politics* 28(1), pp. 57-72.

AHARONI, SARA AND MEIR AHARONI (EDS.)

2000   *Israel 2000*. Miksam, Kfar-Sava.

KATRIEL, TAMAR

1986   *Talking Straight: Dugri Speech in Israeli Sabra Culture*. Cambridge University Press, Cambridge.

KERR, CLARK ET AL.

1962   *Industrialism and Industrial Man: the Problems of Labor and Managememnt in Economic Growth*. Heinemann, London.

KIMMERLING, BARUCH

1985   *The Interrupted System: Israeli Civilians in Wars and Routine Times*. Transaction Books, New Brunswick (in collaboration with Irit Becker).

LERNER, DANIEL
1958   *The Passing of Traditional Society: Modernizing the Middle East.* Free Press, New York.

LESHEM, ELAZAR AND JUDITH T. SHUVAL (EDS.)
1998   *Immigration to Israel — Sociological Perspectives.* Studies of Israeli Society, Volume VIII, Transaction Publishers, New Brunswick.

LIEBMAN, CHARLES AND ELIEZER DON-YEHIYA
1983   *Civil Religion in Israel.* University of California Press, Berkeley.

LISSAK, MOSHE
1999   *The Mass Immigration in the Fifties: The Failure of the Melting Pot Policy.* The Bialik Institute, Jerusalem (Hebrew).

NATIONAL SCIENCE BOARD
1996   *Science and Engineering Indicators.* Washington DC: US Government Printing Office (NSB-96-21), App. A, p. 65.

PERES, YOCHANAN AND EPHRAIM YUCHTMAN-YA'AR
1992   *Trends in Israeli Democracy: The Public View.* Lynne Rienner, Boulder.

REGEV, MOTTI
1996   "Musica Mizrakhit, Israeli Rock and National Culture in Israel." *Popular Music* 15, pp. 275-284.

2000   "To Have a Culture of Our Own: On Israeliness and it's Variants." *Ethnic and Racial Studies* 23(2), pp. 223-247.

SCHMELTZ, UZIEL, SERGIO DELLAPERGOLA AND URI AVNER
1991   *Ethnic Differences Among Israeli Jews: A New Look.* The Institute of Contemporary Jewry, The Hebrew University of Jerusalem, American Jewish Yearbook, The American Jewish Committee, Jerusalem.

SHAMIR, JACOB AND MICHAL SHAMIR
1993   *The Dynamics of Israeli Public Opinion on Peace and the Territories.* The Tami Steinmetz Center for Peace Research, Tel Aviv.

SHAVIT ZOHAR (ED.)
2002   *The Construction of Hebrew Culture in Eretz Ysarel.* The Israeli Academy for Sciences and the Humanities, The Bialik Insitute, Jerusalem.

SICRON, MOSHE AND ELAZAR LESHEM (EDS.)
1998   *Profile of an Immigration Wave: The Absorption Process of Immigrants from the Former Soviet Union, 1990-1995.* The Magness Press, The Hebrew University, Jerusalem.

SMOOHA, SAMI
1978   *Israel: Pluralism and Conflict.* Routledge & Kegan Paul, London.

SPRINZAK, EHUD AND LARRY DIAMOND
1993   *Democracy Under Stress.* Lynne Rienner, Boulder.

WEBER, MAX
1904   *The Protestant Ethic and the Spirit of Capitalism.* Unwin, London.

WISTRICH, ROBERT AND DAVID OHANA, (EDS.)
1995   *The Shaping of Israeli Identity, Myth, and Trauma.* F. Cass, London.

YUCHTMAN-YAAR, EPHRAIM
1987   "Economic Culture in Post-Industrial Society: Orientation towards Growth, Work and Technology." *International Sociology*, Vol. 2(1), pp. 77-101.

YUCHTMAN-YAAR, EPHRAIM AND AVI, GOTTLIEB
1985   "Technological Development and the Meaning of Work: A Cross Cultural Comparison." *Human Relations*, Vol. 38(7), pp. 603-621.

YUCHTMAN-YA'AR, EPHRAIM AND YOCHANAN, PERES
2000   *Between Consent and Dissent: Democracy and Peace in the Israeli Mind.* Rowman and
            Littlefield, Lanham.
ZRUBAVEL, YAEL
1995   *Recovered Roots: Collective Memory and the Making of Israeli National Tradition.*
            Chicago University Press, Chicago.

Social Relations and Social Capital in Vietnam: Findings from the 2001 World Values Survey[*]

Russell J. Dalton[**], Pham Minh Hac[***], Pham Thanh Nghi[***] and Nhu-Ngoc T. Ong[**]

It is almost an understatement to say that Vietnam has experienced dramatic social, economic, and political changes in recent years. Following decades of war, North Vietnam and South Vietnam became the Socialist Republic of Vietnam in 1975, and has been ruled since then by the Vietnamese Communist Party. But in 1986, the Vietnamese government introduced extensive renovation (*doi moi*) policies that were extended even farther by the 1992 constitution (Turley and Selden 1993). These reforms allowed prices to float, introduced private sectors into business, decollectivized farmlands, and liberalized foreign trade and investment. A series of economic, social and legal reforms have followed from the marketization of the economy. In 1999 Vietnam and the United States normalized trade relations, and Vietnamese participation in the international economy has grown steadily over the past decade. The Vietnamese are also experiencing improving living standards, with the World Bank reporting impressive gains in the late 1990s, with rising incomes and reduced rates of poverty (World Bank 2001). Much remains to be done, but significant change has occurred over the past decade.

[*] We would like to thank Ronald Inglehart and the Swedish Agency for International Development for their support of the Vietnamese survey. We also gratefully acknowledge Dorothy Solinger's advice on the interpretation of some of our findings.

[**] University of California at Irvine.

[***] National Center of Social Sciences and Humanities, Hanoi.

This article examines patterns of social relations and social capital in Vietnam. We inquire into whether the ongoing changes in Vietnam's economic and political situation are related to changes in social life (Gertler and Litvack 1998; Le Thi 1999; Pham Minh Hac 2001; Pham Van Bich 1999; Dollar et al. 1998). The agricultural share of the economy is decreasing, for example, while industry and manufacturing grow in economic importance (Anderson 1999). People are migrating from rural areas to the urban centers in the North and South (Central Census Steering Committee 2000). Our research asks whether these societal changes are apparently affecting how individuals are socially connected, the nature of their social group ties, and whether new forms of social capital are developing in Vietnam. We also examine attitudes toward family and gender as a possible consequence of these trends. Social change has the potential to shape the future course of Vietnamese social and political attitudes — and that is the focus of this essay.

Our analyses are based on the first scientifically sampled national survey of public opinion in Vietnam, the World Values Survey 2001 (WVS), which was conducted by the Institute of Human Studies in Vietnam (see methodological appendix). This survey replicated the core questionnaire of the international WVS project, and also extended the Institute's own research program on "People: Goals and Driving Forces for Socio-Economic Development." This opinion survey is an especially valuable research resource because so little is scientifically known about Vietnamese attitudes on social and political issues. Among other topics, the 2001 World Values Survey inquired about family and social relations, membership and participation in social groups, and satisfaction with life conditions. This research focuses on these areas, describing contemporary opinions in Vietnam and examining how social change may affect such key features of society.

Social Relations and Social Networks

One indicator of social development comes from the patterns of social relations in a nation. Social networks are mechanisms to connect the individual to society, providing patterns of social interaction, social cues, and social identities (Inkeles and Smith 1974; Inkeles 1983; Inglehart and Baker 2000). A traditional East Asian agrarian society, for example, is normally focused around family relations (Pham Van Bich 1999). The family plays a role as a survival value, and familial ties and traditional authority patterns are emphasized within such networks. As societies modernize, work networks often become more important, as fellow employees become the significant peers in ones life. Another feature of social modernization might be the development of institutionalized social networks, such as through community groups, sports clubs or cultural groups, or other such associations. Placed against these expectations are the cultural traditions of Vietnam, in which the family plays a large and apparently continuing role as the focal point of social life. Scholars suggest that family, village and nation are closely interrelated in creating a basic structure for Vietnamese society (Hickey 1964; Nguyen Van Huyen 1944).

To map the broad contours of the actual social networks in Vietnam today, the WVS asked respondents how often they engaged in various social activities.[1] We find that the family is the central point of social life in Vietnam. A full 59% said they spend time with their parents or relatives on a weekly basis, compared to only 32% who weekly spend time with work colleagues, or 17% with social friends. These results reaffirm Hirschman and Vu's (1996) findings that more than three quarters of Vietnamese with living parents saw them on a weekly basis; these authors concluded that this was "an extraordinary pattern of intimate family ties" (Hirschman and Vu 1996:243). Weekly interactions in institutional social networks, such as through clubs or associations (9%) or religious groups (5%) are much less frequent.

As the other national surveys in the 2000-01 WVS are completed this will provide a better cross-national context for interpreting the Vietnamese findings, but recent WVS surveys for a set of East Asian nations provide some context. The gap between family activity and participation in any other network is greater in Vietnam than in China, Japan or the Philippines — but these other nations also rank the family as the most central network.[2] The Chinese also emphasize work networks (62%), because of the importance of work cooperatives and occupational issues; but participation in work networks is roughly comparable in Vietnam, Japan (21%) and the Philippines (34%). Friendship networks appear noticeably less important in Vietnam than in the other three nations; for instance, the Vietnamese are half as likely as Chinese and Philippine respondents to say they weekly meet with friends. It is also striking that religious networks are less often cited in Vietnam and Japan, and these networks are actually more active in China and the Philippines.

---

[1] The question wording is: "I'm going to ask how of often you do various things. For each activity, would you say you do them every week or nearly every week; once or twice a month; only a few times a year; or not at all? Spend time with a) parents or other relatives, b) with friends, c) socially with colleagues from work or your profession, d) with people at your church, mosque or synagogue, or e) socially with people at sports clubs or voluntary or service organization.

[2] The family is cited as a weekly activity by 90% of the Chinese, 50% of the Philippine sample, and 49% of the Japanese respondents.

One way to assess the potential effects of social development on these social networks is to examine whether these patterns vary systematically across demographic groups. For example, if there are systematic differences by income and education levels, then we might speculate that rising social status might shift patterns of social relations in predictable ways. Similarly, we expect that farmers would follow more family-center patterns of social relations than urban workers. We also might hypothesize that younger Vietnamese might place less reliance on family ties, and be more integrated to work and friendship networks. Moreover, because Vietnam still has a largely agrarian population with modest living standards, we are able to observe a nation that is relatively early in the social modernization process. What are the likely consequences if social modernization continues?

Table 1 presents the relationship between a standard set of social characteristics and the frequency of activity within each separate social network. The income and education relationships are most directly related to the social modernization theme. These analyses show that higher levels of income and affluence tend to increase involvement in *all social networks*; family activity is higher among the better educated, as well as participation in work and friendship networks. To give a reference framework for these relationships: 55 percent of respondents with a primary schooling say they meet with their parents or relatives on a weekly basis, compared to 66 percent among with at least some college education (taub = .08 in Table 1). Those in middle class occupations also tend to be more active in friendship, work and social group networks. The only exception to the general social status pattern is religious activity, which displays contrasting relationships with the social status measures. Another theoretically important predictor is age, and here again we find relatively consistent results. Participation in most social networks is more common among younger Vietnamese; the only exception is the religious sector, where older respondents report more activity. There are also modest regional differences, residents of the North are relatively more likely to engage in family or friendship network activities.

The low level of religious attachments and the pattern of relationships present a complex picture of the role of religion in Vietnamese society. On the one hand, there is a move from traditional religious values to secular-rational values among the young and better educated resulting from the Marxist-based ideology of education and the policies of the regime. On the other hand, religious activities have endured. People still talk about religious beliefs; traditional festivals are reestablished in the countryside. Most families, including communists and the intelligentsia, have "spirituality of dwelling" or "sacred place." Table 1 also indicates that religious networks are relatively more active in the Southern region of

Table 1

The Relationships between Social Characteristics and Social Network Activity

Predictor	Family	Friends	Work	Religious	Groups
Income	.05	.08*	.02	.09*	.15*
Education	.08*	.13*	.14*	−.08*	.03
R's occupation	.00	.08	.09	.04	.06
Age	−.15*	−.09*	−.12*	.09*	−.04
Male	.04	.14	.05*	−.11*	.14*
North	.08*	.10*	−.02	−.17*	.01

Source: 2001 World Values Survey, Vietnam.
Most table entries are tau-b correlations; the occupation correlation is an eta statistic.
Correlations significant at the .05 level are denoted by an asterisk.

Vietnam. These data suggest that the role of religion may not be dependent on agrarian, industrial, postindustrial or knowledge-based economies.

These are intriguing results if they reflect a general example of the early stages of social development. Higher levels of income and education in Vietnam increase participation in an array of social networks. Development does not lead away from traditional family networks, and may actually increase the density of these networks; but at the same time there is an even greater increase in participation in work, friendship and social group networks. Thus further development in Vietnam is not so likely to exchange on set of social networks for another, but to expand the number and activity levels of the networks that connect individuals to society, and which help form their social and political identities.

Group Memberships

Another important theme in the literature on social development is the degree of social involvement within a society, or what is often described as a civil society (Yamamoto 1996; Abuza 2001: 12-15; Shi 1998). Participation in social groups develops the interpersonal skills that are part of the evolution of a modern society, and helps to broaden the life experiences and perspectives of group members. An active civil society also provides a training ground for developing political skills, and diverse groups may serve as agents of interest articulation within society and politics.

The Western literature on Vietnam is divided on the extent of such civil society activity in the nation. Membership in social groups has apparently ebbed and flowed over time, in part in reaction to the government's efforts to mobilize the public to participate in such organizations. While some scholars suggest that *doi moi* has led to the expansion of civil society as new organizations emerge to represent new interests in society (Thayer 1995; Lockhart 1997), others maintain that such social forces in Vietnam are less autonomous and assertive than the comparable social groups in Eastern Europe (Womack 1993).

To provide empirical evidence on these points, the World Values Survey asked respondents whether they were a member of a group in 14 different areas (and an additional "other" category). Figure 1 describes a Vietnamese population that is engaged in an active social life. A fifth or more of the public report they are members of a sport/recreation group, a local community group, a social welfare organization, a women's group, or a political group. There is also substantial involvement in educational/cultural groups, unions, professional association, and youth groups. The typical Vietnamese respondent reports belonging to 2.33 groups, which is significantly higher than the Chinese (.91), Japanese (1.41), or the Philippine (1.93) survey findings. [3]

At least in part, these patterns of group membership reflect the past efforts of the Vietnamese government to actively engage the public in social groups that were initiated and directed by the government. The

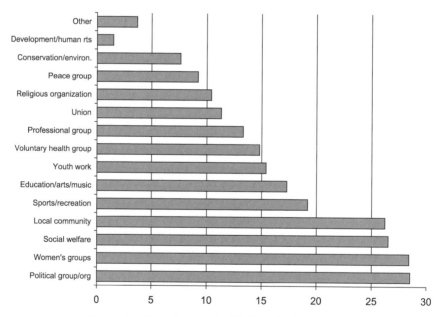

Figure 1.   Membership in Various Social Groups.

---

[3] We should also note that membership in a group does not mean that all members are actively participating in group activities. In Vietnam and the other WVS nations it is common for only about 10 percent of group members to describe themselves as active participants.

Vietnamese Women's Association, the Ho Chi Minh Youth Union, the Vietnam Farmers Association, the Vietnamese Confederation of Labor and other groups have historically served as avenues for the government to communicate with key social sectors in Vietnam, and often these groups claimed large national memberships (Porter 1993: ch. 3). Participation in the Youth Union, for example, was often a route to career advancement, and participation in such groups was encouraged. More recently the government encouraged various local cooperatives to address certain community issues. The result is a high degree of social engagement, even if it does not fully match the civil society model of democratic theory.

If we simply count the number of groups to which an individual belongs, we again find evidence that social development increases the density of social networks and civil society participation within Vietnam. Group membership is significantly higher among those who are better educated (taub = .13) and those with higher incomes (taub = .13). While it is often the case that group membership increases with age and the accumulation of family responsibilities and a career,[4] there is no such age relationship in Vietnam (taub = .02). This suggests that younger Vietnamese are engaging in social groups with increasing frequency as part of the social development of the nation, thus group membership may grow even more in the future.

Social Trust

One of the theorized consequences of expanding social networks is that they break down parochial attitudes and lead to more cosmopolitan views of the world. In addition, extensive social network participation may weaken traditional ascriptive patterns of authority, as individuals work with others to address common interests. Of course, such effects depend on the nature and content of the interactions that occur within social networks, some of which may reinforce or diminish such patterns.

Research frequently focuses on social trust as an indicator of the content of social relations in a nation, and a potential byproduct of patterns of social capital formation. Ronald Inglehart (1997) and Robert Putnam (2002), for example, emphasize that trust in others is a key element in developing a civic culture. But it is less clear what might be expected in Vietnamese attitudes of social trust. Traditional agrarian and Confucian traditions often encourage trust in a relatively narrow circle of family and close friends, and caution about the unknown stranger. The cultural legacy of communism is also unclear, since prior research demonstrates that levels of social trust vary widely across East European nations in the

---

[4] For example, there is a significant positive relationship between age and group membership in Japan (.19) and the United States (.07).

1990s (Inglehart 1997; Newton 1999). Vietnam's changing socio-economic conditions and increased interaction with the international community may also affect these orientations.

The World Values Survey contains a standard survey question tapping trust in others. [5] The Vietnamese respondents are somewhat skeptical about their fellow man: only 41% think that most people can be trusted, while 59% say that one needs to be careful in dealing with other people. But these results should be interpreted in the context of other cross-national findings. In all the combined nations of the 1995-98 World Values Survey, only 26% of respondents said that most people could be trusted. In terms of other East Asian nations, 42% of Japanese respondents, 41% of the Taiwanese, 52% of the Chinese and only 6% of the Philippine respondents say they trust others. Thus the Vietnamese national level of social trust appears higher than some other nations at Vietnam's stage of economic development.

In exploring the potential impact of social modernization on trust, we found that education and income differences in trust are very slight, not rising to the level of statistical significance. Age patterns are also not statistically significant. Expressions of interpersonal trust are, however, much more common in northern provinces (55%) than in central (28%) or southern (37%) Vietnam. Finally, we find a complex non-linear relationship between social capital, as represented by the number of group memberships, and social trust. Social trust is low among those who do not belong to any social group, and increases with membership in one or two groups. But among the hyperactive — those who belong to five or more groups — social trust dips to its lowest level (27% trustful). We suspect that further analyses can isolate the characteristics of the hyperactive and provide an explanation for these results.

In summary, our findings suggest that social modernization in Vietnam is affecting the pattern of social relations among the public. Although the traditional orientations toward family and community remain, modernization is broadening social networks. In addition, perhaps as the residue of the political mobilization of the past, the levels of social capital and social trust are relatively high among the Vietnamese public, especially in comparison to nations at the same level of economic development.

Family Relations and Authority Patterns

The importance of family is a historic aspect of Vietnamese society, as with many Confucian societies in East Asia. The family is a basis of economic

---

[5] The question wording is as follows: "Generally speaking, would you say that most people can be trusted or that you need to be very careful in dealing with people?"

organization in an agrarian economy, the role of the father and parents in general is reinforced by cultural traditions, and family relations provide a general model for authority relations (Pham 1999; Pye 1985). Through history and changes in political and social regimes, the centrality of the family appears to be an enduring feature of Vietnamese society.

Even though such patterns are widely cited in the literature on Vietnam, there is limited empirical research on family relations and attitudes toward the family. Thus the World Values Survey provides a valuable opportunity to systematically examine public opinion on this aspect of social life. For example, one question asked about the importance of several life domains. The family is ranked as "very important" by 82% of the Vietnamese; this is roughly comparable to the other East Asian nations in the 1995-98 World Values Survey: China (77%), Taiwan (77%), Korea (90%), and Japan (91%). [6] Another survey question shows that most respondents (88%) think a greater emphasis on family life would be a good thing. The centrality of the family in social life and social relations is apparent throughout our survey.

However, to go beyond general impressions of the importance of family life the survey probed deeper into the values attached to family and parents, and how these orientations are translated into authority relations more generally. The Vietnamese believe in filial piety (*hieu de*) as the children's duty toward their parents. Traditions of ancestor worship and the acceptance of patrilineal authority further deepened the importance of the family as basis for social life. Thus, we find that almost all respondents (99%) say that parents are to be respected regardless of their qualities and faults. In another question, 97% state that "one of my main goals in life has been to make my parents proud." Indeed, even in comparison to other East Asian nations in the 1995-98 WVS, Vietnam ranks the highest on respect for parents (see Figure 2). At the same time, 87% of Vietnamese say that it is the "parents' duty is to do their best for their children even at the expense of their own well-being." [7]

A common question throughout East Asia asks how social modernization might interact with the traditional importance of the family, and the images of hierarchical (and paternalistic) authority that this implies. Exposure to outside media, the pressures of contemporary economics, and other

---

[6] The percent who said other life domains were very important is as follows: work (57%), politics (39%), friends (22%), religion (10%), and leisure (7%).

[7] The question wording is as follows: "Which of the following statements best describes your views about parents' responsibilities to their children: a) Parents' duty is to do their best for their children even at the expense of their own well-being, b) Parents have a life of their own and should not be asked to sacrifice their own well-being for the sake of their children, or c) Neither?

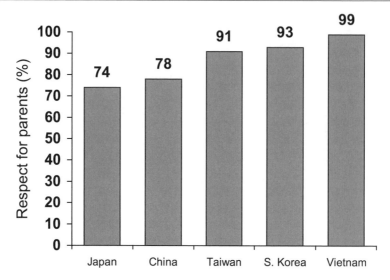

Figure 2.   Respect for Parents in East Asian Countries.

social forces are generally seen as eroding the traditional role of the family in nations across the globe, as well as East Asia.

A series of correlational analyses (not shown), suggest that social modernization has a complex relationship to family attitudes in Vietnam. Much as we observed for activity in social networks, the ascribed importance of the family actually is higher among the better-educated and higher income Vietnamese, and there is no erosion of these sentiments among the young. However, other patterns in these data suggest that the content of family relations may change — if not the importance of these relationships. The "strongest" measure of commitment to the parental family structure is the belief that parents have a duty to their children; these sentiments are significantly less common among the better-educated and younger Vietnamese. For instance, the percentage saying parents should have a life of their own rises from 4.5% among those over age 60 to 14.2% among those younger than age 30.

Changing family relations also have the potential impact to shape other social and political relationships that may have developed to reflect the hierarchical structures of the family. We find, for example, that those who believe it is a parent's duty to sacrifice for their children are slightly more likely to approve of respect for authority (81%) than those who think parents should live their own lives (73%). Similarly, the former are more likely to believe that parents should emphasize obedience in raising children (57%) compared to the latter group (45%). In addition, a belief in parental duty is strongly related to social trust (taub = .12). This final relationship occurs, perhaps, because a belief in parental duty and the importance of family may be linked to a view that social relationships should also be family based, and one can trust those within the family network (e.g., Pye 1985:80). In contrast, those who are less centered on family relations may also be more cautious about the larger social network in which interactions will occur.

In summary, with continued social modernization these trends may gradually erode the authority structure of family relations, even while the social importance of family may prove more durable. And as a consequence, other aspects of Vietnamese society and politics that are connected to family authority patterns may also change.

Gender Relations

Another element of family life concerns the role of women in Vietnamese society. Although there is some archeological evidence that early Vietnamese tribal society was matrilineal and matrilocal, this changed with the Chinese colonization (Frenier and Mancini 1996). When Chinese warlords conquered and annexed Vietnam in 111 B.C., Chinese culture began to force itself into Vietnam, including Confucian teachings. Many Chinese traditions of restricting women's roles were adopted within Vietnamese society. In a classic study of Vietnamese culture, Dao Duy Anh (1938/1998) characterized the roles of the Vietnamese women in the 1930s as quite limited. Vietnamese folklore and literature also stereotype the women's roles and place in the society: Chastity was prized; marriages were arranged; a married woman had to serve her husband and his family by maintaining housework; women ought to bear children because such is their duty (Cong Huyen Ton Nu 1973).

As Vietnamese society modernizes, it is expected that differences in gender roles will narrow. Communist ideology as well as the Laws on Marriage and the Family have attempted to promote gender equality within Vietnamese society (Pham 1999). Especially during the recent years of economic reform, women have made up a vital portion of the labor force, from agriculture to the business sector. The 1999 Census indicates that women constitute the majority of the labor force in the rural (72%) and urban areas (56%) (Central Census Steering Committee 2000). The gap between the male and female proportion of the labor force is also narrowing within the younger generations. This trend is probably due to more men shifting toward the private sector after *doi moi* or the closing gender gap in education (Central Census Steering Committee 2000). For instance, in the year 1997-98, the ratio of female to male students in college was 44 percent for public and 48 percent for private universities (Pham Xuan Nam 2001).

The WVS examined gender attitudes in several areas. Several questions focused on support for a traditional role for women. For instance, a plurality (48%) believes that a man has more right to a job when employment is scarce. At the same time, a large majority claim that a woman needs to have children in order to fulfill her role (86%); however, only 16% approve of a woman being single parent. Furthermore, being a housewife is seen as just as fulfilling as working for pay (86%). Indeed, the Census finds that 50% of the urban women who were economically inactive described themselves as carrying out home duties (Central Census Steering Committee 2000). On the other hand, nearly all Vietnamese (97%) think that both husband and wife should contribute to the household income. This finding reflects somewhat the push for gender equality in the socialist regime. However, more women entering the work force does not mean their home duties are alleviated; rather, many women carry double responsibilities because they not only earn a living from work but also fulfill their traditional roles as a mother and a wife at home (Gammeltoft 1999; Trinh Minh-ha 1992).

These attitudes are not limited to Vietnam. Adherence to a traditional role for women is also common among East Asian nations based on the 1995-98 WVS. For example, a significant number of people believe that men have more right to a job than women in Japan (33%), South Korea (43%), China (42%), and Taiwan (52%). Meanwhile, the need for both spouses' contribution to the household incomes is perceived highly in Japan (59%), South Korea (79%), China (89%), and Taiwan (90%). These sentiments reflect in part economic needs that push both spouses into the work force in both developed and developing East Asian countries.

Although the Vietnamese are more likely to think that a woman needs to have children, the majority in other East Asian nations share these views: Taiwan (52%), China (67%), to Japan (72%) and South Korea (72%). On the same note, approval of women as single parents is still low in these nations, while belief that being a fulfilling role remains common. [8]

Another aspect of gender roles involves politics. The majority of Vietnamese WVS respondents say that men are better politicians (56%). These biases in opinions also appear in the composition of political elites. For the term 1997-2002, for example, only 118 out of the 450 Congress representatives (26%) are women. Female local officials for the term 1999-2004 are still scant with 23% at the provincial level, 21% at the district level, and only 16% at the ward level (Pham Xuan Nam 2001).

---

[8] Approval of single parenthood is low in China (6%), Taiwain (11%), Japan (17%) and South Korea (31%); while that a housewife is a fulfilling role is common: China (69%), South Korea (89%), Taiwan (86%), and Japan (90%).

Several communist nations of Eastern Europe had a quota on women's representation, but there is not yet such quota in the Vietnamese political system.

Despite the conservative outlooks on women's roles in the Vietnamese society, the WVS also found strong rejection of the statement that education is more important for boys than for girls (76%), compared to 63% in Japan, 63% in South Korea, 76% in China, and 78% in Taiwan. This may reflect the high value attributed to education by social norms in East Asian nations, which transcend gender lines. Yet, recent Vietnamese census results still show a significantly higher proportion of females are illiterate or hold only a general level of education, and the number of females without an education is nearly twice that of males (Central Census Steering Committee 2000). In short, gender equality in education falls short of social norms in Vietnam.

We speculated that social modernization may attenuate support for a traditional role for women; and we test this hypothesis in Table 2. Education is clearly related to perceptions of gender relations. Among those with no or little education, for example, up to 54% think that men have more right to a job, and this drops to only 33% among the college-educated (tau-b = −.11). Other relationships in terms of social class, income, and gender are less clear. Age differences are also surprisingly modest; only on issues of the political role of women and education for women are younger Vietnamese distinctly more supportive of women. North/South regional differences are often statistically significant, but their pattern is varied. We suspect that more detailed multivariate analyses, including urban/rural differences and occupational patterns, may underlie some of these regional variations. In general, traditional sentiments toward women's place in the Vietnamese society remain rigid but tend to soften in some areas among the better educated and the more affluent.

Conclusion

Vietnam is a society and political system in the midst of change. While Vietnam's economic development remains limited, the *doi moi* reforms have begun to transform the structure of the Vietnamese economy and social structure. With these reforms have come a steady growth of the private economy, a movement from the countryside into the cities, and growing trade and social exchanges with the rest of the world (Dollar et al. 1998). This article described some of the structural features of contemporary Vietnamese society through the 2001 World Values Survey, and examines how these social forces are affecting the Vietnamese public.

Reflecting the traditions of many other East Asian societies, we find clear evidence of the continuing centrality of the family in Vietnam today.

Table 2

The Relationships between Social Characteristics and Gender Relations

Predictor	Men right to job	Women need children	Approve single parent	Women house-work	Both spouses contribute	Men better pols.	Educate boys
Income	−.01	−.02	.06*	.06*	−.03	−.10*	−.07*
Education	−.11*	−.05	.06*	−.03	−.09*	−.05*	−.15*
R's Occupation	.08*	.07*	.02	.07*	.07*	.01	.05
Age	.03	.04	−.02	−.02	.03	.06*	−.09*
Male	.09*	−.05	−.07*	−.03	−.10*	.03	−.04
North	−.08*	.13*	.00	.05	−.23*	−.10*	−.02

Source: 2001 World Values Survey, Vietnam.
All table entries are tau-b correlations; the occupation correlation is an eta statistic.
Correlations significant at the .05 level are denoted by an asterisk.

Family ties remain the center of social networks for many individuals, and respect for parents is virtually universal. Our data suggests that social modernization is not so much eroding these traditional family-based networks, but expanding social relations to include other social networks, such as work and social group networks. The better educated and the young, for example, are more densely connected in a range of social networks including and extending beyond the family. Indeed, one of the striking cross-national patterns is the extensive level of group membership reported by the Vietnamese. Even though scholars remain divided on the social and political implications of these group networks, their importance is likely to increase as a consequence of Vietnam's continuing social modernization. Group membership does not necessarily fit the civil society model found in other developing nations, but the existence of such extensive networks creates such a potential.

The strength of family traditions in Vietnam may also explain attitudes toward gender relations. Despite the economic and social advances that women have made in the past generation, support for full gender equality is still lacking. Most Vietnamese, including both men and women, still ascribe to a traditional role for women: believing that a man has more right to a job and that housework for a wife is just as fulfilling as paid employment. The majority of Vietnamese also say that men are better politicians. Although there is some evidence that social modernization will attenuate these orientations, the evidence of even more limited than for our social network analyses. These patterns may underscore Pham's (1999: ch. 5) conclusions that the concept of gender equality may be difficult to develop in a society that accepts Confucian traditions, the centrality of family, and the associated patterns of authority relations.

The social bases of these attitudes suggest that the continued social modernization of Vietnam will change many of these attitudes and values, albeit in complex ways that do not signal a single pattern of change. For instance, modernization may not diminish the importance of the family social network in absolute terms, but it many stimulate other social connections that begin to rival the influence of family. Moreover, many of the differences in these attitudes across social groups are quite modest, as Vietnam remains a relatively homogeneous society. But the long-term impact of *doi moi* and social modernization may be to increase this diversity, accentuating the trends we have described here.

References

ABUZA, ZACHARY
2001   *Renovating Politics in Contemporary Vietnam*. Boulder, CO: Lynne Rienner.
ANDERSON, KYM
1999   *Vietnam's Transforming Economy and WTO Accession*. Singapore: Institute for Southeast Asian Studies.
CENTRAL CENSUS STEERING COMMITTEE
2000   *1999 Population and Housing Census: Sample Results*. Hanoi, Vietnam: The Gioi Publishers.
CONG HUYEN TON NU, NHA TRANG
1973   *The Traditional Roles of Women as Reflected in Oral and Written Vietnamese Literature*. Dissertation. University of California, Berkeley.
DAO, DUY ANH
1998   *Viet Nam Van Hoa Su Cuong*. [Vietnamese Cultural Factbook]. Dong Thap, Vietnam: NXB Dong Thap, 1998.
DOLLAR, DAVID, GLEWWE, PAUL, AND JENNIE LITVACK
1998   *Household Welfare and Vietnam's Transition* (World Bank Regional and Sectoral Studies). Washington, D.C.: The World Bank.
FRENIER, MARIAM DARCE AND MANCINI, KIMBERLY
1996   "Vietnamese Women in a Confucian Setting: The Causes of the Initial Decline in the Status of East Asian Women." In Kathleen Barry, ed., *Vietnam's Women in Transition*. New York, NY: St. Martin's Press.
GAMMELTOFT, TINE
1999   *Women's Bodies, Women's Worries: Health and Family Planning in a Vietnamese Rural Community*. Surrey, Britain: Curzon Press.
GERTLER, PAUL AND LITVACK, JENNIE
1998   "Access to health care during transition: The role of the private sector in Vietnam." In David Dollar, Paul Glewwe, and Jennie Litvack, eds., *Household Welfare and Vietnam's Transition*. Washington, D.C.: World Bank, pp. 61-98.
HICKEY, GERALD CANNON
1964   *Village in Vietnam*. Cambridge, MA: Yale University Press.
HIRSCHMAN, CHARLES AND VU MANH LOI
1996   Family and household structure in Vietnam: Some glimpses from a recent survey. *Pacific Affairs* 69 (2): 229-249.

INGLEHART, RONALD
1997   *Modernization and Postmodernization: Cultural, Economic and Political Change in 43 Nations*. Princeton, NJ: Princeton University Press.
INGLEHART, RONALD AND W. BAKER
2000   Modernization, cultural change, and the persistence of traditional values. *American Sociological Review* 65: 19-51.
INKELES, ALEX
1983   *Exploring Individual Modernity*. New York: Columbia University Press.
INKELES, ALEX AND DAVID SMITH
1974   *Becoming Modern Individual Change in Six Developing Countries*. Cambridge, MA: Harvard University Press.
LE, THI
1999   *The Role of the Family in the Formation of Vietnamese Personality*. Hanoi, Vietnam: The Gioi Publishers.
LOCKART, GREG
1997   Mass Mobilization in Contemporary Vietnam. *Asian Studies Review* 21 (November).
NEWTON, KENNETH
1999   "Social and Political Trust in Established Democracies." In Pippa Norris, ed., *Critical Citizens*. Oxford, Great Britain: Oxford University Press.
NGUYEN VAN HUYEN
1944   *The Civilisation of Vietnam*.
PHAM, KIM VINH
1992   *Vietnam: A Comprehensive History*. California: Pham Kim Vinh Research Institute.
PHAM MINH HAC
1994   *Human Factors in the Renovation Cause*. Hanoi, Vietnam. KX-07.
PHAM MINH HAC
2001   *Human and Human Resource Studies in Industrialization and Modernization*. Hanoi, Vietnam: Political Publishing House.
PHAM, VAN BICH
1999   *The Vietnamese Family in Change: The Case of the Red River Delta*. Surrey, Great Britain: Curzon Press.
PHAM, VAN SON
1960   *Viet Su Toan Thu*. [Vietnamese Complete History]. Saigon, Vietnam: Thu Lam.
PHAM, XUAN NAM
2001   *Quan Ly Su Phat Trien Xa Hoi Tren Nguyen Tac Tien Bo va Cong Bang*. [Managing Society's Development on Principles of Progress and Justice]. Hanoi.
PORTER, GARETH
1993   *The Politics of Bureaucratic Socialism*. Cornell University Press.
PUTNAM, ROBERT, ED.
2002   *Democracies in Flux*. New York, NY: Oxford University Press.
SHI, TIANJIN
1997   *Political Participation in Beijing*. Cambridge, MA: Harvard University Press.
THAYER, CARLYLE
1995   "Mono-organizational Socialism." In Benedict Tria Kerkvleit and Doug Porter, eds., *Vietnam's Rural Transformation*. Boulder, CO: Westview Press.

TRINH, MINH-HA
1992   *Framer Framed.* New York, NY: Routledge.
TURLEY, WILLIAM AND MARK SELDEN, EDS.
1992   *Reinventing Vietnamese Socialism: Doi Moi in Comparative Perspective.* Boulder, CO:
            Westview Press.
WEINS, THOMAS B.
1998   "Agriculture and rural poverty in Vietnam." In David Dollar, Paul Glewwe,
            and Jennie Litvack, eds., *Household Welfare and Vietnam's Transition.* Washington,
            D.C.: World Bank, pp. 61-98.
WOMACK, BRANTLY
1993   "Political Reform and Political Change in Communist Countries: Implications
            for Vietnam." In William Turley and Mark Selden, eds., *Reinventing Vietnamese
            Socialism* Boulder, CO: Westview.
WORLD BANK
2001   *World Development Report.* Washington, D.C.: World Bank.
YAMAMOTO, TADASHI
1996   *Integrative Report. Emerging Civil Society in the Asia Pacific Community.* Institute
            of Southeast Asian Studies, Singapore, and Japan Center for International
            Exchange, Japan, pp. 1-40.

Methodological Appendix

The survey was conducted in September-October 2001 using a multi-stage area probability sample with a designated random walk household selection at the last stage. The Institute for Human Studies in Vietnam conducted the project and fieldwork under the direction of Dr. Pham Minh Hac.

In the first stage, we stratified provinces by the eight census regions and selected twenty provinces on a basis proportional to population. Within these provinces 99 districts were randomly selected, and two villages or town were selected from each district. In the final stage there were 200 primary sampling units; within each sampling unit the interviewer conducted a designated "random walk" to select five households. Within each household the interviewer selected the adult with the nearest birthday. The response rate was approximately 83 percent. The sample consists of 1,000 respondents distributed proportionately throughout Vietnam to be representative of the adult population. In comparison to 1999 census statistics (Central Census Steering Committee 2000), the survey closely represents the population on several standard demographic measures:

	Survey	Census		Survey	Census
Red River Delta	19.9%	19.4%	18-19 years	5.2%	6.5
Northeast	14.4	14.2	20-29	17.5	29.1
Northwest	2.9	2.9	30-39	23.2	25.4
North Central	8.1	13.1	40-49	23.9	16.7
Central Coast	13.2	8.6	50+ years	30.2	22.3
Central Highland	6.5	4.0			
Southeast	12.8	16.6	No education	4.2%	9.8
Mekong River Delta	22.2	21.2	Primary	32.0	50.3
			Lower sec.	33.7	26.7
Male	49.1%	48.4	Upper sec.	23.2	10.4
Female	50.9	51.6	College	6.9	2.7

The statistical sampling error of this study is approximately 3 to 4 percent. This means that national percentages in this report are likely (95 percent of the time) to be within ±4 percent of the actual population percentages. In addition, one should also consider that this was the first application of national probability sampling on a political attitude survey in Vietnam. The Vietnamese population also is unfamiliar with the survey methodology, and some respondents may feel hesitant to express their opinions fully. So it is possible that non-sampling errors are also present in these data even though the Institute for Human Studies expressed their willingness to take extraordinary care to follow scientific procedures.

Additional information on the Vietnamese survey, the English and Vietnamese language questionnaires, sampling design, and information on the World Values Survey project is available on our project website:
www.democ.uci.edu/democ/archive/vietnam.htm

Authority Orientations and Political Support: A Cross-national Analysis of Satisfaction with Governments and Democracy[*]

NEIL NEVITTE[**] AND MEBS KANJI[**]

Introduction

In the mid 1970's Samuel Huntington predicted that the new middle classes in many advanced industrial states would become more restless and "post-industrial politics" less benign (1974; also Crozier, Huntington and Watanuki 1975). The accumulated evidence provides some support for that prediction; citizens in a number of states have become more inclined to publicly express their dissatisfaction with governments (Inglehart 1997; Klingemann 1999; Dalton 1999). Occasional citizen dissatisfaction with a particular government is neither unusual nor necessarily problematic. More problematical is the possibility that deep and sustained dissatisfaction might corrode regime support. The worry is that dissatisfaction with particular governments might turn into dissatisfaction with the workings of democracy more generally.

What are the determinants of dissatisfaction with governments? And, what is the connection between citizens' evaluations of government performance and their satisfaction or dissatisfaction with the workings of democracy more generally? This analysis examines these two separate but closely related questions. Neither research question is new, but we depart from

[*] We gratefully acknowledge the financial support of the Social Sciences and Humanities Research Council of Canada, Research Grant # 829991010. The Research Council is not responsible for the interpretation of the findings reported in this article.

[**] Department of Political Science, University of Toronto, Canada.

conventional approaches in three respects. First, we argue that contemporary explanations for dissatisfaction with governments may pay insufficient attention to the structure of authority patterns. Following Eckstein (1966, 1969), we explore the possibility that discrepancies in authority patterns have significant independent effects on levels of citizen satisfaction and dissatisfaction with governments.

Second, prevailing explanations of variations in diffuse support focus primarily on the importance of institutions (Newton and Norris 2000). Citizens' assessments of their political systems may not always be "of a piece." As Norris observes, publics can, and do, "distinguish between different levels of the regime, often believing strongly in democratic values, for example, while proving critical of the way that democratic governments work in practice" (1999a:9). Public confidence in political institutions undoubtedly is crucial to the vitality of democratic life, but so are political actors. What is less certain, and what is open to investigation, is whether it is outlooks towards political institutions rather than political actors that are more important determinants of citizen satisfaction with the workings of democracy.

Researchers investigating these two broad questions have relied primarily on empirical evidence from advanced industrial states. There is no reason to suppose that the dynamics driving citizen satisfaction and dissatisfaction in wealthy well established democratic states would be the same as those driving citizens' evaluations of their governments in poorer countries with briefer experiences with democratic practices. The third goal of this analysis, then, is to broaden the field of investigation and to use data from the 2000 World Values Surveys to test the extent to which hypotheses derived from different theoretical perspectives hold up in both advanced industrial states and less wealthy ones.

Theoretical Orientation

Most analysts of contemporary democratic life in western states do not claim that democracy is in crisis (Norris 1999; Klingemann and Fuchs 1995; Kaase and Newton 1995), but they do suggest that most citizens believe that all is not well (Putnam, Pharr and Dalton 2000:27). A variety of explanations have been suggested to account for the most critical sources of citizen discontent.

Some explanations focus on value change. In one of the most prominent variations of this line of reasoning, Ronald Inglehart argues that "mass values and attitudes are a major influence on whether or not democratic institutions survive in a given society" (2000:225). Much of Inglehart's research indicates that the core values of publics are changing and these changes have consequences for what people want out of life and what citizens expect of governments. Raised under conditions of material and physical security, post-war generations have shifted away from a preoccupation with basic material needs towards postmaterialist concerns (Inglehart 1990, 1997). Postmaterialist values embrace a variety of "higher order" concerns including a preference for more open government. The sheer volume and consistency of the evidence in support of this value change theory is impressive. The same basic finding emerges in nearly every country for which there are systematic data: those segments of the publics holding postmaterialist values are more critical of traditional hierarchical institutions and consistently more likely to engage in elite challenging behaviors. Moreover, Inglehart's account goes considerable distance towards explaining why the relationship between levels of material wealth in a society and levels of public satisfaction with governments is not a simple linear one.

A second explanation focuses more on how structural changes (Clarke and Rempel 1997) have contributed to rising levels of cognitive mobilization (Dalton 1984, 2002; Inglehart 1990). The cognitive mobilization explanation draws attention to how the accumulation of skills and resources of an increasingly well educated middle class and the combined effects of these changes promote rising levels of citizen engagement (Dalton 1984:267). Wider access to higher levels of formal education is particularly significant because higher levels of formal education have important consequences for citizen outlooks and behavior (Nie, Junn and Stehlik-Barry 1996). One is that they provide individuals with a greater capacity to organize information and to be more independent in the interpretation and use of that information (see also, Dalton and Wattenberg, 1993). Higher levels of formal education are also associated with greater interest in politics, and greater interest supplies the motivation to seek out more information. These publics are not only more interested in, and knowledgeable about, their civic worlds, they are also more inclined to be active and critical.

A third socio-cultural explanation for why public satisfaction with governments and politics might be in short supply is the erosion in levels of social capital (Putnam 1995, 2000; Norris 2001). Social capital concerns both social networks and the norms of reciprocity that lubricate those networks, in particular interpersonal trust. Putnam argues that it is the technological transformation of leisure that is responsible for declining levels of civic engagement and undermining social trust, and the effects of these transformations have made it even more difficult for governments to govern. Regardless of whether the erosion of social capital is directly attributable to new modes of leisure, the evidence showing that citizens with weak social capital, low interpersonal trust, exhibit levels of satisfaction with government that are significantly lower than those where people enjoy higher levels of social capital is remarkably consistent (Putnam 1993, 1995, 2000).

These three accounts of the changing dynamics between citizens and government have become well-established explanations for good reasons. They are plausible, they are firmly grounded in well-established theory, and each is backed by an impressive body of empirical evidence. Even so, it is not clear that these accounts exhaust all of the explanatory possibilities and, in our view, there is a fourth possible explanation that warrants some consideration. The origins of this alternative explanation reach back to the seminal work of Harry Eckstein (1966, 1969).

Eckstein's theorizing began with the observation that authority orientations are a fundamental axis of political life. Drawing upon configurative case studies of Norway, Britain and Germany, Eckstein argued that an explanation for the presence of democratic stability in some countries, but not others, is attributable to the presence or absence of congruence in the authority patterns in society.[1] Eckstein's initial preoccupation was in demonstrating that the roots of democratic stability could be explained by the extent to which family and political authority patterns were congruent. Pateman (1970) later demonstrated that this general line of reasoning could also be extended and applied to the link between authority patterns in the workplace and those in the polity. And other research more recently suggests that authority patterns in the workplace are also systematically connected to those in the family (Nevitte 1996).

It is Eckstein and Gurr's (1975) later investigations that turned to focus on what consequences discrepant authority patterns might have for support for governments and legitimacy, and these directly inform the core hypothesis explored here. Congruent authority patterns, Eckstein and Gurr contend, foster allegiance to governments whereas inconsistencies in authority patterns have the potential to undermine public satisfaction with governments and imperil that allegiance (Eckstein and Gurr 1975:450). This innovative theorizing about authority patterns represented an important advance in empirical democratic theory, but the empirical foundations of these claims were almost entirely grounded in case studies. While quite specific hypotheses about variations in citizen satisfaction can be readily deduced from this theory, these hypotheses have not, to our knowledge, been subject to rigorous empirical testing with systematic cross-national evidence. Our goals are to draw on the insights from this earlier body of theory, to recast the central propositions

---

[1] As Eckstein and Gurr put it later "a government will tend to be stable, if its authority pattern is congruent with the other authority patterns of the society of which it is a part (1975:234).

in the form of testable hypotheses, and to investigate those hypotheses using recent WVS data from multiple countries. We evaluate the contribution of this alternative perspective by placing the empirical findings inspired by the Eckstein perspective in the context of those coming from the three more contemporary theories outlined above.

Data and Methods

The World Values Surveys (WVS) are a useful data source for testing hypotheses about authority orientations, views about government performance and democratic satisfaction for a combination of reasons. First, these surveys contain data from multiple countries and the same core set of questions asked in each country has been designed to ensure cross-national equivalence. The WVS include well-tested measures for each of the theoretical concepts that are central to this analysis. Furthermore, the WVS use the same standard methodologies for sampling and data collection techniques, and the timing of the data collection was deliberately coordinated to maximize comparability. Consequently, we can be reasonably confident that the WVS yield data that meet the necessary standards of cross national comparability.

Eckstein and Gurr's claim that discrepancies in authority orientations contribute to dissatisfaction in citizen evaluations of a government's performance is not a proposition they limit to advanced industrial states. To test the generalizabilty of that claim, we examine data from eight countries (n = 11,739) that vary significantly with respect to their institutional make-up, the extent of their experience with democratic practices, and levels of wealth: Argentina, Canada, Chile, Japan, Mexico, Nigeria, Spain, and the United States. [2] The details of how each variable is operationalized are documented in Appendix A. The baseline measure of people's orientations to political authority is operationalized by using the five-item political action index (Marsh and Kaase 1979). The assumption is that people's views toward political authority are reflected in their willingness to challenge political authority. For comparative purposes, the scale scores are standardized (range from 0 to 1, where 1 = a strong willingness to challenge political authority). To compare whether, and how, citizens' orientations towards authority vary across different domains we consider five additional measures all of which are standardized (0 = a high level of deference, to 1 = low level of deference). These codings correspond to that used in the baseline index. The first indicator, is

---

[2] The results reported here are based on the unweighted data. In all cases, the unweighted results are virtually identical to the weighted results; they produce no substantive differences in interpretation.

greater respect for authority in the future a good thing or a bad thing, taps general orientations toward authority. Two indicators tap attitudes toward authority in the family: Do respondents feel it is important to teach children about obedience in the home? And should one always love and respect their parents, or only when they have earned it? The two remaining indicators measure orientations toward authority in the workplace: Who should own and participate in the management of business and industry — owners and government, or employees? And, when should one follow instructions at work — always, even when one does not fully agree with them, or only when one is convinced they are right?

Findings

The place to begin is with the basic aggregate data. As Figure 1 shows, there are significant cross-national variations with respect to citizens' orientations towards the baseline measure of political authority. The willingness of publics to challenge political authority is positively related to aggregate income levels. In effect, every $10,000 increase in GDP/capita, corresponds to a .3 increase on the willingness to challenge political authority index. These results are entirely consistent with other findings (Welzel and Inglehart 2001; Welzel, Inglehart and Klingemann 2001) and they suggest that citizen inclinations to challenge political authority is a basic trait of open societies, and open societies tend to be more prosperous. Significantly, however, the willingness of publics to challenge political authority is not a proxy for public satisfaction with democracy. These WVS data show, for example, that the highest levels of public satisfaction with democracy are found in Spain, but the Spanish rank fourth, well behind publics in the United States, Canada and Japan, on their willingness to challenge authority. Similarly, Japan ranks third on willingness to challenge authority but they rank well below publics in six other countries in their levels of satisfaction with democracy.

Variations in aggregate outlooks toward authority clearly do distinguish publics in less developed countries from their counterparts in advanced industrial states, but the core component of the Eckstein and Gurr hypothesis that relates authority orientations to levels of satisfaction with governments is primarily concerned with discrepancies between political authority orientations and authority orientations in other domains. The first point to establish is: To what extent, in each of these eight countries, is there evidence of discrepancies between orientations towards political authority and such other authority orientations as those in the family and the workplace? Figure 2 reports the aggregate mean differences between each country's average score on the baseline index — willingness to challenge political authority — and their national average scores on each

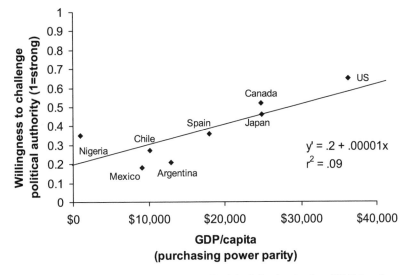

Figure 1.   Willingness to Challenge Political Authority by GDP/capita.

Note: willingness to challenge political authority is measured using a standardized 5-item additive index.
See Appendix A for question wording and coding.
Source: 2000 World Values Surveys and The World Factbook, 2001.

of the five additional indicators of authority orientations. Several relevant findings emerge.

First, the presence of discrepancies in authority orientations is clearly not atypical. In fact, there are statistically significant differences between orientations towards political authority and authority orientations in other domains in about 95% of the cases examined.[3]

Second, the data indicate significant cross-national variations in the scale of these discrepancies. The greater the distance between each mean score and the intersection of the vertical axis, the greater the discrepancy. Equally significant is the clear evidence indicating that not all discrepancies in authority orientations operate in the same direction. Mean scores arrayed to the left of the vertical axis, *negative* discrepancies, indicate that most citizens in that country are less deferential in their political authority outlooks than they are in their general, workplace and family authority outlooks. Points distributed along the right side of the vertical axis, *positive* discrepancies, signify precisely the opposite; most citizens are

---

[3] Eckstein and Gurr supply no empirical guideline for indicating when authority orientations do, or do not qualify as "congruent" or "discrepant." For that reason, we rely on the convention of statistically significant differences.

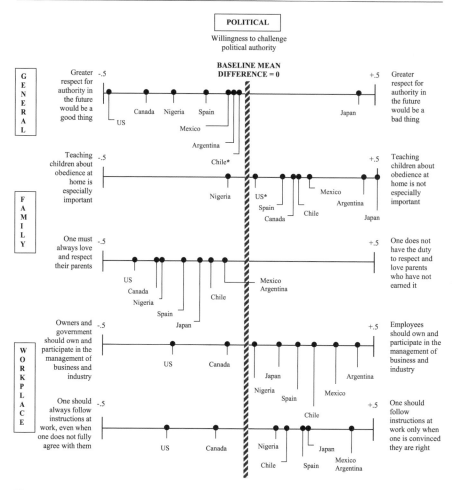

Figure 2. Aggregate Discrepancies — Willingness to Challenge Political Authority Compared to Authority Orientations in General, in the Family, and in the Workplace by Country (Average score on authority orientations in the family and in the workplace MINUS the average score on willingness to challenge political authority).

*p > .05; all other differences are statistically significant.
Note: see Appendix A for question wording and coding.
Sourse: 2000 World Values Surveys.

more deferential to political authority than they are in their outlooks to authority in the other domains.

Third, given the wide variations in cultural settings and regime styles of the eight countries, there are some remarkably consistent cross-national patterns with respect to the distributions of some outlooks. For example, regardless of national setting, most people exhibit greater respect for parental figures, and for authority in general, than they do for political authority. When it comes to child rearing and workplace participation, however, the opposite pattern typically holds. There is also some evidence of cultural affinities. The American and Canadian cases, for example, are nearly always closely clustered together, and in these two instances nearly all of the discrepancies have a negative valence. The Mexican and Argentinean findings also typically cluster together but more often than not they cluster towards the positive polarity; they are positive discrepancies

These aggregate mean scores, of course, mask the extent to which there are variations in distributions of authority orientations within national populations. A more detailed portrait of national variations, however, points to important nuances (see Appendix B). In every society, regardless of which combination of authority patterns are considered, there is usually a balance of positive and negative discrepancies. Thus, although most Spaniards are generally more inclined to support greater employee participation in workplace decision-making than they are likely to challenge political authority (Figure 2), there is nonetheless a healthy proportion of Spaniards (16%) who indicate that they are less supportive of greater worker participation in the workplace (Appendix B). In no country is there complete unanimity on these authority dimensions.

These findings provide empirical grounding for the claims made by Eckstein and others that authority patterns vary significantly across different societies and domains. But significantly, Eckstein and his colleagues provide no commentary about the possibility that there may be different varieties of discrepant authority patterns. Consequently, they provide no guidance on the possibility that different kinds of discrepancies might have different consequences.

It is quite conceivable, for instance, that qualitative differences in the disjuncture of authority patterns could have quite different effects on citizen evaluations of government performance. For example, citizens who are less deferential outside of the polity (multiple positive discrepancies) may be more likely than others to express greater dissatisfaction with government because political authority patterns are more constraining than those experienced in the family and workplace. Conversely, citizens who are more inclined to defer to authority in their everyday lives (multiple negative discrepancies) may be less inclined than others to feel, and express, their dissatisfaction with governments or challenge the status quo. The implication is that there are at least two variations of the core hypothesis worth investigating:

Hypothesis 1a: *Citizens with a pattern of multiple positive discrepancies (who are less deferential in the workplace, the family, and in general authority outlooks, than in the polity) will express less satisfaction with the performance of governments.*

Alternatively:

Hypothesis 1b: *Citizens with a pattern of multiple negative discrepancies (who are more deferential in the workplace, the family, and in general authority outlooks, than in the polity) will express greater satisfaction with the performance of governments.*

The findings reported in Figure 3 provide support for both of these hypotheses. The 2000 WVS asked respondents about their satisfaction with the way that people in (government) were handling their country's affairs. The data show that variations in citizens' satisfaction with governments depends not only on the scope but also on the direction of the discrepancies in authority patterns. The greater the number of positive discrepancies the less satisfaction there is with government performance, and the greater the number of negative discrepancies, the greater the level of satisfaction with government performance. Indeed, the magnitude of these differences is striking; multiple discrepancies in either direction appear to have the potential of influencing evaluations of government performance by a considerable amount. These results is striking consistent in two respects. First, the very same patterns emerge regardless of which combination of authority orientations are compared. And second, these findings consistently hold up regardless of whether citizens live in wealthy advanced industrial states with long democratic traditions or in poorer countries with briefer experiences with democratic practices (see Appendix C).

What is required, however, is a direct test of the second hypothesis, namely, that discrepant authority patterns contribute to variations in levels of public satisfaction with governments. But the clear evidence indicating that the two different types of discrepancies have identifiably different effects, suggests that separate hypotheses, one for each type of discrepancy, should be specified and tested. As follows:

Hypothesis 2a: *Positive discrepancies in authority patterns will have an independent effect that decreases citizen satisfaction with the performance of governments.*

And,

Hypothesis 2b: *Negative discrepancies in authority patterns will have an independent effect that increases citizen satisfaction with the performance of governments.*

It is possible, of course, that the apparent links between discrepancies in authority patterns and variations in satisfaction with governments are confounded and mediated by, or just derivative of, other sources of variation in levels of satisfaction with governments. For instance, the bivariate relationships between discrepant authority orientations and dissatisfaction with government might simply be attributable to more complex relationships between authority orientations and the distributions

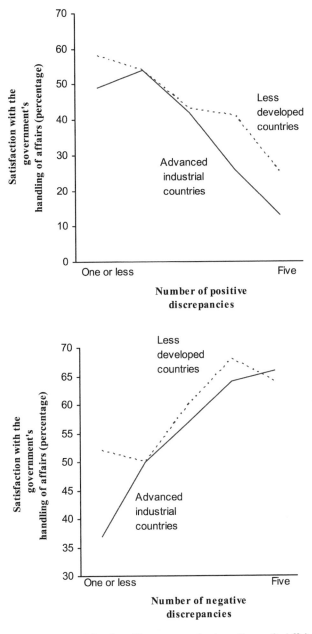

Figure 3. Satisfaction with the Government's handing of Affairs[†] by The Number of Positive and Negative Discrepancies.

[†]Includes those who are "very satisfied" and "fairly satisfied."
Note: less developed countries include Mexico, Argentina, Nigeria and Chile. Advanced industrial countries include Spain, US, Canada and Japan.
See Appendix A for question wording and coding.
Source: 2000 World Values Surveys.

of postmaterialist value orientations, cognitive mobility or social capital. The only convincing way to show that authority orientations provide a credible alternative explanation for variations in satisfaction with governments is to demonstrate that discrepant authority orientations have significant net effects on variations in satisfaction with governments. That is, it must be demonstrated that discrepancies in authority patterns have a significant impact on citizen satisfaction with governments after the effects of such other explanations as postmaterialist orientations, cognitive mobility, and social capital, have been taken into account. To evaluate that proposition we turn to a multivariate model to isolate the impact of discrepancies in authority patterns on levels of satisfaction with government performance. The model controls both for the effects that might be attributable to other explanations and for such other individual attributes as age, sex and income.

The results reported in Table 1 indicate a number of important findings. First, both positive and negative discrepancies turn out to have significant effects on evaluations of government performance, after the impact of other explanations and various socio-demographic factors are taken into account. In effect, with each additional positive discrepancy, the odds of that individual being satisfied with their government's performance decrease by as much as 39%. Conversely, with each additional negative discrepancy, the chances of being more satisfied with government performance more than double. Second, when the model is unpacked and the same tests are performed separately for both publics in advanced industrial states and less developed countries, the same general findings emerge. Not surprisingly, there is some evidence of variation in the extent to which the same predictors have an impact on satisfaction with governments in wealthier or poorer settings. But the general finding is quite clear. The absence of congruence in authority patterns consistently emerges as a significant predictor of variations in support for governments even after the effects of other explanations and individual socio-economic characteristics are accounted for. In short, these data provide substantial support for the Eckstein and Gurr theory that authority patterns shape citizen satisfaction with governments.

To this point, the analysis has focused on sharpening our understanding of what factors explain variations in a certain type of specific support, citizens' levels of satisfaction or dissatisfaction with the performance of people in government. But to what extent do variations in this type of specific support help to account for variations in citizens' diffuse support (Easton 1965; Kornberg and Clarke 1992; Norris 1999; Nevitte 2002)? The prevailing perception is that citizens' evaluations of how people in government perform is less important to their satisfaction with the workings

Table 1

Logistic Regression — Determinants of Government Satisfaction

Dependent variable: satisfaction with the government's handling of affairs (1 = satisfied)

Independent variables	All countries merged			Less developed countries			Advanced industrial states		
	B	S.E.	Exp (B)	B	S.E.	Exp (B)	B	S.E.	Exp (B)
Discrepancies:									
number of positive discrepancies (multiple = 1)	-.50**	.10	.61	-.60**	.17	.55	-.33**	.14	.72
number of negative discrepancies (multiple = 1)	.85**	.08	2.33	.21	.14	1.23	1.20**	.11	3.31
Alternative explanations:									
value change (postmaterialism = 1)	-.17*	.08	.84	-.39**	.11	.68	.01	.11	1.02
cognitive mobilization (high = 1)	-.13*	.07	.87	.43**	.10	1.53	-.46**	.09	.63
social capital:									
- interpersonal trust (low = 1)	-.22**	.05	.80	-.33**	.09	.72	-.22**	.06	.80
- voluntary association membership (no involvement = 1)	-.50**	.06	.60	-.14	.10	.87	-.72**	.08	.49
Socio-demographics:									
age (senior = 1)	.01	.06	1.01	.10	.09	1.11	.03	.08	1.03
sex (male = 1)	-.02	.05	.98	.001	.07	1.00	-.05	.06	.95
income (high = 1)	.09	.06	1.10	-.15	.09	.86	.21*	.08	1.23
Constant	.37**	.10		.29	.15		.37**	.14	
Model Chi-Square	346.33; p < .001			78.64; p < .001			367.04; p < .001		
N	7,827			3,263			4,564		

* significant at p < .05; **significant at p < .01.

Note: see Appendix A for question wording and coding.

Source: 2000 World Values Surveys.

of democracy than is confidence in government institutions. The argument is that because political actors are transient, what really counts when it comes to regime support is strong public confidence in government institutions. According to Norris and Newton, "politicians come and go with swings of the electoral pendulum," but a "loss of confidence in institutions may well be a better indicator of public disaffection with the modern world because they are the basic pillars of society. If they begin to crumble, then there is, indeed, cause for concern" (Newton and Norris 2000:53). The hypothesis expressing this expectation would be:

Hypothesis 3: *Citizen confidence in governmental institutions is a better predictor of their satisfaction with the way democracy works than are citizen evaluations of how well people in government handle the affairs of the country.*

The 2000 WVS data allow us to test that hypothesis and, once again, the appropriate test requires a multivariate test. In this model (Table 2), government satisfaction becomes a key independent variable, along with confidence in government institutions. Two additional controls are imported into the model. The "life satisfaction" control is introduced to minimize the variation attributable to generalized feeling of satisfaction, and the "feelings towards democracy" control is entered for similar reasons (see Abramson and Inglehart 1998).

The results reported in Table 2 show public confidence in political institutions is a significant predictor of democratic satisfaction. They also show that satisfaction with how people in government "handle the country's affairs" has a significant effect on democratic satisfaction overall. Indeed, the impact of the "people in government" variable turns out to be a much stronger predictor of democratic satisfaction than is citizen confidence in various governmental institutions (parliament, the civil service and parties) after contextual and sociodemographic factors are taken into account. Satisfaction with government officials increases the chances of democratic satisfaction by more than five times, more than three times the impact of confidence in institutions. Moreover, these same general patterns hold when the same tests are conducted separately for advanced industrial states and for less developed countries albeit with minor variations. Some intriguing differences emerge when the data for advanced industrial states are compared with those for less developed countries (LDC) are probed in greater detail. The confidence in institutions variable is routinely used as an additive index of responses to questions about confidence in three different governmental institutions — parliament, civil service, and political parties. When the index is disaggregated and multivariate tests are conducted separately for each institution, the results show that confidence in political parties is a significantly stronger predictor of democratic satisfaction

Table 2
Logistic Regression — Determinants of Democratic Satisfaction

Independent variables	Dependent variable: democratic satisfaction (1 = satisfied)								
	All countries merged			Less developed countries			Advanced industrial states		
	B	S.E.	Exp (B)	B	S.E.	Exp (B)	B	S.E.	Exp (B)
Political authorities:									
satisfaction with the government's handling of affairs (satisfied = 1)	1.75**	.05	5.73	1.92**	.07	6.82	1.66**	.08	5.28
Political institutions:									
parliament, civil service and political parties (confidence in all three = 1)	.73**	.07	2.08	.46**	.09	1.58	1.13**	.11	3.09
Context:									
life satisfaction (high = 1)	.35**	.08	1.42	.35**	.11	1.42	.30**	.13	1.35
feelings toward democracy (very good system = 1)	1.35**	.10	3.87	1.15**	.14	3.16	1.68**	.15	5.34
Socio-demographics:									
age (senior = 1)	.40**	.07	1.49	.17	.10	1.19	.10	.10	1.11
sex (male = 1)	-.04	.05	.96	-.08	.07	.92	.02	.07	1.02
income (high = 1)	.05	.07	1.05	.01	.09	1.01	.28**	.10	1.33
education (post-secondary = 1)	.002	.07	1.00	-.14	.10	.87	-.29**	.10	.75
Constant	-2.27**	.12		-2.18**	.16		-2.03**	.18	
Model Chi-Square	2129.70; p < .001			1193.07; p < .001			1033.74; p < .001		
N	8,784			4,692			4,092		

* significant p < .05; ** significant p < .01.

Note: see Appendix A for question wording and coding. Source: 2000 World Values Surveys.

in LDC whereas confidence in parliament is a stronger predictor of democratic satisfaction in advanced industrial states. The implication is that party building is a more effective strategy for promoting general regime support in LDC. On balance, however, these findings lead us to reject the third hypothesis.

Concluding Discussion

We began by indicating that theories of value change, cognitive mobilization, and social capital, all provide compelling explanations for the changing dynamics between citizens and their governments. But we also suggested that another explanation for citizen dissatisfaction with governments can be deduced from an earlier theoretical framework developed by Eckstein and his colleagues, and that this explanation requires some investigation. Eckstein's core expectation was that citizens will be less satisfied with government when political authority patterns are not congruent with the authority patterns elsewhere in society.

Our empirical test of that proposition provides general support for Eckstein's theory. Using WVS data from eight countries, it is clear that there are significant discrepancies in the authority orientations of publics in these countries. But the evidence also suggests that the original formulation of Eckstein's theory requires respecification in at least one important respect. The findings indicate there are two different kinds of discrepancies in authority patterns; negative discrepancies and positive discrepancies. In the case of negative discrepancies, citizens are less deferential in their political authority orientations than in their authority orientations towards the family and workplace. In the case of positive discrepancies, citizens are more deferential in the political domain than they are in others. It is not clear that Eckstein and colleagues anticipated these qualitative differences in types of discrepancies, but they turn out to have substantively important consequences for citizens' evaluations of governments.

The second set of significant findings indicate that where there are positive discrepancies in authority patterns, citizen satisfaction with the performance of governments declines. And where there are negative discrepancies, citizen satisfaction with the performance of governments increases. These results are remarkably consistent. They apply equally to publics in advanced industrial states and LDC. Each pattern has the same impact on citizen's evaluations of government performance regardless of whether the national setting is more or less prosperous. The implication is that the re-specified theory is a generalizable one.

The results indicate, generally, that the value change, cognitive mobilization and social capital explanations for variations in public support for governments work as one would predict. The findings are not identical in every detail in every national setting, but the overall pattern is consistent. The evidence also suggests that discrepant authority orientations is an explanation that does not compete with others; it is an explanation that complements others. Empirically, discrepant authority orientations clearly account for significant additional variation in citizen dissatisfaction with governments even after other explanations are taken into account.

There is virtually no conclusive evidence indicating that public support for democratic principles has eroded (Fuchs, Guidorossi and Stevensson 1995; Fuchs and Klingemann 1995). Nonetheless, many analysts continue to express concern about public support for, and confidence in, the core institutions of democratic government (Newton and Norris 2000; Norris 1999a; Nye, Zelikow and King 1997). The reasonable presumption is that these institutions mediate citizens' evaluations of regime support. One inference that might be made from our findings is that public satisfaction with the quality of democratic life might be improved by institutional design, by adjusting governmental institutions to correspond with social authority patterns. The prospect is an intriguing one. But it is not at all clear that priming public confidence in governmental institutions is a sufficient remedy. Confidence in governmental institutions does shape citizen satisfaction with democratic life. But our data also show that citizen satisfaction with the quality of democratic life is affected even more powerfully by their evaluations of how "people in government are handling the country's affairs." The implication is that while institutions matter, so do political actors.

References

ABRAMSON, P. AND R. INGLEHART
1999   "Comparing European Publics." *American Political Science Review*, Vol. 92, No. 1, 185-190.
CLARK, T. AND M. REMPEL
1997   *Citizen Politics in Post-Industrial Societies.* Boulder, Colorado: Westview Press.
CROZIER, M., S., HUNTINGTON AND J. WATANUKI
1975   *The Crisis of Democracy: Report on the Governability of Democracies to the Trilateral Commission.* New York: New York University Press.
DALTON, R.
2002   *Citizen Politics: Public Opinion and Political Parties in Advanced Industrial Democracies,* Third Edition. Seven Bridges Press, Inc.: Chatham House Publishers.
1984   "Cognitive Mobilization and Partisan Dealignment in Advanced Industrial Democracies." *Journal of Politics*, Vol. 46: 264-84.
DALTON, R. AND M. WATTENBERG
1993   "The Not So Simple Act of Voting," in A. Finifter, *Political Science: The State of the Discipline.* Washington, D.C.: The American Political Science Association.
EASTON, D.
1965   *A Systems Analysis of Political Life.* New York: Wiley.

ECKSTEIN, H.
1969   "Authority Relations and Governmental Performance." *Comparative Political Studies*, 2: 269-325.
1966   *Division and Cohesion in Democracy*. Princeton: Princeton University Press.
ECKSTEIN, H. AND T.R. GURR
1975   *Patterns of Authority: A Structural Basis for Political Inquiry*. New York: John Wiley and Sons.
FUCHS, D., G. GUIDOROSSI AND P. SVENSSON
1995   "Support for the Democratic System," in Klingemann, H. and D. Fuchs, *Citizens and the State*. Oxford, U.K.: Oxford University Press.
HUNTINGTON, S.
2000   "Forward," in Pharr, S. and R. Putnam, *Disaffected Democracies: What's Troubling the Trilateral Countries?* Princeton, NJ: Princeton University Press.
1991   *The Third Wave*. London: University of Oklahoma Press.
1974   "Post-Industrial Politics: How Benign Will It Be?" *Comparative Politics* 6: 147-77.
INGLEHART, R.
2000   "Globalization and Postmodern Values," *The Washington Quarterly*, Vol. 23, No. 1, Winter, 215-228.
1997   *Modernization and Postmodernization: Cultural, Economic, and Political Change in 43 Societies*. Princeton, NJ: Princeton University Press.
1990   *Cultural Shift in Advanced Industrial Society*. Princeton, NJ: Princeton University Press.
KAASE, M. AND K. NEWTON
1995   *Beliefs in Government*, Oxford, U.K.: Oxford University Press.
KLINGEMANN, H. AND D. FUCHS
1995   *Citizens and the State*. Oxford, U.K.: Oxford University Press.
KORNBERG, A. AND H. CLARKE
1992   *Citizens and Community: Political Support in a Representative Democracy*. Cambridge, U.K.: Cambridge University Press.
LIPSET, S.M. AND W. SCHNEIDER
1987   *The Confidence Gap*. Baltimore: Johns Hopkins University Press.
MARSH, A. AND M. KAASE
1979   "Political Action: A Theoretical Perspective," in Barnes, S., M. Kaase et al., *Political Action: Mass Participation in Five Western Democracies*. Beverly Hills, CA: Sage Publications, 27-56.
NEWTON, K. AND P. NORRIS
2000   "Confidence in Public Institutions: Faith, Culture, or Performance?" in Pharr, S. and R. Putnam, *Disaffected Democracies: What's Troubling the Trilateral Countries?* Princeton, NJ: Princeton University Press.
NEVITTE, N.
2002   *Value Change and Governance in Canada*. Toronto, ON: University of Toronto Press.
1996   *The Decline of Deference: Canadian Value Change in Cross-National Perspective*. Peterborough, ON: Broadview Press.
NIE, N., J. JUNN AND K. STEHLIK-BARRY
1996   *Education and Democratic Citizenship in America*. Chicago, Illinois: The University of Chicago Press.

NORRIS, P.
2000   "Making Democracies Work: Social Capital and Civil Engagement in 47 Societies." Paper for the European Science Foundation EURESCO Conference on Social Capital: Interdisciplinary Perspectives at the University of Exeter, September 15-20.

1999   *Critical Citizens: Global Support for Democratic Governance.* Oxford: Oxford University Press.

1999a   "Introduction: The Growth of Critical Citizens?" in P. Norris, *Critical Citizens: Global Support for Democratic Governance.* Oxford: Oxford University Press.

1999b   "Conclusions: The Growth of Critical Citizens and its Consequences," in P. Norris, *Critical Citizens: Global Support for Democratic Governance.* Oxford: Oxford University Press.

NYE J.S. JR., P.D. ZELIKOW AND D.C. KING
1997   *Why People Don't Trust Government.* Cambridge, Mass: Harvard University Press.

PATEMAN, C.
1970   *Participation and Democratic Theory.* Cambridge: Cambridge University Press.

PHARR, S. AND R. PUTNAM
2000   *Disaffected Democracies: What's Troubling the Trilateral Countries?* Princeton, NJ: Princeton University Press.

PUTNAM, R.
2000   *Bowling Alone: The Collapse and Revival of American Community.* New York: Simon and Schuster.

1995   "Bowling Alone: America's Declining Social Capital." *Journal of Democracy,* Vol. 6, No. 1 (January), 65-78.

1993   *Making Democracy Work: Civic Traditions in Modern Italy.* Princeton: Princeton University Press.

PUTNAM. R., S. PHARR AND R. DALTON
2000   "Introduction: What's Troubling the Trilateral Democracies," in Pharr, S. and R. Putnam, *Disaffected Democracies: What's Troubling the Trilateral Countries?* Princeton, NJ: Princeton University Press.

THE WORLD FACTBOOK
2001   Washington, D.C.: Central Intelligence Agency; Bartleby.com, www.bartleby.com/151/.

WELZEL, C. AND R. INGLEHART
2001   Human Development and the 'Explosion' of Democracy: Variations of Regime Change Across 60 Societies, Discussion Paper FS III 01-202, Wissenschaftszentrum Berlin für Sozialforschung (WZB), Berlin.

WELZEL, C., R. INGLEHART AND HANS-DIETER KLINGEMANN
2001   "Human Development as a General Theory of Social Change: A Multi-Level and Cross-Cultural Perspective." Discussion Paper FS III 01-201, Wissenschaftszentrum Berlin für Sozialforschung (WZB), Berlin.

Appendix A: Question Wording and Coding

Dependent Variables
INDICATOR: Willingness to Challenge Political Authority

QUESTION WORDING/CODING:
I'm going to read out some different forms of political action that people can take, and I'd like you to tell me, for each one, whether you have actually done any of these things, whether you might do it or would never, under any circumstances, do it.

   Signing a petition (have done/might do = 1; never do = 0)
   Joining in boycotts (have done/might do = 1; never do = 0)
   Attending lawful demonstrations (have done/might do = 1; never do = 0)
   Joining lawful demonstrations (have done/might do = 1; never do = 0)
   Occupying buildings or factories (have done/might do = 1; never do = 0)

INDEX RELIABILITY:
All countries merged (Alpha = .7); Spain (Alpha = .8); United States (Alpha = .6); Canada (Alpha = .7); Japan (Alpha = .7); Mexico (Alpha = .8); Argentina (Alpha = .7); Nigeria (Alpha = .7); Chile (Alpha = .8)

INDICATOR: Satisfaction with the Government's handling of Affairs

QUESTION WORDING/CODING:
How satisfied are you with the way the people in the federal government are handling the country's affairs? Would you say you are very satisfied, fairly satisfied, fairly dissatisfied or very dissatisfied?
   (very satisfied and fairly satisfied = 1; fairly dissatisfied and very dissatisfied = 0)

INDICATOR: Democratic satisfaction

QUESTION WORDING/CODING:
On the whole are you very satisfied, rather satisfied, not very satisfied or not at all satisfied with the way democracy is developing in our country?
   (very satisfied or rather satisfied = 1; not very satisfied or not at all satisfied = 0)

Independent/Control Variables
INDICATOR: Authority Orientations in General

QUESTION WORDING/CODING:
I'm going to read out a list of various changes in our way of life that might take place in the near future. Please tell me for each one, if it were to happen, whether you think it would be a good thing, a bad thing, or don't you mind?
   Greater respect for authority (bad thing = 1; don't mind = .5; good thing = 0)

INDICATOR: Authority Orientations in the Family

QUESTION WORDING/CODING:
Here is a list of qualities that children can be encouraged to learn at home. Which, if any, do you consider to be especially important? Please choose up to five.

Obedience (not mentioned = 1; mentioned as important = 0)
With which of these two statements do you tend to agree?
  A. Regardless of what the qualities and faults of one's parents are, one must always love and respect them
  B. One does not have the duty to respect and love parents who have not earned it by their behavior and attitudes
    (agree with statement B = 1; agree with statement A = 0)

INDICATOR: Authority Orientations in the Workplace

QUESTION WORDING/CODING:
There is a lot of discussion about how business and industry should be managed. Which of these four statements comes closest to your opinion?
  1. The owners should run their business or appoint the managers
  2. The owners and the employees should participate in the selection of managers
  3. The government should be the owner and appoint the managers
  4. The employees should own the business and should elect the managers
    (statements 2 or 4 = 1; statements 1 or 3 = 0)
People have different ideas about following instructions at work. Some say that one should follow one's superior's instructions even when one does not fully agree with them. Others say that one should follow one's superior's instructions only when one is convinced that they are right. With which of these two opinions do you agree?
    (must be convinced first or depends = 1; should follow instructions = 0)

INDICATOR: Number of positive discrepancies

NOTE:
— A 5-item additive index compiling the aggregate number positive discrepancies per respondent.
    (multiple discrepancies = 1; 1 or less positive discrepancies = 0)

INDEX RELIABILITY:
All countries merged (Alpha = .6); Less developed states (Alpha = .53); Advanced industrial states (Alpha = .6)

INDICATOR: Number of negative discrepancies

NOTE:
— A 5-item additive index compiling the aggregate number of negative discrepancies per respondent.
    (multiple negative discrepancies = 1; 1 or less negative discrepancies = 0)

INDEX RELIABILITY:
All countries merged (Alpha = .8); Less developed states (Alpha = .8); Advanced industrial states (Alpha = .8)

INDICATOR: Value change

NOTE:
— Inglehart's standard 4-item materialism/postmaterialism index.
(postmaterialism = 1; mixed = .5; materialism = 0)

INDICATOR: Cognitive mobilization

NOTE:
— A 3-item additive index measuring respondents' level of interest in politics, the frequency with which they discuss politics and their level of education.
(highly cognitively mobile = 1; moderately cognitively mobile = .5; low level of cognitive mobility = 0)

INDEX RELIABILITY:
All countries merged (Alpha = .55); Less developed states (Alpha = .52); Advanced industrial states (Alpha = .6)

INDICATOR: Social capital

Interpersonal trust
QUESTION WORDING/CODING:
Generally speaking, would you say that most people can be trusted or that you need to be very careful in dealing with people?
(need to be very careful = 1; most people can be trusted = 0)

Voluntary association membership
QUESTION WORDING/CODING:
Please look carefully at the following list of voluntary organizations and activities and say which, if any, do you belong to?
Social welfare services for elderly, handicapped or deprived people
(belong = 1; not mentioned = 0)
Religious or church organizations (belong = 1; not mentioned = 0)
Education, arts, music or cultural activities (belong = 1; not mentioned = 0)
Labor unions (belong = 1; not mentioned = 0)
Political parties or groups (belong = 1; not mentioned = 0)
Local community action on issues like poverty, employment, housing, racial equality (belong = 1; not mentioned = 0)
Third world development or human rights (belong = 1; not mentioned = 0)
Conservation, the environment, ecology, animal rights
(belong = 1; not mentioned = 0)
Professional associations (belong = 1; not mentioned = 0)
Youth work (e.g. scouts, guides, youth clubs etc.) (belong = 1; not mentioned = 0)
Sports or recreation (belong = 1; not mentioned = 0)
Women's groups (belong = 1; not mentioned = 0)
Peace movement (belong = 1; not mentioned = 0)
Voluntary organizations concerned with health (belong = 1; not mentioned = 0)
Other groups (belong = 1; not mentioned = 0)

INDEX RELIABILITY:

All countries merged (Alpha = .7); Less developed states (Alpha = .6); Advanced industrial states (Alpha = .7)

INDICATOR: Political institutions – parliament, civil service and political parties

QUESTION WORDING/CODING:
I am going to name a number of organizations. For each one, could you tell me how much confidence you have in them: is it a great deal of confidence, quite a lot of confidence, not very much confidence or none at all?
   Parliament (a great deal or quite a lot = 1; not very much or none at all = 0)
   The civil service (a great deal or quite a lot = 1; not very much or none at all = 0)
   Political parties (a great deal or quite a lot = 1; not very much or none at all = 0)

INDEX RELIABILITY:
All countries merged (Alpha = .7); Less developed states (Alpha = .8); Advanced industrial states (Alpha = .7)

INDICATOR: Life satisfaction

QUESTION WORDING/CODING:
All things considered, how satisfied are you with your life as a whole these days? (high level of satisfaction = 1; moderate level of satisfaction = .5; low level of satisfaction = 0)

INDICATOR: Feelings toward democracy

QUESTION WORDING/CODING:
I'm going to describe various types of political systems and ask what you think about each as a way of governing this country. For each one, would you say it is very good, fairly good, fairly bad or very bad way of governing this country?
   Having a democratic political system (very good = 1; fairly good = .66; fairly bad = .33; very bad = 0)

INDICATOR: Age

QUESTION WORDING/CODING:
This means you are _____ years old?
   (51yrs+ = 1; 31yrs-50yrs = .5; 18yrs-30yrs = 0)

INDICATOR: Sex

QUESTION WORDING/CODING:
   Sex of respondent (1 = male; 0 = female)

INDICATOR: Income

QUESTION WORDING/CODING:
Here is a scale of incomes. We would like to know in what group your household is counting all wages, salaries, pensions and other incomes that come in. Just give the letter of the group your household falls into, before taxes and other deductions.

($50,001+ = 1; $27,501-50,000 = .5; $27,000 or less = 0)

INDICATOR: Education

QUESTION WORDING/CODING:
What is the highest education level that you have attained?
    (post-secondary = 1; secondary = .5; primary = 0)

Appendix B: Positive and Negative Discrepancies at the Individual Level

(Authority orientations in general, in the family, and in the workplace MINUS willingness to challenge political authority)

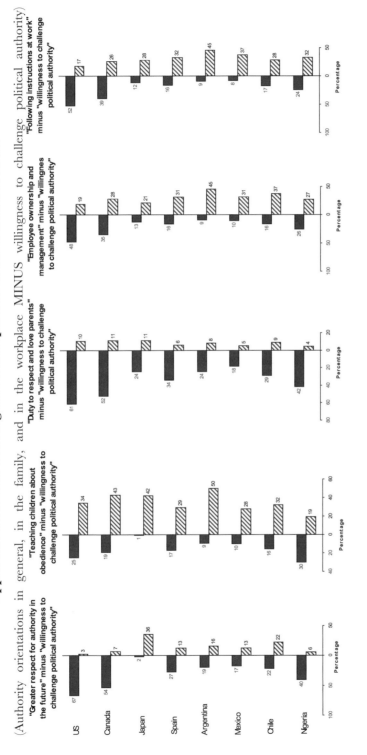

Source: 2000 World Values Surveys.

Appendix C: Satisfaction with the Government's Handling of Affairs by the Number of Positive and Negative Discrepancies by Domain

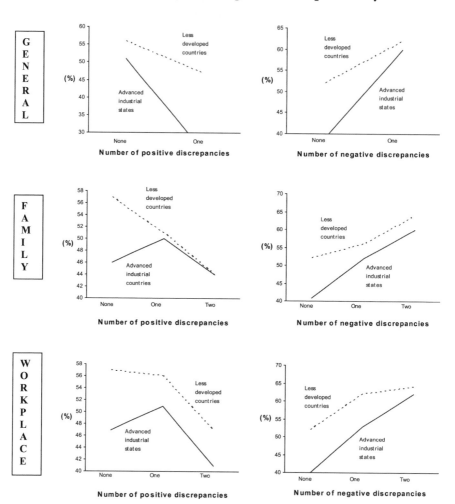

Source: 2000 World Values Surveys.

Revising the Value Shift Hypothesis: A Descriptive Analysis of South Africa's Value Priorities between 1990 and 2001

HENNIE KOTZÉ AND KARIN LOMBARD[*]

Since 1990 South Africa has been characterized by intense restructuring in the political, social, cultural and economic sphere, and this monumental transformation has had a multifarious impact on South African society. Much of this impact and the resultant changes have been assessed in recent academic and political debate, yet there has been little extensive and systematic research to assess the direction, magnitude and nature of these changing dynamics of South Africa's values. Although the World Values Survey (WVS) has proven invaluable for research in this field of mass public values, most of the research has been fashioned in a manner to tap values in industrialized and western states, arguably rendering some aspects of the theoretical models of explanation less relevant for developing nations. This article therefore aims to advance an understanding of value change within the South African context, particularly in light of the expansive political, social and economic changes to have transpired since 1990, whilst simultaneously proposing one possibility of an expansion to the model currently used to measure value change. The aim of this study is to determine whether South African value priorities are changing, and, if so, what is the direction and magnitude of this change. The change will be measured in terms of the materialist/post-materialist dimension between 1991 and 2001, and a separate pre-materialist/materialist continuum,

* Department of Political Science, University of Stellenbosch. This article is a shortened and reworked version of a paper delivered at the International Conference on World Values Studies, Stellenbosch, South Africa, November 2001.

between 1995 and 2001, after which a comparison will be drawn to determine which dimension proves more pertinent.

On the grounds of the socio-economic and historical context of South Africa, it can be hypothesized that the pre-materialist/materialist continuum offered will prove more applicable than the original Inglehart materialist/post-materialist dimension, rendering it a better instrument for the measurement and consequent analysis of South Africa's and potentially other developing countries' values. The more relevant measurement scale will then be utilized to determine whether value change has occurred, and the results will be extrapolated. Ideally this article would then follow with an extensive comparison of values amongst the various population sub-groups, to show whether the divisions of South African society are reflected in its values, but unfortunately only one division in South African society will be focused upon.

Questions to be addressed are therefore: What does South Africa's value dimension look like? What have been the most pervasive changes in public values? What are possible explanations for these changes? What are the implications of the dynamics of this value change for the present? In which way will these implications influence South Africa's future? The principal significance of the article lies in starting to fill a knowledge gap concerning the direction, degree and nature of the dynamics of value change within South Africa, as well as testing an alternative model for value measurement in developing countries.

The capacity of this article should not, however, be overestimated. It should simply be seen as one step in the process of understanding the jigsaw of South African values, as well as the extension of a largely western-industrialized nation model to greater universal applicability and use. This article is therefore also significant in that it attempts to formalize the first few steps taken towards an expansion of a potentially relevant and insightful theory to incorporate most of the developing world.

Socio-Economic and Political Background

Before the results of the 1990, 1995 and 2001 WVS can be compared, it is crucial that the differing backdrops against which the three surveys were conducted be examined. This measurement and comparison of socio-economic and political settings is imperative to establish a context in which to analyze the changes in South Africa's value dimension. To achieve this a framework of indicators of the most pervasive external changes has been selected.

The 1991 South African World Values Survey was conducted on the very eve of nationwide transition. The international community had imposed formal sanctions since 1988, and President PW Botha had been succeeded by FW De Klerk, whilst Nelson Mandela had been released from Prison after serving 27 years. Although change appeared imminent, there was great uncertainty and much apprehension.[1] The October 1995 WVS, although conducted in the post-Apartheid era, took place a mere 18 months after the first democratic elections. Most South Africans were still trying to internalize the expansive changes to have occurred within the country over the last five years. Although many of the broad political changes had been enacted, many South Africans were still awaiting the implications of these on the broader socio-economic environment. Uncertainty for the future loomed.[2] Since then much has changed. A relatively peaceful transition has occurred and South Africa has held its second democratic elections in June 1999. The euphoria of the first elections had subsided. Economically and socially a certain degree of consolidation has occurred and much of the uncertainty has dissipated. A completely different political milieu has been entered into with the African National Congress (ANC) almost attaining a two-thirds majority in Parliament.[3] It is thus necessary to determine South Africa's value structure in this new environment. The different context against which the 2001 World Values Survey was conducted will no doubt be reflected in the results of the survey.

In terms of the economy, the last decade has revealed a mixed bag of changes. With regard to macro-economic policy, there has been a shift from the 1994 Reconstruction and Development Programme (RDP), with its emphasis on growth through reconstruction, to the Growth Employment and Redistribution (GEAR) macro-economic strategy, with a greater emphasis on Gross Domestic Product (GDP) growth, increased job creation, lower inflation, increased non-gold exports, increased inflows of foreign investment and a rise in domestic savings (Adelzadeh 1999:3). This change in macro-economic policy has been accompanied by a relatively dismal growth rate, a comparatively low GDP per capita[4] and increasing levels of unemployment.[5] Escalating unemployment has clearly

---

[1] Also see Liebenberg (1994), Van Zyl Slabbert (1992), Friedman and Atkinson (1994), Giliomee and Schlemmer (1994), Habib and Moodley (1993).

[2] Also see Giliomee (1995), Johnson and Schlemmer (1996), Shaw (2001), Giliomee and Schlemmer (1994), Sisk (1994).

[3] Also see Friedman (1999), Lodge (1999), Maharaj (1999), Woods (2000), Southhall (2001).

[4] SARB, South African National Accounts 1946-1998, June 1999 and SARB, Quarterly Bulletin, March 2000.

[5] CSS, *October Household Surveys*, 1994, 1995, 1996, 1997, 1998, 1999. Idasa's Budget Information Service, also claims that 36% of the potential workforce is unemployed in 2001 (*The Mail & Guardian*, 23 March 2001).

become one of the biggest problems facing the country. Another leading challenge facing South Africa is its gross income inequality, with a recent report ranking South Africa as the country with the most skewed income distribution, second only to Brazil (*Mail and Guardian*, 28 July 2000).

Although financial indicators are important, the significance of economic development levels should not be underestimated. In 1995 South Africa ranked 86th on the Human Development Index (HDI), whilst in 2000 South Africa ranked 103rd (Human Development Report 2000). Despite this apparent drop in standards of living, the quality of life of many South Africans has improved through the provision of free or affordable basic goods and services, examples of which include the provision of water, electricity and shelter. The provision of health care and education have revealed both progress and deterioration (*Cape Argus*, 31 March 2001; *Mail & Guardian*, 21 January 1999).

The Inglehart Model

The end product of a number of years of research by, amongst others Ronald Inglehart, was the construction of two indexes to classify 12 items into underlying materialist and post-materialist values (Inlgehart 1977:40). Inglehart's theoretical justification of classification along this values continuum was partially founded on Abraham Maslow's hierarchy of needs (1954),[6] which states that there is a specific direction in which the change of needs will move, given a set of definate conditions. Employing the complimentary and interdependent hypotheses of *scarcity* and *socialization*,[7] he asserted that when one category of needs had been fulfilled the next hierarchical category would take precedence. Consequently, in societies where conditions of physical and economic security become more consolidated, "a potentially universal process should occur" (Inglehart 1995:6), a process that results in the ever greater prevalence of post-materialists in many industrialized nations (Inglehart 1977, 1997; Abramson and Inglehart 1995). The *socialization* hypothesis has since been recast into a mould of 'formative security' (Inglehart 1990:121-124). Inglehart's hypotheses have not, however, gone without

---

[6] See Abraham Maslow, *Motivation and Personality*, New York: Harper, 1954.

[7] The *scarcity* hypothesis is built upon the premise that the greatest demand will be made for those entities for which there is the scarcest supply. Inglehart (1985:103) states that "an individual's priorities thus reflect one's socioeconomic environment". The *socialization* hypothesis focuses on the idea of generational replacement, whereby values are relatively stable and specific to a certain age group within a specific population. He asserted that exposure to a specific socialization process and socio-economic environment during one's formative years has a lasting effect, and can impact equally seriously on one's choice of priorities at a later stage (Abramson and Inglehart 1987:184).

criticism,[8] but this article will attempt to discuss one possibility of how this model can be amended for greater relevance in the measurement of the values of industrializing nations.

The South African Three Index Model

As already mentioned, the locus of most of the research conducted by Inglehart and his colleagues has been the industrialized world. Although some recent adaptations have allowed, to a limited degree, for the developing world to be included in the research (Abramson and Inglehart 1995:11), a classification that only allows for a materialist/post-materialist dimension does not prove very relevant for most of the developing world, where basic survival needs are often not even met. The South African World Values Survey executed in 1995 and 2001 include a battery containing the 12 original items, as well as the 18 different options of national priorities, a new and unique addition being the inclusion of 6 items that are concerned with basic survival needs. The pre-materialist items are as follows: *"Providing shelter for all People"; "Providing clean water for all people"; "Making sure that everyone is adequately clothed"; "Making sure that everyone can go to school"; "Providing land for all people"; "Providing everyone with enough food to eat"*.

The inclusion of the six extra items by the principal investigators of the 1995 WVS, which allow for the adding of the so-called pre-materialist dimension, can be justified on the grounds of "the complexity and diversity of the South African population as far as values are concerned and the extent that poverty is affecting value orientations" (Lategan 2000:410). The inadequacy of a dimension without a pre-materialist index does not, however, simply rest with the fact that some fundamental needs are not represented by the existing items, but that certain post-materialist items are wrongly interpreted to express certain pre-materialist or materialist needs, thereby skewing the results towards increased post-materialism, when this is not the case. One example is the item regarding *"giving people more say in their work and in their community"*, which can be wrongly interpreted as pertaining to the employment situation and could in fact be focusing on such materialist needs as greater job security. The questionnaires for 1995 and 2001 have also replaced the item regarding 'maintaining a stable economy' with one pertaining to employment levels, possibly due to

---

[8] For criticism see Duch and Taylor (1993), Clarke and Dutt (1991), Clarke, Kornberg, McIntyre, Bauer-Kaase and Kaase (1999), Davis and Davenport (1999), Davis, Dowley and Silver (1999), Marks (1997), Davis (2000), Flanagan (1987).

increasing levels of unemployment already proving themselves a potential problem to the principal investigators of the 1995 leg of the WVS.[9]

Research Design

The study utilizes existing attitudinal data obtained from the World Values Survey for the years 1990, 1995 and 2001.[10] Although a longer time period would have been preferable, data of the original 12-item model only spans 11 years, whilst data for the 18-item model only spans 5. The questionnaire was offered in a number of indigenous languages. The sample sizes were approximately 3 000 in all three legs, and were drawn from all inhabitants of South Africa over the age of 16, by a process of stratifying the entire population into four groupings, namely by province, gender, population group and community size.

During data analysis various statistical procedures were utilized to monitor and analyze the nature of the value priorities of the South African population according to the two dimensions, in order to ascertain which measure is most relevant in a South African context. A comparison of the results will entail analyzing the impact of the addition of a pre-materialist index on the distribution of value priorities, thereby revealing a possible alternative to the standard model. This will be followed by an analysis to ascertain the direction and degree of the change to have transpired over the specified period of time, also involving a speculative empirical analysis to determine the causes of value change in South Africa.

The Materialist/Post-materialist Dimension

Figure 1 depicts the location of the South African population along the original dimension first proposed by Inglehart in 1973. (See Appendix A for information on the construction of the indexes.) The figure can be interpreted in terms of a score of −10 and 10, denoting 'highly polarised' materialist or post-materialist types, with scores of between −2 and 2 denoting 'neutral' or 'mixed' types, who express both materialist and post-materialist values in roughly equal proportions. Those scoring between 4 and 8 (or −4 and −8) can be thought of as mixed types with greater emphasis on either materialist or post-materialist needs. From Figure 1 it becomes clear that there has been very little shift in the portion of pure materialists and pure post-materialist between 1990 and 2001, whilst a substantial increase in the number of mixed typed materialists (i.e. those scoring −6 and −8) is discernible.

---

[9] See section regarding the magnitude of unemployment as a national problem.

[10] The 1981 samples did not include rural Blacks, and is therefore not deemed representative enough to be included in the study.

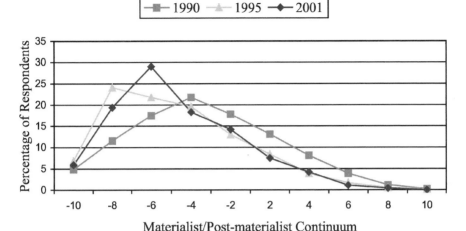

Figure 1. Scores on the Materialist/Post-materialist Continuum.

The increasing prioritization of one type of value is inevitably linked to a decrease in the prioritization of another, whereby the increased prioritization of materialist values is paralleled with an overall reduction of respondents on the more neutral and post-materialist side of the scale. Any further analysis of the data in the format of the materialist/post-materialist dimension shall be foregone in favor of analysis according to the pre-materialist/materialist dimension, primarily on the grounds of the previously described socio-economic situation in the country.

The Pre-materialist/Materialist Dimension

Figure 2 portrays the value orientations of the South African population between 1995 and 2001. Overall there is a higher portion of respondents that prioritize pre-materialist needs in 1995 than in 2001, and this situation appears to be compensated for by the large percentage of respondents with weak to medium materialist underpinnings in 2001.

Taken as a whole, there does appear to be a trend of slight increase in the emphasis on materialist, as opposed to pre-materialist, needs over the last five years. The overall decrease, albeit a slight one, in pre-materialists of varying polarizations, could be attributed to a number of factors.

Although the classic political behaviour debate of 'affect' versus 'cognition' in the formulation of judgments has been noted, this article will be built on the premise that most people rely on both 'affect' and 'cognition'[11] in the making of decisions, and will therefore utilize at

---

[11] See Kuklinski et al. 1991.

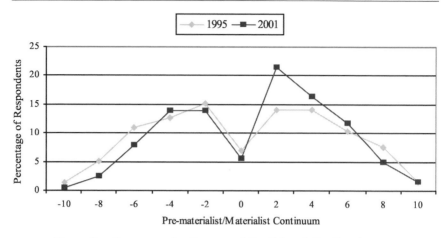

Figure 2.   Scores on the Pre-materialist/Materialist Continuum.

least some objective facts in the processing and substantiating of their opinions. In the following sections various potential paths of reasoning will be extrapolated, and examples of corroborative information, that people could have utilized, provided.

The first plausible rationale involves a general perception that the basic survival needs of the people are being catered for, rendering the provision of basic needs a progressively less pre-occupying need. There is a multitude of plausible reasons for this change. The most obvious reasoning would entail a real improvement in state delivery of basic services and infrastructure. A workable economic platform was put in place, need assessments were conducted, target policies drafted and finances, according to some to the tune of approximately R100 billion, made available (*Indicator SA* 2000:80). This alone could go some distance to explaining why pre-materialist needs reveal a declining prioritization. Kinder and Kiewiet (1981:129-161) asserted that people make electoral decisions on socio-tropic assessment, and this argument could be transported to the assessment of general conditions. People not in need of state provision of these goods and services, could be lead to believe that once these previously mentioned steps have been taken, the issue has been sufficiently addressed.

If one speculates that most citizens, even those not in direct contact, are more critical, relying on results and not promises to make judgments, there is indeed sufficient evidence to suggest that primary needs are increasingly being met, once again allowing for other values to be prioritized. A recent report in *Indicator SA*, which monitored infrastructure delivery, revealed that in some areas the delivery of social services has improved dramatically. Examples include the approximately one million housing subsidies that have been granted, the improvements made in terms of the provision, access and equity of education, the large number of clinics that have been built, as well as the progress in water delivery (Education:Achieving... 2000:78).

Statistics quoted in Møller (2000:22), portray how South Africans feel in terms of whether they have perceived a change for the better in their lives since 1994. The fact that four of the top five fields in which South Africans perceived the most pronounced changes for the better, represent basic survival needs (housing, electricity, health care, education), would imply that a large portion of South Africans feel that their basic needs are being fulfilled to greater satisfaction now, then was the case 6 years ago. The perception of improvements in other fields, such as the creation of jobs or increased crime prevention, is far smaller, leaving much room for these types of needs to be prioritized. According to a recent longitudinal study conducted by the Human Sciences Research Council (HSRC), dissatisfaction with, amongst others educational opportunities, health care and standard of living, has declined for Blacks, while Whites, Coloureds and Indians have shown increasing levels of dissatisfaction. The end status is, however, that with regard to the seven facets under investigation, people as a whole were more satisfied in the year 2000, than they were in 1994 (Klandermans, Roefs and Olivier 2001:48-54).

Another plausible argument to explain the apparent public perception of basic needs having been better met in 2001 than in 1995, could be that, although social service delivery may not have improved, people have greater access to the services and infrastructure provided by the state. Very often it is insufficient to simply look at the statistics, one actually needs to look at the accessibility and distribution of the resources. It is possible that these resources have become increasingly accessible over time, leading to this decrease in the prioritization in pre-materialist values. Particularly in the field of water and electricity provision, more effort has been made to reach the poor, rural and disenfranchised. More than 1.3 million rural people now have access to clean water within 200 metres of their house, and over 1.5 million houses have been electrified (*Indicator SA* 2000:79). The fact that women and children, two of the sectors of society most disadvantaged in the past and most in need at present, are the only ones given free health could further substantiate the perception that basic needs are being better met.

An alternative explanation is based on a more even distribution of basic social services and infrastructure, independent of the increasing income inequality gap. This would mean that although people do not have more income available, they have experienced a higher standard of living due to benefits handed out in kind and not in cash. Examples include free education (Van Den Berg 2000, quoted in Nattrass and Seekings 2001:56) free health care to pregnant women and children under the age of 6, as well as food stamps or producer subsidies (*Indicator SA* 2000:82). This situation would be further augmented by the fact that the higher income groups pay more tax than they receive social delivery goods or services, whether in cash or kind, whilst the opposite is true for the poorest categories, whose benefits greatly exceeded the amounts of tax they pay (Nattrass and Seekings 2001:56).

Consequently, it would appear that there is a wealth of statistics to substantiate the perception that perfunctory survival needs are being increasingly met. There is, however, just as large an amount of literature and statistics that all but prove the exact opposite. [12] The argument of more equal access to social services is disputed by indications such as the situation where the main beneficiaries of a reformed housing policy were the urban poor, with the rural poor being largely excluded from the process, leaving many worse off than at the outset (Nattrass and Seekings 2001:59). Another case in point is the provision of non-grid electricity, which does not allow for the use of electric stoves, which means that women, who are largely responsible for the cooking, still do not benefit from this service (Hassen 2000:15), and will therefore not consider their needs better met.

Critical citizens could easily find a host of information substantiating the notion that increasing financial and personnel allocation does not guarantee a better output of social services and goods. More money having been spent on schools, children nutrition schemes and housing subsidies does not ensure that people received the goods and services. Some of the reasons for this include implementation problems and corruption. A case in point would be the large number of rural clinics that have been built since 1994, of which many have suddenly had to contend with 30% staff cuts (*The Mail & Guardian*, 6 February 1998). Further, many people may have originally received access to resources, but due to a lack of maintenance and proper upkeep, only experienced the spoils for a short while. An example here would be the more than 50% of water faucets that have been broken since the implementation of the thousands of communal taps since 1994 (Bond 2000:18).

The decline of the prioritization of pre-materialist needs could, however, also be based on completely different notions, one possibility being that poor and needy people are increasingly looking to other sources for the provision of basic needs, and finding them there. Superior social

---

[12] For an overview of the two positions on the delivery of basic social services and goods see Bond, P. (2000) "Infrastructure Delivery: Class Apartheid" in *Indicator SA*, Vol. 17, No. 3 and Hassen, E. (2000) "Are Bricks and Mortar enough: Infrastructure Delivery" in *Indicator SA*, Vol 17, No 3.

networks facilitating community and family delivery of perfunctory goods and services is simply one example. Statistics regarding this would be near impossible to attain, but one could argue that extended family networks are becoming increasingly important as people opt out of the system of relying on the state. Other non-state actors, such as NGOs, churches, community and foreign aid organizations could be fulfilling the needs of people more successfully in 2001 than in 1995. An example in this instance would be some of the houses that have been built by women's self-help groups, in conjunction with *stokvels*, or the Protea scheme, which is helped by an NGO called the South African Homeless People's Federation, which builds houses with the use of second hand materials, collective labour and finances them with moneys made available by the rotation of financial assets (*The Star*, 25 February 1998). People could however, increasingly be opting for the private provision of goods, as is being seen in the increasing reliance on the provision of private security and health care.[13] Here, once again, aggregate statistics (if any could be unearthed), would not be truly representative of the real situation, and consequently the argument that people are increasingly seeing their primary needs met by non-state sources must remain simply speculative.

A different plausible route is to reconceptualize why pre-materialist values would be deemed less important, and three conceivable arguments shall be examined. The first scenario asserts that the de-prioritization of pre-materialist needs could be due to excessive and ever-escalating levels of crime and unemployment, coupled with the perceptions that the state is performing worse in these fields than in others. This scenario could mean that South Africans are increasingly prioritizing the items regarding the fighting of crime and on the economic security side, the item dealing with employment to such a degree as to skew the results. Thus although the respondents would score very low on the other materialist items, the scores on these two are very high, thereby falsely designating people as materialists instead of the pre-materialists that they truly are. Hence, although primary needs may be far from adequately met, the unnaturally high levels of crime results in pre-materialists selecting this item, rather than important pre-materialist items in the battery. Although crime levels are very high by international standards, crime has become an even more critical issue as a consequence of the framing it has undergone. The popular media, in particular, has been largely guilty of sensationalizing violent crimes to increase viewer figures, whilst the national government has increasingly framed crime as one of the potentially biggest obstacles to democratic

---

[13] For a detailed analysis of the increased reliance on private security, see Schonteich (1999).

consolidation (Shaw and Gastrow 2001:253). Various political parties and media sources have utilized crime to realize political agendas and maintain specific support bases, in terms of White conservative parties framing white farmers as under constant fatal threat from black criminals. A testing of this argument could yield very interesting results, and could be done in much the same format as the experimental research conducted by Clarke and Dutt (1991:905), in which the perceived shift towards post-materialism observed by Inglehart and his colleagues was, in fact, unsubstantiated if a question on employment was inserted to replace one of the questions in the original battery. By replacing the item regarding crime or unemployment with other items, such as reducing the income inequality (if the economic security item is left out), or improving the criminal justice system (if the physical security item is left out), more real results could possibly be computed. For the moment we will simply have to bear in mind that this possibility exists, and thus the results may not necessarily be as representative of real value underpinnings as expected due to measurement error.

Based upon the same premise, namely that materialist values are not being prioritized on the grounds of pre-materialist needs having been more satisfactorily met, the second alternative concerns another possible measurement error. The specific phrasing of the question asked of respondents could be less than reliable in testing underlying value priorities, and more adequate at testing people's evaluations of which parts of government policy are still inadequate, requiring more work. The exact wording of the question is as follows: "People sometimes talk about what the aims of this country should be for the next ten years. On this card are listed some of the goals which different people would give top priority. Would you please say which one of these you, yourself, consider the most important?" It is possible that people could interpret this question, not in terms of what the national needs are, but in terms of the weaknesses in government policy. The statistics regarding people's perceptions of the most prominent changes, quoted previously, highlights those fields in which people have seen a marked improvement. There is only one materialist item listed, with 5% of South Africans feeling that there has been an increase in the provision of jobs and job prospects (Moller 2000:22). Thus it would seem that most South Africans feel that the government has focused to a greater extent (and with much more success), on items of pre-materialist foundation, than on items of materialist underpinning. Hence they could rationalize that these 'materialist' items need to be accorded more attention in the future, despite pre-materialist needs largely still inadequately met.

Another alternative could be that South Africans are undergoing a conceptual overhaul, a mind shift exemplified by the move from the RDP to GEAR. This would entail that people no longer think in the order of needs as postulated by Maslow (1954), whereby the fulfillment of basic survival needs is a pre-requisite for the prioritization of security needs. It is possible that South Africans are increasingly re-organizing their needs, whereby the *modus operandi* to fulfilling basic survival needs is to have economic and physical security and safety. High levels of economic growth, low inflation and full employment may thus be prioritized ahead of items such as the provision of food, clothing, land and water, as people could rationalize that these can be bought, once money has been earned. The item regarding shelter, and to a greater degree that regarding education, will probably be exceptions, explaining why these are the two most mentioned pre-materialist items.

Shelter could represent an exception because such large portions of South Africans are still without a shelter fit for human habitation. Another reason could be that this item may also have certain post-materialist and materialist underpinnings. Many South Africans lay great emotional claim to owning their own homes, a conviction conceivably amplified by the forced removals under the Apartheid government. The positive self-reinforcement experienced when owning your own home is not easily paralleled, and therefore the item regarding shelter could cater to post-materialist needs for some. Further, the item may reveal materialist values, in terms of the ownership of a home representing some kind of financial stability, in terms of it being a costly commodity, which can be sold if large debts were to be incurred, as well as it functioning as collateral when applying for loans. The item regarding schooling may also be an exception because a solid education may be perceived as the ticket to employment, bringing with it financial security. Consequently South Africans could be prioritizing economic security needs in a value trade-off between present and future gain. People could be willing to compromise on the prioritization of certain pre-materialist needs on the grounds that these will be automatically met, if economic stability and prosperity has been established.

It becomes clear that there are a multitude of motivations for the visible decrease in the emphasis of pre-materialist values, in favor of low-polarized materialist items. Different respondents will employ various motivations, often no doubt in interaction with each other, to come to the conclusions demonstrated in the results. Most probably it is the dynamics of the duel effects of decreasing pre-materialism and increasing materialism that can be held liable for these findings. The fact that most of the increase is experienced amongst the least-polarized materialists (those scoring 2) highlights the fact that the results have been altered by just one or two fewer pre-materialist and one or two more materialist items being selecting in 2001 than in 1995. Thus it would seem that this change is very short-term, and that the orientations in the South African case are still very fluid, and far from any kind of crystallization.

The Disaggregated Pre-materialist/Materialist Dimension

The value change discussed above may not, however, be representative of the value fluidity of all the population sub-groups in South Africa's highly heterogeneous population. As mentioned, it is impossible to discuss the value change in each separate socio-economic and demographic group, and hence the essay will focus on the four main racial groups (see Figures 3 and 4), although this research also measured value change in the population as disaggregated according to education, income, age and gender. Amongst the black population the strong and weak pre-materialists-, as well as mixed and weak materialist types, have experienced a decrease since 1995, whilst the weak materialist types have displayed an increase over the same period of time. Plausible causes of this increasing coalescing around the weak materialist pole have already been speculated upon previously, and will therefore not be addressed in great detail. Suffice to say that it is probably the dual interaction of increasing emphasis being laid on physical security needs, with Africans being the primary victims of crime (Shaw and Gastrow 2001:243) and the possibility of perfunctory survival needs having been better met.

A slightly divergent pattern is visible in the Coloured groups, who, whilst displaying a slight decrease in strong pre-materialist types, reveal a slight upsurge in all three the weak pre-materialist, mixed and weak materialist types. They also reveal a marked decline in the portion of strong materialists. Coloured people therefore seem to be exhibiting this trend of escalating convergence around the middle-of-the-range value types to a far greater extent than Blacks. A strikingly different trend is visible amongst Indians. The visible decline in weak and strong pre-materialists appears offset by an increase in mixed types. This picture appears replicated once again, by a drop in weak materialists being compensated for by an increase amongst strongly polarized materialists.

The White group, however, portrays a scenario unlike that of any of the other groups, starting with a marginal increase in both the strong and weak pre-materialists. No longer protected by a favorable Apartheid state and having to content with affirmative action policies, white people are increasingly feeling the pinch. Together with the situation of greater integration since 1994 having dispelled some of the ignorance of the poverty stricken situation amongst other, largely non-white, groups, Whites

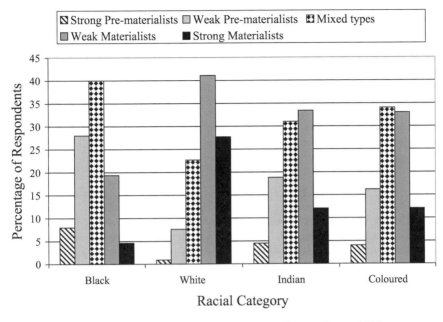

Figure 3.   Value-type Distribution according to Race: 1995.

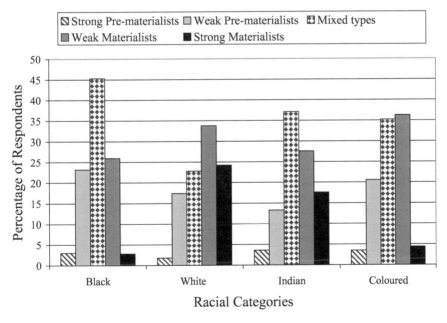

Figure 4.   Value-type Distribution according to Race: 2001.

could be more aware of pre-materialist needs of the country as a whole. The largest determinants in terms of the increase in pre-materialists is probably, however, the increasingly experienced threat to white ownership of land and White pre-occupation with the perceived deterioration of the national education system. This increase in pre-materialists must then be offset by a decrease elsewhere. Despite the much lauded emphasis on security needs amongst the white population, the greater prioritization of the previously mentioned pre-materialist needs outstrips this concern with security, resulting in a situation where a value trade-off reveals a decrease in materialists amongst the white population.

The 18-item Materialist/Post-materialist Dimension

The pre-materialist/materialist dimension having been exhaustively examined, it is now necessary to return to a speculative analysis of the population located on the 18-item materialist/post-materialist spectrum. In the first section of the analysis, in which the population was situated on the original Inglehart materialist/post-materialist dimension, it was revealed that only a very small portion of South Africans actually prioritize post-materialist values. It has, subsequently, been concluded that the batteries containing the pre-materialist items represent an improved method of tapping underlying value structures. For this reason it is imperative that the movement along the materialist/post-materialist dimension of this model, as opposed to the original Inglehart model, be evaluated. Right from the outset of the analysis of Figure 5, it is quite clear that there has only been marginal change in terms of this dimension over the last five years. The orientation of the population along the materialist/post-materialist dimension reveals little change, with only very slight deviations at some points. Due to the results of the analysis of the Inglehart materialist/post-materialist dimension, a very even distribution about the median was not expected, but these only serve to reinforce the reduced applicability and relevance of the materialist/post-materialist continuum.

South Africa does not, however, appear to be moving away from post-materialist to materialist prioritization, as the greater coalescing around the materialist pole is largely determined by a decreasing emphasis on pre-materialist values. Hence it would seem that the primary location of value trade-offs appear to be the interface between pre-materialist and materialist values, with post-materialist values simply remaining quite irrelevant. Table 1 demonstrates the fact that there is no overall increase in post-materialists, but that a slight increase in the prioritization of separate materialist items, accompanied by a slight decrease in the prioritization of post-materialist items, resulted in a situation of a 2% decrease amongst the mixed types. The possible reasons for an increased prioritization of

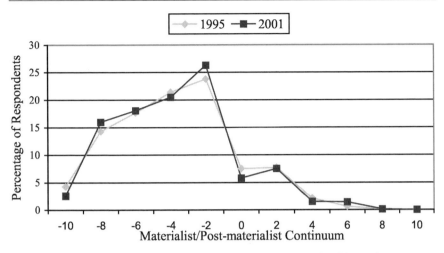

Figure 5.   Scores on the Materialist/Post-materialist Dimension.

Table 1

Percentage Change in Materialist/Post-materialist Dimension

	1995	2001
Materialists	81.5	83.5
Materialist/Post-materialist Mixed Types	7.5	5.8
Post-materialists	10.5	10.5

materialist needs have been expanded upon during the analysis section, and will not be addressed again.

In terms of the post-materialist values, the Apartheid government having being replaced by a democratic one, could catalyze a subconscious decline in the perceptual importance of certain post-materialist needs. This move could have brought about the perception that the abolition of repressive Apartheid laws, the inception of an electoral liberal democracy and an exemplary constitution, makes it unnecessary to pre-occupy oneself with a number of the post-materialist items, such as the freedom of speech and more say in important government decisions. With the change in institutional and legal structure, and many protective measures enshrining and guaranteeing many important rights and freedoms, these items may be receiving less attention. Speculation of the possible reasons aside, the value shift hypothesis — entailing a redistribution of values towards increased post-materialism, is definitely not observable in the South African context, with post-materialist values remaining rather marginal in the bigger picture of South Africa's value orientation.

Are South Africa's Values Changing?

Despite the absence of a shift towards increased post-materialism, South Africa's values appear to be undergoing a slight reorganization along the pre-materialist/materialist dimension. This value movement has, however, not been as large as might have been expected, in light of the massive restructuring that has occurred within the country over the period under review.

A superficial observation of the end statistics provided in Table 2, could result in deductions that South Africa's values are not undergoing systematic change. Conclusions of such a nature could be arrived at, as the largest visible change entails a decrease in pre-materialists, in conjunction with an approximately equal increase amongst mixed types, denoting a moderation in polarization, and not a 'real' change, with the percentage increase in materialists being a marginal 1.1%. Such an interpretation would, however, not be reflective of the real extent of movement occurring within various sub-groups of the population. South Africa's values are therefore undergoing relatively dramatic fluctuations, mainly reflected when the data are disaggregated for the various population sub-groups, despite the end results not always reflecting this. There does, however, appear to be a decrease in pre-materialism, with an ever so slight increase in the portion of materialists, with levels of post-materialism remaining unchanged, and still relatively insignificant. On the whole a process of incrementally more convergent value orientations becomes apparent. Whilst very few isolated groups display an increasing polarization towards the extremes, the majority is increasingly representing middle-of-the-range alternatives, with an ever-increasing portion prioritizing both materialist and pre-materialist values. Further, value change appears to be undergoing a plethora of fluctuations within the various population sub-groups, indicating that the short-term value priorities of most South Africans are in no way crystallized, but are likely to undergo further change.

Table 2

Percentage Change in the Pre-materialist/Materialist Dimension

	1995	2001
Pre-materialists	30.1	24.6
Pre-materialist/Materialist Mixed Types	36.2	40.9
Materialists	33.4	34.3

The Appropriateness of the Three-Index Model

Most of these findings and consequent deductions would not have been possible without the introduction of the pre-materialist index. The original materialist-post-materialist dimension proved inappropriate in tapping South Africa's true value orientations, primarily because the interface of value change in South Africa is located within the pre-materialist/materialist dimension, with the importance of post-materialist values remaining marginal. The inclusion of pre-materialist items in two successive waves of the South African WVS, proved to be a crucial element in attaining a true portrayal of South Africa's value orientations, creating the possibility that a revised model may also prove more applicable for other developing countries. The drawing of any decisive conclusions, regarding the universally greater appropriateness of this amended model, would have to be preceded with applications to the data of other African, developing and even industrialized nations.

Conclusion

In conclusion one can assert that the expansive external political, social and economic changes to have transpired since 1990 and 1995 respectively, have brought about internal fluidity in the value dimension of South Africa as a whole, as well as for the various population sub-groups individually. The assertion made by Rescher (1969:118), that the "change in the operational sphere — in the whole range of social, cultural, demographic, economic, and technological factors that comprise the way of life in that society — has enormous repercussions for values-providing tremendous opportunities for the enhancement of some of our traditional ideals and aspirations, and great threats to the realization of other," appears validated. As predicted the value shift hypothesis promulgated by Inglehart appears largely uncorroborated, whilst an overall trend away from pre-materialism towards increased mixed type value priorities, with a slight increase in materialists, has become evident.

In the process of this analysis, the article has also begun to situate a global, but still largely Western theory, in a South African and developing world context, denoting a small step towards expanding knowledge regarding the direction, degree and nature of the dynamics of universal value priorities. The opportunity for further advancement of this knowledge could thus be presenting itself in the form of the development of an expanded conceptual framework that demonstrates greater applicability to the socio-economic and cultural reality of South Africa, Africa, and much of the developing world.

Appendix 1

Table 3 demonstrates the factor loadings of the uniquely South African 18-item model in 1995. Most of the loadings appear acceptably high, with the item regarding keeping the countryside beautiful even loading in this application of the 18-item model. The only problem appears to be the item regarding employment, which loads onto the component which houses all the post-materialist items, but doing so with a negative prefix.

The table of 2001 factor loadings (Table 4) reveals predictable results, except, once again, in the case of the item regarding "unemployment". In both data sets the item regarding unemployment appears to simultaneously encompass pre-materialist, materialist and post-materialist needs. One could speculate that in the South African mindset, having a job is cognitized as a basic survival need, primarily because without the means of income derived from employment, most of the other basic needs will not be met, thus involving an almost direct link. The item will, of course, represent materialist needs to some degree, in terms of being included in the group of financial and economic factors, which, both on an individual and national level, affect economic security. Unemployment

Table 3

Factor Loadings of Principal Components Analysis of 18-item Model: 1995[14]

	Component 1	Component 2
Providing Shelter for all People	*0.52*	
Making sure that Everyone is adequately clothed	*0.47*	
Providing clean Water for all People	*0.45*	
Making sure that Everyone can go to School	*0.38*	
Providing Land for all People	*0.36*	
Providing enough Food for all People	*0.33*	
Maintaining Law and Order	−0.66	
Maintaining a high Rate of Economic Growth	−0.55	
Fighting Crime	−0.50	
Maintaining a strong Defence Force	−0.29	
Fighting Rising Prices	−0.26	
Making sure all People are fully employed		**−0.74**
Keeping the Countryside beautiful		**0.42**
Protecting Freedom of Speech		**0.34**
A Society where Ideas count more		**0.28**
More say at Work and in their Communities		**0.25**
A more Humane and less Impersonal society		**0.19**
More say in Government Decisions		**0.15**

Extraction Method: Principal Component Analysis. Rotation Method: Varimax with Kaiser Normalization. Rotation converged in 3 iterations.

---

[14] On the basis of the results of the principal components analysis in Taylor (1998:88), only two factors were extracted.

Table 4

Factor Loadings of Principal Components Analysis of 18-item Model: 2001

	Component 1	Component 2 [15]
Providing Shelter for all People	0.69	
Providing Land for all People	0.46	
Providing clean Water for all People	0.30	
Making sure that Everyone is adequately clothed	0.28	
Providing enough Food for all People	0.18	
Making sure that Everyone can go to School	0.12	
Fighting Crime	−0.69	
Maintaining Law and Order	−0.59	
Fighting Rising Prices	−0.36	
Maintaining a high Rate of Economic Growth	−0.26	
Maintaining a strong Defence Force	−0.24	
Making sure all People are fully employed	0.21	
More say in Government Decisions		**−0.76**
More say at Work and in their Communities		**0.54**
A more Humane and less Impersonal society		**0.53**
A Society where Ideas count more		**0.34**
Protecting Freedom of Speech		**0.31**
Keeping the Countryside beautiful		**0.19**

Extraction Method: Principal Component Analysis. Rotation Method: Varimax with Kaiser Normalization. Rotation converged in 3 iterations.

may, however, also entail certain post-materialist underpinnings, by means of the psychologically damaging effects of unemployment, an example of which would include the loss of feelings of self-worth as a result of being unemployed. Although this somewhat complex item appears to reveal a host of underlying values, for the purpose of the continuity of the analysis, it will still be included in the materialist index.

The theoretical and empirical validity and reliability sufficiently expanded upon, the indexes can be constructed. In both the 12-item and the 18-item model the indexes were created in much the same way. The construction of the index began by adding all the respective materialist and respective post-materialist items together. Utilizing the SPSS computing function, the scores that each respondent attained were tallied up, resulting in a materialist and post-materialist index, each with a scale of 0 to 9. This scale came into being as two items from each table were combined, and as respondents were only allowed one first- and one second-option, with a first option scoring two points and a second option 1, whilst any item not selected scored 0.

A variable with a scale of 0 to 9 is less than practical in terms of index construction, making it imperative that the variable be converted to one ranging

---

[15] Factor loadings were clearer on component 3 than component 2.

from 0 to 10. This was facilitated by multiplying all the scores by 1.1 recurring, which, thereby creating a variable with a scale of 0 to 10. Index construction complete, it was possible to assemble a continuum on which to map the population. In the instance of the 12-item model, only one continuum needed to be constructed, with the materialist pole on the left and the post-materialist on the right. The 18-item model requires the construction of two continuums, one along a pre-materialist/materialist spectrum, and one along a materialist/post-materialist spectrum. All three were constructed by theoretically placing the 'lower-order' pole at the left end of the scale, running in the negative numbers, with the 'higher order' index falling on the right. Mathematically this entailed multiplying the 'lower order' index by negative 1, and the 'higher order' index by positive 1, and then simply adding up the products.

References

ABRAHAMSON, P.R., S. ELLIS AND R. INGLEHART
1997   "Research in Context: Measuring Value Change". *Political Behaviour*, Vol. 19, No. 1, 41-59.
ABRAMSON, P.R. AND R. INGLEHART
1995   *Value Change in Global Perspective*. Ann Arbor: University of Michigan Press.
ADELZADEH, A.
1999   "The Costs of staying the Course". *NGQO — An Economic Bulletin published by the National Institute of Economic Policy*, Vol. 1, No. 1, 1-6.
BLAKE, M.
1998   "Are the Poor being heard?" in Barberton, C. et al. (eds), *Creating Action Space: The Challenge of Poverty and Democracy in South Africa*. Cape Town: David Philips.
BOND, P.
2000   "Infrastructure Delivery: Class Apartheid". *Indicator SA*, Vol. 17, No. 3, 18-21.
CLARKE, H.D., N. DUTT AND J. RAPKIN
1997   "Conversations in Context: The (Mis)Measurement of Value Change in Advanced Industrial Societies". *Political Behavior*, Vol. 19, No. 1, 19-39.
CLARKE, H.D., A. KORNBERG, C. MCINTYRE, P. BAUER-KAASE AND M. KAAS
1999   "The Effect of Economic Priorities on the Measurement of Value Change: New Experimental Evidence". *American Political Science Review*, Vol. 93, No. 3, 637-647.
DAVIS, D.W., K.M. DOWLEY AND B.D. SILVER
1999   "Postmaterialism in World Societies: Is it really a Value Dimension". *American Journal of Political Science*, Vol. 43, No. 3, 935-962.
DAVIS, D. AND D. DAVENPORT
1999   "Assessing the Validity of the Postmaterialist Index". *American Political Science Review*, Vol. 93, No. 3, 649-664.
DUCH, R.M. AND M.A. TAYLOR
1993   "Postmaterialism and the Economic Condition". *American Journal of Political Science*, Vol. 37, No. 3, 747-779.
1994   "A Reply to Abramson and Inglehart's 'Education, Security, and Postmaterialism'". *American Journal of Political Science*, Vol. 38, No. 3, 815-824.

FLANAGAN, S.
1987   "Value Change in Industrial Societies". *American Political Science Review*, Vol. 81, No. 4, 1289-1319.
FRIEDMAN, S.
1999   "South Africa: Entering the Post-Mandela Era". *Journal of Democracy*, Vol. 10, No. 4.
GILIOMEE, H.
1995   "Democratization in South Africa". *Political Science Quarterly*, Vol. 101, No. 1.
GILIOMEE, H. AND L. SCHLEMMER
1994   "Overview: Can a South African Democracy become consolidated". H. Giliomee et al. (eds), *The Bold Experiment*. Johannesburg: Southern.
GRANATO, J., R. INGLEHART AND D. LEBLANG
1996   "The Effect of Cultural Values on Economic Development: Theory, Hypotheses, and Some Empirical Tests". *American Political Science Review*, Vol. 40, No. 3, 607-631.
HABIB, A. AND K. MOODLEY
1993   *The Negotiated Revolution*. Johannesburg: Jonathan Ball.
HOROWITZ, D.
1991   *A Democratic South Africa*. Oxford University Press.
HASSEN, E.
2000   "Are Bricks and Mortar enough: Infrastructure Delivery?" *Indicator SA*, Vol. 17, No. 3. 13-16.
Indicator
2000   "Education: Achieving Equality?" *Indicator SA*, Vol. 17, No. 2, 40-44.
INGLEHART, R.
1977   *The Silent Revolution: Changing Values and Political Styles amongst Western Publics*. Princeton: Princeton University Press.
1990   *Culture Shift in Advanced Industrial Society*. Princeton, NJ: Princeton University Press.
1997   *Modernization and Postmodernization: Cultural, Economic and Political Change in 43 Societies*. Princeton: Princeton University Press.
2000   "Globalization and Postmodern Values". *The Washington Quarterly*, Vol. 23, No. 1, 215-228.
INGLEHART, R. AND P.R. ABRAMSON
1992   "Generational Replacement and Value Change in Eight West European Societies". *British Journal of Political Science*, Vol. 22, 183-228.
1994   "Economic Security and Value Change". *American Political Science Review*, Vol. 88, No. 2, 336-354.
1999   "Measuring Postmaterialism". *American Political Science Review*, Vol. 93, No. 3, 665-677.
INGLEHART, R. AND J. RABIER
1986   "Political Realignment in Advanced Industrial Society: From Class-Based Politics to Quality-of-Life Politics". *Government and Opposition*, Vol. 21, 456-479.
KLANDERMANS, B., M. ROEFS AND J. OLIVIER (EDS)
2001   *The State of the People: Citizens, Civil Society and Governance in South Africa, 1994-2000*. Pretoria: Human Sciences Research Council.
KOTZÉ, H.
2000   "Shared Values in South Africa: A selection of value orientations in the field of personal ethics". *Scriptura*, Vol. 75, 409-420.

KUKLINSKI, J.H., E. RIGGLE, V. OTTATI, N. SCHWARZ AND R.S. WYER
1991   "The Cognitive and Affective Bases of Political tolerance Judgments". *American Political Science Review*, Vol. 35, No. 1, 1-27.

LATEGAN, B.C.
2000   "Extending the Materialist/Post-materialist distinction: Some remarks on the classification of values from a South African perspective". *Scriptura*, Vol. 75, 409-420.

LIEBENBERG, I. (ED.)
1994   *The Long March — The Story of the Struggle for Liberation in South Africa*. HAUM.

LODGE, T.
1999   *South African Politics since 1994*. Cape Town: David Philip.

MAHARAJ, G.
1999   *Between Unity and Diversity: essays on nation building in Post-Apartheid South Africa*. Cape Town: IDASA.

MARKS, G.N.
1997   "The Formation of Materialist and Postmaterialist Values". *Social Science Research*, Vol. 26, 52-68.

MASLOW, A.
1945   *Motivation and Personality*. New York: Harper.

MARAIS, H.
1998   "The battleground of the economy" in *South African Limits to Change: The Political Economy of Transformation*. London: Zed Books.

MOLLER, V.
2000   "Democracy and Happiness: Quality of Life Trends". *Indicator South Africa*, Vol. 17, No. 3.

NATTRASS, N. AND J. SEEKINGS
2001   "Race and Economic Inequality in South Africa". *Daedalus*, Winter 2001, 45-72.

RESCHER, N.
1969   *Introduction to Value Change*. Prentice-Hall, Inc., Englewood Cliffs, New Jersey.

ROKEACH, M.
1973   *The Nature of Human Values*. The Free Press, New York.
1979   *Understanding Human Values*. The Free Press, New York.

SCHONTEICH, M.
1999   "Fighting Crime with private muscle: the private sector and crime prevention". *African Security review*, Vol. 8, No. 5, 65-75.

SHAW, M. AND P. GASTROW
2001   "Stealing the Show? Crime and its Impact in Post-Apartheid South Africa". *Daedalus*, Winter 2001, 235-258.

SHAW, S.
2001   *South Africa's Transition to Democracy: An African Success Story*. Cape Town.

SISK, T.
1994   "Review Article: Perspectives on South Africa's Transition: Implications for Democratic Consolidation". *Politikon*, Vol. 21, No. 1, 66-75.

SLABBER, E.
2000   "Black Rich get richer". *Finance Week*, 25 February 2000, 28.

SOUTHALL, R. (ED.)
2001   *Opposition and Democracy in South Africa*. London: Portland.

TAYLOR, H.
1998   *Squaring the Circle: Towards a Valid Values Dimension for South Africa.* Unpublished MA Thesis, University of Stellenbosch.
VAN DETH, J.W. AND E. SCARBROUGH
1995   *The Impact of Values.* Oxford University Press.
VAN ZYL SLABBERT, F.
1992   *The Quest for Democracy.* Penguin.
WHITEFORD, A.
1996   "Economic and Human Development" in *A Socio-Economic Atlas of South Africa: A demographic, Socio-economic and Cultural Profile of South Africa.* Pretoria: HSRC Publishers.
WOODS, D.
2000   *Rainbow revisited: South Africa's decade of democracy.* London: Andre Deutsch.

Individual Values and Global Governance

A Comparative Analysis of Orientations towards the United Nations

THORLEIF PETTERSSON[*]

In an increasingly globalized world, the domestic and the foreign, the national and the international become more and more intertwined. As Rosenau (1997:4) put it, "Domestic and foreign affairs have always formed a seamless web, and the need to treat them as such is urgent in this time of enormous transformation." The World Values Survey (WVS) may supply interesting data for such required investigations of the interconnectedness of the national and international. In this paper, peoples' orientations toward one of the most important organizations for global governance, the U.N., will be analyzed, using the evidence from a new battery of questions on this topic, which was developed for the most recent WVS questionnaire.

The UN is taking on greater significance in world affairs. When the UN and its Secretary-General, Kofi Annan, were awarded the 2001 Nobel Peace Price, the Nobel committee said that the end of the Cold War "has at last made it possible for the U.N. to perform more fully the part it was originally intended to play. Today the organization is at the forefront of efforts to achieve peace and security in the world, and of the international mobilization aimed at meeting the world's economic, social and environmental challenges" (Norwegian Nobel Peace Prize Committee 2001). A recent scholarly analysis has found that the contemporary UN is the "prime global mechanism for simultaneously maintaining historic patterns and absorbing profound changes" (Rosenau 1997:389). In the face of tremendous obstacles, the UN manages to persist and even in some respects to thrive. The increased importance of the UN since the end of

[*] Uppsala University, Sweden.

the Cold War is illustrated by the fact that in 1987, the UN assigned about 10,000 peace-keepers to 5 operations on an annual budget of 233 million dollars. In 1994, the number of troops rose to 72,000 peace-keepers in 18 different operations at an annual budget of more than 53 billion dollars. Furthermore, during the mid-eighties, the Security Council met on a monthly basis, while 10 years later, the Council was meeting on a daily schedule (Rosenau & Durfee 2000:154).

There have however been few studies of how common people view the UN. "In summarizing the findings on attitudes towards the United Nations, the point to be emphasized is the inadequacy of the available data" (Everts 1998:422). However, some results suggest that attitudes towards the UN constitute a separate dimension of orientations towards internationalized governance, that there is a comparatively high awareness of the UN, a high degree of interest in several of the key problems it tackles, and an overall positive attitude towards the institution itself. It has also been suggested that attitudes towards the UN are uncertain and that peoples' knowledge about the complexity of its programs and organizational structure is limited. But we possess surprisingly little empirical evidence on the subject. As Everts (1998:423) put it, "a comprehensive study of attitudes towards the United Nations is imperative." The WVS provides valuable material for this purpose.

Public Opinion and Global Governance

Some have argued that is pointless to examine the linkages between a system for global governance like the UN, and the values and social orientations of ordinary citizens. This is a hotly debated question between the three main schools in International Relations (IR) theory. The Realist school tends to take into account only those individuals who occupy high government positions, take mass publics for granted, and see the ordinary citizen as ready to submit to state leadership in international politics. Liberal theory grants the citizens a certain role, especially with regard to the ways their multiple interests may generate collective organizations which may have an impact on public officials. According to postinternationalist theory, individuals are central, and their skills and world views are assumed to have a substantial impact on international politics. To this school of thought, "macro collectivities and institutions derive their sustenance from the individuals they embrace" (Rosenau & Durfee 2000:81). Therefore, "any transformation at the micro level is bound to find expression in the aggregated dynamics that give shape and direction to global life" (ibid). In recent years, a swing of the pendulum towards culture and identity is "strikingly evident in post-Cold War IR theorizing" (Lapid 1996:3). The swing even includes religious beliefs and values as an intrinsic aspect of international relations (Dark 2000:VII). In this sense, new developments in IR theory have extended both the number and kinds of actors who play a key role for global governance, and among the key actors are now found both individuals and mass publics (Rosenau 1997:275-311; Sinnott 1998). Due to the expanded systems for public education and peoples' increased political skills (cf. Inglehart 1990; 1997), "people have become increasingly more competent in assessing where they fit in international affairs and how their behavior can be aggregated into significant collective outcomes" (Rosenau 1997:59). The concept of citizenship is changing and cosmopolitan orientations have become increasingly common.

The thesis that individual level values and skills are important to world affairs is based on three equally important premises. "One is that citizens have become more analytically and emotionally skillful and a second is that this skill revolution at the micro level matters, that through perceptual and aggregate processes citizens are shaping macro outcomes more extensively than they have in the past. The third is the presumption that the macro system of world politics has entered a period of prolonged turbulence that is especially vulnerable to micro inputs" (Rosenau 1997:279f). Thus, peoples' competence in international affairs has increased, and because of the enhanced turbulence in the system for world politics, the system has become more liable to peoples' efforts to influence the system. Therefore, in order to reach a proper understanding of the multi-faceted phenomenon of global governance, peoples' values and social orientations should be considered. Although it may be true that mass publics do not know much about the many detailed aspects of The International Food Regime, the Law of Sea, or even the UN, these regimes can be related to a set of so called diffuse values, which enable their creation and persistence (Sinnott 1998:26). The principle of sovereignty and the notion of exclusive control within a specific geographic area are examples of such diffuse values. Even if the main repository for such diffuse values may be various international institutions, they also "exist in a broad cultural milieu *of which public opinion is a part*" (ibid, italics added here). By such arguments, interesting theoretical linkages between public opinion and various institutions for internationalized governance can be established.

In this manner, it has been concluded that "far from regarding public opinion as something remote and irrelevant, regime theory, particularly in its more recent manifestations, strongly implies that domestic public opinion may impel or constrain moves towards internationalized governance, whether these moves are comprehensive and robust as in the case of European integration, or partial and tentative, as in the case of most international regimes" (Sinnott 1998:29). In contrast to a "permissive-consensus-understanding," which assumes public opinion to be of little importance in most areas of internationalized governance (Lindberg & Scheingold 1970), it has been argued that the more peoples' orientations towards internationalized governance relate to their deeply held values, the more likely the impact of public opinion on élite action, and the less likely the success of élite efforts to lead public opinion away (cf. Inglehart 1997: Chap 6). Consequently, in order to assess the importance of public opinion with regard to an organization for internationalized governance, the relationship between peoples' orientations towards that organization and their basic values is a key issue. The stronger the relationships, the more influential their orientations may be. However, it should also be noted that such relationships do not automatically yield the formation of publics which can bring about change in the systems for global governance. "Individuals are restless, their loyalties are in flux; their inclinations to shift into apathetic, self-centered, ideological, or democratic forms of citizenship have been intensified; but how and why these tendencies among individuals have been transformed into spontaneous and effective publics is not easily explained" (Rosenau 1997:299). In order to improve the knowledge in such matters, answers to the question of "which kinds of basic values are related to which kinds of orientations towards which kinds of internationalized governance" may prove valuable. This paper is an effort to start answering this complicated question.

It should furthermore be noted that the relationships between peoples' basic values and their orientations towards internationalized governance are not only of interest to the understanding of international affairs. These relationships are also important to cultural sociology and the efforts to get a comprehensive understanding of the relevance and scope of peoples' basic values and cultural convictions, both at the local, the regional, the national, and the international levels. To an overwhelming degree, comparative analyses of WVS data have until now investigated the relationships between peoples basic values and their views on various domestic concerns, for instance socio-economical issues, political issues, moral issues, issues with regard to social relations, family issues, etc. Thus, to extend these analyses to include the relationships between peoples' basic values and their orientations towards different kinds of international relations, is of key interest also from a value study approach.

A Comparative Analytical Strategy

In order to clarify the many factors which may condition the relationships between peoples' basic values and their orientations towards international-ized governance, these relationships should be investigated in a variety of different economical, political, social, and cultural contexts. This paper will report on such a comparative investigation of WVS data from 10 countries, which are chosen to yield as great variation as possible in cultural, social, economical, and political matters. In case the relationships between peoples' basic values and their orientations towards the UN should be similar in these different contexts, then the factors which differentiate between the contexts can be regarded as irrelevant to the relationships. Thus, the comparative strategy known as the "most different systems design" (Przeworski & Teune 1970) will be used. The more a certain relationship can be found on an international scale, the lesser the possibility that the relationship is conditioned by the specific characteristics of a given context (Dogan & Pelassy 1990:21). If on the other hand the relationships should vary between the different contexts, further analyses of the country differences in cultural, social, economical, and political matters, may clarify the causes for the different relationships.

For this comparative investigation, 10 countries from Africa, Asia, Europe, and North and South America, respectively, have been chosen. Needless to say, the selected countries can only be taken from the group of countries which have completed their participation in the latest WVS round. Therefore, from pure theoretical arguments, one may advocate to compare other countries than the ones selected. Disregarding such problems, the following 10 countries have been chosen: South Africa and Zimbabwe from Africa, Japan and Vietnam from Asia, Sweden and Serbia from Europe, US and Canada from North America, and Mexico and Argentina from Latin America. Previous WVS research has demonstrated that these countries belong to different cultural zones. Thus, South Africa has been located in the African cultural zone, Japan in the Confucian, Sweden in the Protestant European, Serbia as part of the former Yugoslavia in the Ex-Communist, Argentina and Mexico in the Latin-American, and Canada and US in the English-speaking cultural zone (Inglehart & Baker 2000). As for Zimbabwe and Vietnam, which did not participate in the previous WVS waves, Zimbabwe can be assumed to be part of the African zone, and Vietnam to belong to either the Confucian, the South Asian, or the Ex-Communist zone. Thus, the countries included in this study differ substantially in basic cultural patterns. That the 10 countries also differ in basic social, political, and economical dimensions can be substantiated by a number of other sources. Some of this information is summarized in Table 1.

Table 1 demonstrates that the 10 countries differ substantially in several basic dimensions. With regard to the size of the populations, there is a vast difference between the largest countries (US and Japan), and the smallest (Zimbabwe, Sweden, and Serbia). In terms of age structure, the percentage young people in Japan is about only half of the percentage in South

Table 1

Socio-economic and political data for 10 countries from 5 continents. Data from CIA World fact book, Freedom House, World Bank statistics, and Country file 2001. All indicators refer to the year of 2000. In the case of missing data for year 2000, data from the most adjacent year is choosen. Data for Serbia includes Montenegro (population of about 600.000)

	Africa:		Asia:		Europe		North America		South America	
	S Afric	Zimbabw	Japan	Vietnam	Sweden	Serbia	US	Canada	Mexico	Argentina
Population in millions	43.586	11.365	126.771	79.939	8.875	10.677	278.058	31.292	101.879	37.384
Population 1-14 years	32.1%	38.7%	14.6%	32.1%	18.2%	19.8%	21.1%	18.9%	33.3%	26.5%
Life expectancy at birth	48.1	37.1	80.8	69.6	79.7	73.5	77.3	76.2	71.8	75.3
GDP ppp per capita USD	8.500	2.500	24.900	1.950	22.200	2.300	36.200	24.800	9.100	12.900
Human development index	697	555	924	671	926	?	929	935	784	837
Power resource index	9.5	3.5	37.4	2.7	45.7	?	51.5	52.1	15.9	33.4
GDP by agriculture	5%	28%	2%	25%	2%	20%	2%	3%	5%	6%
GDP by services	65%	40%	63%	40%	74%	30%	80%	66%	68%	62%
Degree of urbanization	50%	35%	79%	20%	83%	52%	77%	77%	74%	90%
Pol. Rights, civil lib. Freed house	1,2	6,5	1,2	7,6	1,1	4,4	1,1	1,1	3,4	2,3
Television sets per capita	.12	.03	.68	.04	.52	.26	.79	.69	.25	.21
Internet users by 100.000	42	2	213	2	507	8	532	420	25	24
Internationalization index	70.6	63.3	101.7	25.9	123.3	?	113.7	120.8	77.5	77.5
Ratified environm agreements	10	10	19	10	24	10	20	21	14	17
Received aid USD per capita	12.8	20.5	0	18.3	0	60.1	0	0	0.4	2.5
Military expend (millions USD)	2.271	239	40.545	631	5.923	?	293.023	18.420	4.718	3.313

Africa, Zimbabwe, Vietnam, and Mexico, while the life expectancy at birth ranges around 75 and 80 in some countries (Japan, Sweden, US, Canada, Argentine), and below 50 in the two African countries. There are also great differences between the poorest and the richest countries, both in terms of GDP per capita, the UN human development index, and the power resource index. The latter is a composite index tapping the urbanization, the non-agricultural population, the number of students, the number of illiterates, the area of family farms, and the degree of decentralization of non-agricultural economic resources (Vanhanen 1997). These differences are also reflected in the amount of received aid per capita. In all these respects, US, Japan, Canada, and Sweden, differ from Zimbabwe, South Africa, Vietnam, Mexico, and Argentina. This difference is also reflected in the developments of information technology (TV, Internet), which is an important dimension of structural globalization (Halman & Pettersson 1999). In terms of the economy, there are also substantial differences with regard to the sizes of the agricultural and service sectors, something affecting the value structures in the various countries (Inglehart & Baker 2000). In countries like Vietnam, Serbia, and Zimbabwe, the agricultural sector reaches about one fourth, as compared to Japan, Sweden, US, and Canada, where this sector is substantially smaller. These differences are paralleled by the differences in the size of the service sector, where the latter group of countries score highest. With regard to political rights and civil liberties (Freedom house ratings), there are marked differences between three groups of countries: 1) Zimbabwe, Vietnam and Serbia, 2) Mexico and Argentina, and 3) South Africa, Japan, Sweden, US, and Canada. It is only the last group of countries which can be described as "fully free." It may be of interest to mention that these differences are partly paralleled by the degree of corruption (Transparency now ratings). Table 1 also presents some data on international issues. With regard to the number of ratified environmental international agreements, Sweden, US, Canada and Japan score higher than the remaining countries, and this difference is also paralleled with regard to the degree of internationalization (Johansson 1997). It can finally be seen that there are vast differences between the 10 countries with regard to the strength of the armed forces. In this regard, the military power of Zimbabwe and Vietnam is only a minimal fraction of the strength of US, Canada, and Japan.

On the basis of such differences, it can be concluded that the 10 countries represent a great variety of cultural, economical, political, and social contexts. Consequently, one of the criteria for the "most different systems design" is met.

WVS Measurements of Two Value Dimensions and Two Orientations towards the UN

Previous comparative research on the EVS/WVS data has focused on two basic value dimensions. The first is the "traditional versus the secular rational value orientation" where "the authority of God, Fatherland and Family are all closely linked" (Inglehart & Baker 2000:25; cf. Inglehart 1997: Chap. 3). The second is the "survival versus the self-expression value orientation", which taps a syndrome of "trust, tolerance, subjective well-being, political activism, and self-expression" (ibid). These basic dimensions correlate with key macro- and micro-level characteristics (see e.g. Inglehart 1997; Inglehart & Baker 2000). For instance, they correlate with the size of the industrial and the service sectors at the macro level, and with age and education at the micro level. Based on considerations from a previous discussion (Pettersson 2000), this paper will use a modified version of the two basic value dimensions. These can shortly be described as follows.

The traditional value orientation taps attachment to religious and traditional family values together with experiences of national identity. The measure of religious values is assessed as a composite score from two components, one concerning the importance of religion, and the other whether one thinks that the churches are giving adequate answers to man's moral, spiritual, social and family problems. The measure of traditional family values is calculated as a composite score from two components, one concerning how important the family is in one's life, and the other whether one adheres or not to a set of traditional opinions on family life concerning e.g. strict parent-child relations, etc. The measure of national identity taps one's sense of national pride and national belonging. More detailed information on the items which are used for the three indicators for the traditional value orientation is given in the Appendix.

The civic orientation is measured by a postmaterialism index, a social capital index, and an index tapping protest proneness. Even if a number of definitions of civic culture and the civic society have been proposed (see e.g. Inglehart 1997: Chap 6; Weintraub 1997), these three facets are often regarded as basic dimensions of civic involvement. The postmaterialism index taps the degree to which the respondents prefer materialist or postmaterialist views on the way society should be organized (Inglehart 1990, 1997). The social capital index is built on two components, one concerning social trust, and the other involvement in social networks, formal as well as informal (cf. Putnam 2000). The measure of protest proneness taps the willingness to engage in various forms of social protests like signing a petition, joining a boycott, etc. More detailed information on the items which are used to measure the civic orientation is given in the Appendix.

Table 2

Varimax rotated factor matrice for 6 indicators for two basic value orientations. Results from the 2000 WVS wave for 10 countries. Each country weighted to n = 1.500

	Factor 1: Traditional values	Factor 2: Civic orientation
Religious values	.67	−.17
Family values	.68	−.20
National identity	.68	.12
Postmaterialism	−.19	.59
Social capital	.20	.73
Protest proness	−.27	.66
Explained variance:	28%	19%

The results from a factor analysis of the six indicators for the two basic value orientations are presented in Table 2. In this analysis, each country is weighted to include 1.500 respondents. The data are also weighted in order to achieve intra-national representability in terms of socio-economic and regional background of the respondents. The results demonstrate that the six indicators relate as expected to the two value dimensions.

As for the *orientations towards the UN*, these may in principle concern all the positions one can take with respect to this organization (Niedermayer & Westle 1998:44). A recent typology of orientations towards international-ized governance distinguishes four modes of orientation towards five differ-ent aspects or elements of such governance (Niedermayer & Westle 1998). These distinctions allow a typology of 32 different orientations. Figure 1 presents a graphical model of the typology. The model underlines that ori-entations towards organizations for internationalized governance include several dimensions, where inferences from one to another may be prob-lematic. What is true for e.g. diffuse evaluations of policy outcomes, need not necessarily hold for behavioral intentions with regard to the organi-zation *in toto*. The model also helps illustrate that the empirical analyses presented in this paper only concern two of the many different orienta-tions towards the UN. These concern attitudes towards the vertical power structure within the UN and general confidence in the UN.

Orientation towards the UN vertical power structure: According to the details of the typology not shown in Figure 1, there are two different dimensions of the power structure within an organization for internationalized governance, namely the horizontal and the vertical. "The horizontal power structure denotes the institutions of the international system of governance

Object of orientation:		Mode of orientation:			
		Psychological involvement	Specific evaluation	Diffuse evaluation	Behavioural intention
Internat. regime as a whole		1	2	3	4
Object components:	Component elements:				
Political collectivity	Territorial	5	6	7	8
	Personal	9	10	11	12
Political order	Values/norms	13	14	15	16
	Power struct	17	18	19	20
Political authorities		21	22	23	24
Policies	Plans/outputs	25	26	27	28
	Funct. scope	29	30	31	32

Figure 1: A typology of 32 different orientations towards internationalized governance. After Niedermayer & Westle 1998.

and the distribution of power between them. The vertical power structure is defined as the distribution of power between the international and national level" (Niedermayer & Whestle 1998:43). Applied to the UN system, the horizontal dimension would refer to the distribution of power among the various parts of the UN like e.g. UNESCO and WHO, while the vertical would concern the distribution of power between the international and the national levels. The vertical power structure within the UN is a topic of key interest. "At the core of the controversies over the UN's expanding roles is the question of whether it remains the servant of the states that created it in 1945 or, instead, is becoming an autonomous actor with its own authority" (Rosenau 2000:150). According to the realist strand of IR theory, the member states "have the capacity in any situation to curb or to end the activities of UN officials deemed to have exceeded the authority granted them by the Security Council" (ibid). Even if the liberalist version of IR theory does not deny that the member states have the ultimate control over the UN, it emphasizes that this control is comparatively seldom used. Thus, this line of thought is more apt to see the UN as a site for cooperation among the member states. The postinternationalist IR perspective on the other hand, interprets many of the UN actions as expressions of an independent autonomy on behalf of the UN, and argues that UN officials "have a leeway that, for all practical purposes, is essential free of supervision and thus amounts to an independent, autonomous authority" (ibid). Over the years, the UN has witnessed a development where the postinternationalist understanding has become more influential (Rosenau 1997:394-396). Therefore, the distribution of vertical power within the UN concerns a theoretically very important issue.

The measure of attitudes towards a centralized vertical power structure within the UN which is used in this paper taps whether people think that problems in relation to international peacekeeping, protection of the environment, aid to developing countries, refugee programs, and human rights, respectively, are best handled by the respective national governments themselves, by the national governments working together with coordination by the UN, or by the UN itself, rather than by the various national governments. A set of factor analyses demonstrate that the views on these five items relate to one and the same dimension. More detailed information on this measure of attitudes towards a centralized vertical power structure within the UN is given in the Appendix. The more the respondents prefer the UN alone as the best handler of the various problem-areas, the more they can be assumed to prefer a centralized vertical power structure, where the UN system is given power and authority over the national level with regard to the various international problem-areas.

Confidence in the UN is measured by only one question, which is part of a battery of questions on confidence in a variety of different institutions and organizations, including the UN. With reference to the typology for orientations towards the UN, this question can be assumed to tap a diffuse evaluation of the UN *in toto*.

Results: National Means for Two Value Dimensions and Two Orientations towards the UN

In each country except Japan, where the WVS survey was performed as a postal survey, the data collection was made by face-to-face interviews. The degree to which this difference has affected the Japanese results can not be assessed. In each country, the sample of interviewees were drawn according to the best available methods. In some countries, this involved quota sampling (e.g. Vietnam), in others random sampling of individual respondents from official population registers (e.g. Sweden). These differences are not assumed to be of substantial importance for the results presented in this paper. The sample sizes for the various countries were: South Africa 3.000, Zimbabwe 1.002, Japan 1.362, Vietnam 995, Sweden 1.015, Serbia 1.200, US 1.200, Canada 1.931, Mexico 1.535, and Argentina 1.280.

Table 3 demonstrates the national means for the various indicators of the two basic value orientations and the two orientations towards the UN. Table 3 also reports the over-all scores for the traditional value orientation, the civic orientation, and the orientation towards centralized vertical power within the UN. These over-all scores are obtained as factor scores (cf. Table 2).

Table 3

Mean values for two basic value orientations and two orientations towards the UN. Results from the 2000 WVS wave for 10 countries from 5 continents

	Africa:		Asia:		Europe		North America		South America	
	S Afric	Zimbabw	Japan	Vietnam	Sweden	Serbia	US	Canada	Mexico	Argentina
Religious values	6.16	6.85	2.36	3.63	3.15	4.45	5.63	4.64	6.25	5.22
Family values	7.63	8.56	6.72	8.20	6.64	7.46	7.52	7.39	7.67	7.51
National identity	4.80	4.90	3.57	5.10	4.14	3.76	4.60	4.62	4.68	4.71
Tradit values: Factor score	.33	.90	-1.27	.37	-.73	-.54	.17	-.09	.25	-.05
Postmaterialism	1.98	1.87	2.42	2.23	2.68	1.74	2.74	2.83	2.24	2.57
Social capital	1.98	2.04	1.63	2.59	2.97	1.70	2.57	2.44	1.70	1.57
Protest proness	2.08	1.23	2.00	1.31	3.42	2.13	3.17	2.65	.99	1.20
Civic orient: Factor score	-.36	-.42	-.22	.08	1.00	-.53	.72	.61	-.43	-.38
Confidence in the UN	2.83	2.87	2.63	2.74	2.83	1.68	2.62	2.72	2.35	2.29
Centralized UN: Devel aid	2.15	2.31	2.12	2.09	2.17	2.12	2.10	2.02	1.90	2.21
Centralized UN: Environm	1.58	1.45	2.12	1.78	1.83	1.51	1.76	1.72	1.66	1.62
Centralized UN: Hum right	1.64	1.64	2.08	1.62	2.26	1.75	1.89	1.88	1.81	1.71
Centralized UN: Peace	2.16	2.35	2.42	2.06	2.16	1.80	2.20	2.22	1.91	2.29
Centralized UN: Refugees	2.08	2.21	2.24	2.00	2.04	2.07	2.02	1.89	1.83	1.48
Centralized UN: Factor score	-.01	.21	.49	-.16	.30	-.27	.01	.01	-.26	-.17

With regard to the traditional values, each of the three indicators rank the 10 countries in roughly the same order (Spearman's rho around .60 to .80). As for the mean values for these indicators, Zimbabwe, South Africa, Vietnam, and to a certain extant the US score high, while Sweden, Japan, and Serbia score low. Concerning the civic orientation, the three indicators rank the 10 countries in a somewhat less consistent manner (Spearman's rho range between .30 to .60; especially weak correspondence between postmaterialism and social capital). With regard to the mean scores, Sweden, US and Canada score high, while Serbia, South Africa, Zimbabwe, Mexico, and Argentina score low. In a general sense, these country differences for the two basic value dimensions are in accordance with the results from previous WVS research (Inglehart 1997; Inglehart & Baker 2000).

Regarding the orientations towards the UN, a previous analysis of EVS/WVS data from more than 50 countries concluded that the non-response rates for the question on confidence in the UN were unexpectedly high (Pettersson 2000). This finding is in line with previous research, which have shown attitudes towards the UN to be vague and uncertain (Everts 1998:422). Among the 10 countries included in this analysis, the non-response rates for confidence in the UN was lowest for Sweden and US (about 4%) and highest for Zimbabwe, Japan, and South Africa (about 37%, 23% and 20%, respectively). Such unusually high non-response rates can be explained in different ways, which need not be mutually excluding. One interpretation may conclude that the high non-response rates demonstrate that people are not apt to take the easy way out and fake an answer when they are confronted with difficult questions. Another interpretation may suggest that in the case of confidence in the UN, the results are less representative, and mainly valid for the subsamples which have enough information and knowledge to state their confidence in this organization for global governance. Since the UN is often seen as a highly prestigious institution, one may also assume peoples' answers to a question about their confidence in the UN to be significantly affected by social desirability.

Disregarding the comparatively high non-response rates, it can be concluded that all countries except Serbia demonstrate a fairly high degree of confidence in the UN (all have mean scores above 2). This is in line with previous findings on orientations towards the UN, which have demonstrated overall positive attitudes (Everts 1998:422). Among the 10 countries, Serbia, Mexico, and Argentina demonstrate somewhat less confidence in the UN as compared to the other countries.

In the case of attitudes towards a centralized vertical power structure within the UN, it should first be noted that the non-response rates for the five questions on this issue are lower as compared to the question for confidence in the UN. In this regard, Argentina, Mexico, and Serbia score systematically higher than the other 7 countries on each of the five questions. Thus, in these three countries, the question of how distribute the vertical power within the UN seems to be more ambiguous and difficult to answer. As for the mean values for this attitude, especially Japan, Sweden, and Zimbabwe demonstrate the most positive orientations, in contrast to Serbia, Mexico, Argentina, and Vietnam. A cluster analysis of the national means for confidence in the UN and attitudes towards the vertical power structure within the UN yields two clusters, with Argentina, Mexico, and Serbia belonging to one, identified by less confidence in the UN together with less positive attitudes towards a centralized vertical power structure within the UN. Thus, the group of countries which are least positive towards the UN and least in favor of a more autonomous UN, have all experienced UN missions and interventions to their countries. Whether these experiences explain their more negative orientations towards the UN can not be assessed from the data at hand.

A Causal Model for the Relations between Basic Values and Orientations towards the UN

The key research question of this paper concerns the multivariate relationships between peoples' orientations towards the UN and their basic value preferences. In the lack of previous research on these relationships, a tentative causal path model will serve as guideline. The model, which includes the social background variables of age, gender, and social class, the two basic value orientations, and the two orientations towards the UN is shown in Figure 2. The model tentatively postulates confidence in the UN to be prior to a positive view towards a centralized vertical power structure within the UN. The assumption is simply that the higher the confidence, the more likely one would be to "allow" the UN a kind of authority beyond the level of the various member states. Thus, confidence in the UN is tentatively assumed to precede the orientations towards the vertical power structure within the UN. It should further be noted that the causal model includes age, gender, and social class as social background variables influencing both the two basic value orientations and the two orientations towards the UN. That the social background variables can be assumed to influence the value orientations is well in line with previous research (see e.g. Inglehart 1997). In the absence of previous research, the assumption that the three social background variables should affect orientations towards the UN is tentative only.

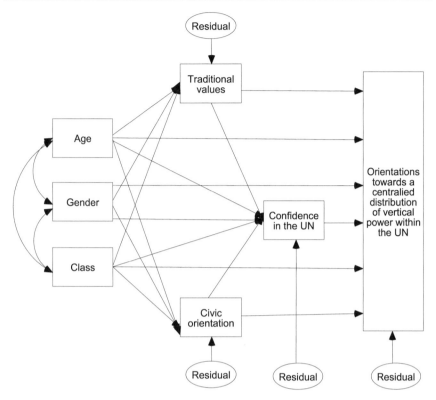

Figure 2.   Tentative causal path model for the relationship between three social background variables, two basic value dimensions, and two orientations towards the UN.

Results for the Causal Model

The causal model is investigated for each of the 10 countries, using structural equation analyses and the AMOS program (see e.g. Arbuckle 1997; Byrne 2001). The results are demonstrated in Table 4. It should be noted that the number of respondents in some countries is markedly affected by the comparatively high internal non-response rates, especially for the question on confidence in the UN. In the empirical analyses, social class is measured by a question about which social class the respondents subjectively associated themselves to. To include an "objective" measure for social stratification in such different societies as e.g. Japan and the US, Zimbabwe and Sweden would involve a number of difficult methodological and practical problems (cf. Dogan & Pelassy 1990: chap 6). The WVS has chosen to tackle this problem by introducing a measure of subjective social class (see Appendix).

Table 4

The relationships between age, gender, and social class, two basic value dimensions, and two orientations towards the UN. Entries are unstandardized multiple regression weights for a casual path model with attitude towards UN centralized vertical power as dependent variable (see Figure 2). Results from the 2000 WVS wave for 10 countries from 5 continents. Regression weights multiplied by 100

	Africa:		Asia:		Europe		North Americas		South Americas	
	S Africa (2187)	Zimbabwe (601)	Japan (686)	Vietnam (706)	Sweden (694)	Serbia (805)	U.S. (990)	Canada (1483)	Mexico (1017)	Argentina (844)
Trad. val. → Confidence UN	10.19***	16.57**	7.45	4.09	5.96a	-8.07*	6.06*	9.71***	11.14*	12.05***
Trad. val. → Centralized UN	-9.52***	-16.31**	-5.59	-6.98	-2.85	-2.86	-5.05a	-4.74*	-5.79	-8.03
Civic orient. → Confid. UN	6.77**	10.45*	-3.78	-3.67	3.27	10.97*	4.08	6.46*	17.61***	6.13a
Civic orient. → Central. UN	6.55**	6.42	10.55**	22.36***	9.97**	2.79	6.95*	10.50***	6.89***	22.76***
Confidence UN → Central. UN	1.50	3.90	16.40**	-.62	8.39*	22.23***	19.74***	11.62***	-4.15	18.53***
Age → Confidence UN	-.75***	.06	-.12	.03	-.43*	.11	-.14	-.24**	.04	-.19
Age → Centralized UN	.11	.84**	.06	.26	.28	-.63*	-.31a	-.26*	-.04	-.52a
Gender → Confidence UN	-9.36*	3.43	9.91*	-.57	3.79	-5.94	-.95	-8.18*	-8.56	-9.84
Gender → Centralized UN	-14.07**	-8.82	1.04	-12.28a	-22.14***	-3.33	-1.54	-9.82	-4.15	-4.69
Class → Confidence UN	-8.66***	-1.32	8.40**	7.25	6.17*	9.64**	8.77**	4.25a	9.84**	5.78
Class → Centralized UN	-1.38	2.15	-2.06	1.12	7.14*	.79	1.97	1.45	3.64	15.81*
Age → Trad. values	.43***	.27	2.20***	.40**	1.02***	1.33***	1.30***	1.45***	.80***	.98***
Age → Civic orientation	-.57***	-.31	.62*	-.65**	-.97***	-1.35***	.08	-.88*	-.70*	-.36*
Gender → Trad. values	9.80**	22.42***	-8.47	8.35a	3.22	9.76*	2.90	9.86***	9.47*	8.65
Gender → Civic orientation	-14.74***	-4.00	-3.36	-4.51	4.34	-6.84a	-11.22*	-6.80	-17.48***	-1.30
Class → Trad. values	1.16	.80	12.10***	-3.10	7.21*	-5.23	7.55***	2.17	-2.70a	.22
Class → Civic orientation	-.01	-1.16	16.59***	-7.52	9.35**	15.84***	2.15	12.89***	17.34***	19.75***

a: p < .10; *: p < .05; **: p < .01; ***: p < .001.

Among the many results displayed in Table 4, some deserve special attention. Thus, the results suggest that although the countries differ in important cultural, economical, social, and political measures, the relations between the two basic value dimensions and the two orientations towards the UN seem to be fairly similar across most of the countries. With the exception of Japan and Vietnam, the civic orientation is positively related to confidence in the UN in all the countries and the relationship is statistically significant in most of them. The civic orientation is furthermore related to a positive view on a centralized vertical power structure within the UN. It is only in Serbia and Zimbabwe where this positive relationship is not statistically significant. Thus, with some exceptions, the civic orientation seems conducive to both confidence in the UN as such and a positive view on a centralized vertical power structure within the UN. The traditional value orientation on the other hand seems to be positively related to confidence in the UN, although Serbia is an exception in this case. In the case of the a centralized vertical power structure within the UN, the regression weights for the traditional value orientation are negative in all countries, although non-significant in some. It can therefore be concluded that the traditional value orientation is positively related to a general confidence in the UN and negatively to a centralized vertical power structure within the UN.

Some of the other results displayed in Table 4 are also worth mentioning. With regard to the impact of social background on the orientations towards the UN, the most striking result seems to be the lack of any uniform pattern. For instance, age is positively related to a positive view on a centralized vertical power structure within the UN in Zimbabwe, and negatively in Serbia and Canada. Similar contrary results can be found for the impact of gender on confidence in the UN. With regard to the views on a centralized vertical power structure within the UN, the results suggest a rather weak tendency for women to be more negative than men, although in many countries, this difference does not reach statistical significance. When it comes to social class, confidence in the UN seems to be more prevalent in the upper classes (note that the class measure is recoded to range from low to high), except for South Africa, where there is a marked tendency in the opposite direction. Whether this exception is explained by UN interventions against the former apartheid policy remains to be investigated. With regard to the impact of social class on views on a centralized vertical power structure within the UN, the absence of significant relations seems to be the most visible pattern. All in all, it can therefore be concluded that the results do not demonstrate any substantial and uniform impact of social background on peoples' orientations towards the UN.

Table 4 also describes the relationships between the social background variables and the two basic value dimensions. These results are more in accordance with previous research. As expected, age appear to be positively related to the traditional values (Zimbabwe the only exception), and negatively to the civic orientation (Japan and US exceptions). In almost all of the countries, women score higher on the traditional values than men, and men higher on the civic orientation than women. However, the impact of social class on the two value dimensions seems less uniform in the various countries. Whether this is the result of a problematic measure of social class, or indicating that social class has different ramifications for the two value dimensions in different countries can not be assessed from the present analyses.

As an important aspect of the causal model, Table 5 demonstrates the multiple correlation coefficients for the various path analyses. The results show generally low coefficients. Thus, the social background variables do not explain much of the variation in the two basic value dimensions, and social background and the two value dimensions explain only a small part

Table 5

Multiple correlation coefficients (R) for traditional values and civic orientation regressed on age, gender and class, confidence in the UN regressed on age, gender and class, traditional values, and civic orientation, respectively, and attitude towards centralized vertical power within the UN regressed on age, gender and class, traditional values, civic orientation and confidence in the UN. Results from the 2000 WVS wave for 10 countries from 5 continents

	Africa		Asia		Europe	
	S Africa (2187)	Zimbabwe (601)	Japan (686)	Vietnam (706)	Sweden (694)	Serbia (805)
Traditional values	.10	.17	.38	.11	.21	.25
Civic orientation	.13	.07	.20	.13	.21	.32
Confidence UN	.21	.17	.17	.07	.16	.21
UN: Centralized power	.12	.14	.14	.19	.25	.22

	North America		South America:	
	US (990)	Canada (1483)	Mexico (1017)	Argentina (844)
Traditional values	.25	.25	.16	.18
Civic orientation	.07	.21	.27	.19
Confidence UN	.13	.17	.23	.16
UN: Centralized power	.23	.21	.17	.25

of the variation in the two orientations towards the UN. In these regards, there are hardly any substantial differences between the 10 countries.

Concluding Remarks

Recent developments in IR theory has witnessed an increased interest in mass public orientations towards internationalized governance. At the same time there is a noticeble lack of empirical studies of orientations towards the UN, maybe the most important organization for global governance. It is therefore of considerable interest to investigate peoples' orientations towards the UN, and especially the relationships between these orientations and their basic value orientations. The stronger the relationships, the more likely that their orientations towards the UN may have an impact. A typology of such orientations has however demonstrated that there is a wide variety of relevant orientations to consider. Of these, only two have been included in this investigation. These were general confidence in the UN as such, and views on the vertical power structure within the UN. The latter is said to concern one of the core controversies over the UN.

Using the 2000 WVS data from 10 countries, representing widely different cultural, economical, social, and political contexts, this paper has suggested a modified version of a well-known model for two basic value dimensions. The model distinguishes between the traditional value orientation on the one hand, tapping religious and traditional family values together with sense of national identity, and the civic orientation on the other, tapping postmaterialism, social capital and protest proness. In summary, the results suggest a general pattern for the relationships between these two value dimensions and the two orientations towards the UN. The traditional value orientation seems negatively related to a centralized vertical power structure within the UN, while the civic orientation appears to be positively related. By contrast, both value orientations seem to be positively related to confidence in the UN *in toto*. In this way, both value orientations seem to be conducive to a positive diffuse evaluation of the UN as such (confidence in the UN), while they differ regarding the kind of UN they "prefer". Those who adhere to the traditional value orientation and find God, Fatherland and Family to be important value authorities, seem to prefer a UN where the final authority over the organization is founded at the level of the various member states. One may say that those who have a strong sense of national identity do not want the authority of the national member states to be taken over by others (like e.g. more or less autonomous UN officials). On the other hand, those who adhere to the civic orientation and value trust, tolerance, political activism, and postmaterialist values, seem to be more in favour of an independent UN, with a kind autonomous authority beyond the level of the (democratic) influence of the various member states.

This is an unexpected and maybe slightly paradoxical complement to the corresponding relationships concerning the attitudes towards governance at the national level. At that level, the civic orientation is usually *not* associated with preferences for autonomous authorities beyond democratic control, while the traditional value orientation usually is *less* tied to the demand for a democratic rule. In this sense, the two basic value orientations seem to have reversed consequences with regard to national and internationalized governance. Disregarding whether this is the case or not, the results reported in this paper for the civic orientation seem more in line with the postinternationalist strand of IR theory, while the results for the traditional value orientation appear closer to the arguments from the realist version. It should however be noted that these tendencies are not especially strong, and that exceptions to the general pattern are not uncommon. In e.g. Serbia, with its recent experiences of wars, internal conflicts, and developmental aid from the international community, the general pattern did not appear.

It is furthermore of interest to note that the civic orientation includes social capital as one component. However, social capital theory is largely silent on the topic of internationalized governance. Therefore, theoretically well grounded assumptions on the impact of social capital on orientations towards internationalized governance are hard to develop, although some arguments in this regard deserve attention. The degree of closure in a social system is often seen as important with regard to the effects of social capital, and a certain degree of closure is seen as a "valuable asset to individuals who must decide whether or not to place trust" (Coleman 1990:318). Almost by definition, the global system covered by the UN would for most people be likely to lack any closure at all. And hence, one might assume orientations towards the UN to be unrelated to social capital (interpersonal trust and social networks) in contrast to confidence in political institutions at the national, regional or local level. Despite such arguments, the results have shown social capital to be part of a value orientation which is positively related to both confidence in the UN and a positive attitude towards a centralized vertical power structure within the UN. This relationship between social capital and internationalized governance is certainly of interest to social capital theory.

However, even if the results have demonstrated a general pattern for the relationships between peoples' orientations towards the UN and their basic value dimensions, it should also be noticed that the latter do not explain much of the variation in the former. Although many of the relationships were statistically significant, their predictive power were not especially strong. Therefore, better theoretical models for the complex relations between peoples' basic value preferences and their orientations towards internationalized governance need to be developed. In a similar manner, there is also a need for the development of better items for the measurement of the many orientations towards such governance. However, given the growing importance of global governance and international relations, the results presented in this paper do suggest that the pursuit of such improved theoretical models and refined measurement tools may be worthwhile to future WVS research.

References

ARBUCKLE, J.
1997   *AMOS Users' Guide. Version 3.6.* Chicago: Smallwaters.
BYRNE, B.
2001   *Structural equation modeling with AMOS. Basic concepts, applications, and programming.* London: Lawrence Erlbaum Associates.
COLEMAN, J.
1990   *Foundations of social theory.* Cambridge, Mass: Harvard University Press.
DARK, K.R.
2000   "Introduction", in K.R. Dark (ed.), *Religion and international relations.* New York: St. Martin's Press.
DOGAN, M. AND PELASSY, D.
1990   *How to compare nations. Strategies in comparative politics.* Chatham; Chatham House Publishers.
EVERTS, PH.
1998   "NATO, the European Community, and the United nations", in O. Niedermayer and R. Sinnott (eds), *Public opinion and internationalized governance.* Paperback edition, Oxford: Oxford university Press.
HALMAN, L. AND VLOET, A.
1994   *Measuring and comparing values in 16 countries of the Western World.* WORC, Tilburg: Tilburg university.
HALMAN, L. AND PETTERSSON, T.
1999   "Globalization and patterns of religious belief systems", in L. Halman and O. Riis (eds), *Religion in secularizing society. The European's religion at the end of the 20th century.* Tilburg: Tilburg University Press.
INGLEHART, R.
1977   Long-term trends in mass support for European unification. *Government and opposition,* 12.
1990   *Culture shift in advanced industrial society.* Princeton: Princeton University Press.
1997   *Modernization and postmodernization.* Princeton: Princeton University Press.
INGLEHART, I. AND BAKER, W.
2000   Modernization, cultural change, and the persistence of traditional values. *American Sociological review,* 65.

JOHANSSON, J.
1997   Internationalisering, mimeo. Lund university: Department of political sciences.

LAPID, Y.
1996   "Culture's ship. Returns and departures in International Relations Theory", in Y. Lapid and F. Kratochwil (eds), *The return of culture and identity in IR theory*. London: Lynne Rienner.

LINDBERG, L.N. AND SCHEINGOLD, S.A.
1970   *Europe's would-be polity: Patterns of change in the European Community*. Englewood Cliffs: Prentice-Hall.

NIEDERMAYER, O. AND WESTLE, B.
1998   "A typology or orientations", in O. Niedermayer and R. Sinnott (eds), *Public opinion and internationalized governance*. Paperback edition, Oxford: Oxford University Press.

NORWEGIAN NOBEL PEACE PRICE COMMITTEE
2001   Motivation for the 2001 Nobel Peace Prize, http://www.nobel.no/eng_lau_announce2001.html, October 31th, 2001.

PETTERSSON, T.
2000   "Basic values and support for international regimes. A comparative analysis of orientations towards the United Nations". Paper presented at the WVS conference, Stellenbosch 2001-11-17-21.

PRZEWORSKI, A. AND TEUNE, H.
1970   *The Logic of Comparative Social Inquiry*. New York: Wiley-Interscience.

PUTNAM, R.
2000   *Bowling alone*. New York: Simon and Schuster.

ROSENAU, J.
1992   "Citizenship in a changing global order", in J. Rosenau and E.O. Czempiel (eds), *Governance without government: Order and Change in World Politics*. Cambridge: Cambridge university Press.
1997   *Along the domestic-foreign frontier*. Cambridge: Cambridge University Press.

ROSENAU, J. AND DURFEE, M.
2000   *Thinking theory thoroughly. Coherent approaches to an incoherent world*. 2nd edit, Boulder: Westview Press.

SINNOTT, R.
1998   "Bringing public opinion back in", in O. Niedermayer and R. Sinnott (eds), *Public opinion and internationalized governance*. Paperback edition, Oxford: Oxford University Press.

WEINTRAUB, J.
1997   "Public and private", in J. Weintraub and K. Kumar (eds), *Private and Public in thought and practice*. Chicago: University of Chicago Press.

Appendix: Measurements

A) The traditional value orientation is measured by three indicators: Religious values, traditional family values, and national identity. Religious values are measured by two components. The first concerns how important religion is in one's life, and is measured by a rating scale with response alternatives ranging from "not very important at all" (value 1) to "very important" (value 4). The second component concerns whether one finds that the churches/the religious leaders/the religious authorities give adequate answers to "the moral problems and needs of the individual", "the problems of family life", "people's spiritual needs", and "the social problems facing our country today". From the answers to these four questions, a "church adequacy score" can be calculated (cf. Halman and Vloet 1994). Those who find that each of the issues is given an adequate answer receive a score of 4, while those who find that none of them is given an adequate answer receive a score of 0. The two components of religious values (the importance of religion, and church adequacy, respectively) are then added into a single measure of religious values.

The measure of family values is likewise calculated as the sum of two different components. The first concerns how important family is in one's life, and is measured by a rating scale ranging from "not very important at all" (value 1) to "very important" (value 4). The second concerns five different expressions of traditional family values. These concern whether one thinks that "one must always love and respect one's parents, irrespective of their qualities and faults," that "it is the parents' duties to do their best for their children, even at the expense of their own well-being," that marriage is not "an outdated institution," that "a child needs a home with both a father and a mother in order to grow up happily," together with a dislike of "a woman who wants to have a child as a single parent but she doesn't want to have a stable relation with a man." Those who adhere to each of these 5 views receive a score of 5, while those who support none of them receive a score of 0. The two components of family values (the importance of family, and traditional family values, respectively) are then added into a single measure of traditional family values.

The measure of national identity is assessed by two components. One taps the respondents' degree of national pride and is decided from a question about how proud one is to be "Swedish," "Mexican," etc. The answers are given on a four point rating scale, ranging from "not at all proud" (value 1) to "very proud" (value 4). The second component concerns the degree to which one feels that one belongs to one's country. This component is assessed from two questions on whether one feels that one belongs first of all or in the second place to "the locality where one lives," "the region," "one's country," "the continent where one lives" (e.g. Europe, South America etc), and "the world as a whole." Those who choose "one's country" in the first place receive a score of 2, those who choose "one's country" in the second place receive a score of 1, while those who don't choose this alternative at all receive a score of 0. The two components of national identity (national pride, and national belonging, respectively), are then added into a single measure of national identity.

B) The civic orientation is measured by a postmaterialism index, a social capital index, and an index tapping protest proness. The postmaterialism index asks the respondents to choose the most and the second most important from the following four opinions: maintaining order in the nation, fighting rising prices (materialist items), giving people more say, and protecting freedom of speech (postmaterialist items). The index ranges from materialist views (value 1) to postmaterialist views (value 4). The social capital index is made up of two components, one concerning social trust, and the other involvement in social networks. The component of social trust is measured by two questions. One asks whether most people can be trusted, or if one needs to be very careful in dealing with others. The other asks if most people would try to take advantage of oneself if they got a chance, or if they would try to be fair. The answers to these two questions are combined into one measure for social trust, ranging between 0 and 2. The component of social networks is measured by two indicators, one for informal social connectedness, and one for the formal. The indicator for informal connectedness is based on four items, which ask how often one spends time with friends, with colleagues outside the workplace, with people belonging to one's church, mosque, or synagogue, and with co-members in clubs and voluntary associations. The answers are collapsed into one single measure, ranging from 0 to 4. Those who say that they meet regularly each month with each of the four categories, receive a score of 4, while those who say that they do not, get a score of 0. The indicator for formal social relations is assessed by a set of questions which ask whether one does voluntary work in 14 different organizations and social movements. The score for formal social relations is simply calculated as the number of organizations in which one is doing voluntary work. In order to get a combined score for social networks, the measures of formal and informal civil connectedness are then added. Since the score for the formal relations can reach a substantially higher number than the score for informal connectedness, the two scores are given equal weight by transforming each to a simple dichotomy, with values 0 and 1 and above. In order to achieve an over-all measure for social capital, the scores for social trust and social networks are then added. This score ranges between 0 and 4.

The degree of protest proneness is assessed by a battery of five questions. These ask whether one "has done," "can imagine to do," or would "never do" each of the following five acts: Sign a petition, join a boycott, attend a lawful demonstration, join an unofficial strike, and occupy a building or factory. The measure of protest proneness captures how many of these acts the respondents has been involved in or can imagine to do. Thus, the index ranges between 0 and 5. The index has been used in previous value research (cf. Halman and Vloet 1994).

C) Orientations towards a centralized power structure within the UN. One battery of items in the WVS questionnaire asks whether problems with regard to international peacekeeping, protection of the environment, aid to developing countries, refugee programs, and human rights, respectively, are best handled by the respective national governments themselves, by the national governments working together with coordination by the UN, or by the UN itself, rather than by the national governments. These questions have not been used in previous research. The answers are given on three-point scales, ranging from the view that the various problems are best handled by the national governments themselves (value 1) to the UN itself (value 3). A set of factor analyses demonstrate that the five items are uni-dimensional and that they relate to and the same dimension. Therefore, the more the respondents prefer the UN alone as the best handler of the various problem-areas, the more they can be assumed to prefer a centralized vertical power structure, where the UN is given power over the national level with regard to the various international problem-areas.

D) Confidence in the UN is measured by one question, which is part of a battery of questions on confidence in a variety of different institutions and organizations, including the UN. The answers were given on four-point response scales, ranging from "None at all" (value 1) to "A great deal" (value 4). With reference to the typology for orientations towards the UN, this question can be assumed to tap a diffuse evaluation of the UN as such.

E) Social class is measured by a question about which social class one belongs to. The responses were given on a five-point scale with answer categories upper class, upper middle class, lower middle class, working class, and lower class. In this paper, the answers have been recoded and range from lower to upper class.

Two Contradictory Hypotheses on Globalization: Societal Convergence or Civilization Differentiation and Clash[*]

JUAN DÍEZ-NICOLÁS[**]

Theoretical Framework

For more than two centuries social scientists have struggled with the hen and egg problem, that is, whether the economic system, the political system or the cultural system determines the other two systems (Marx 1904; Weber 1946; Pareto 1921; Lasswell 1977). From social ecosystem theory, economic, political and cultural organizations are instrumental responses that human populations develop to adapt to their (natural and social) environment within a given state of the arts (technology) (Hawley 1986; Duncan 1964). From this theoretical perspective, social ecosystems have expanded through time on the basis of the interaction of the four elements of the ecosystem: population, environment, social organization and value systems (non-material culture) and technology (material culture) (Hawley 1986; Díez-Nicolás 1982, 1995, 1999). The history of mankind has been a continuous process of expansion from small autarchic independent communities to large interdependent communities. In this process, isomorphic processes tend to produce similar social organizational structures to facilitate exchange and communication among increasingly interdependent social systems. Obviously, isomorphism takes place earlier with respect to economic systems (because exchange and

---

[*] A first attempt to refute Fukuyama's and Huntington's theories (or more precisely, ideologies) was presented at the UN sponsored FOURTH INTERNATIONAL FORUM ON URBAN POVERTY held in Marrakech in October 2001 (Díez-Nicolás 2001).

[**] Complutense University, Madrid.

interaction among societies generally comes first, and because of economic interdependence), which explains why economic systems have historically been relatively homogeneous within wide world regions, while showing great political and cultural variation within them.

Fukuyama (1991) has rightly observed a general trend of societies to adopt a single economic system model and a single political system model. After the Berlin wall fell in 1989, and with it the Soviet Empire, its alternative economic and political systems disappeared. Free market economy (capitalism) and parliamentary democratic systems (based on the existence of competing political parties) today seem to be the only viable economic and political models, in such a way that virtually all societies either claim to have attained them, or to be in the process of attaining them. But Fukuyama is wrong in deriving from that fact that capitalist liberal democracy will be "the end of history," just as other utopias have failed in assuming that nothing could come after them. Plato's ideal polis, Campanella's City of the Sun, More's Utopia, and Marx and Lenin's "classless society" are a few examples of this phenomenon. Even though we cannot foresee when, how, why and what will substitute for parliamentary democracy and free market economy, it is probable that new forms of economic and political organizations will develop, as the other three elements of the ecosystem change over time. Even today criticisms of the performance of both free market economy and parliamentary democracy (Shearmur 1996; Giddens 2000; Beck 1999; Hutton & Giddens 2000) are increasingly common. But Fukuyama has not taken into account the role of culture, of belief and value systems, which as Weber rightly demonstrated, influence economic and political systems. Most societies today claim to have attained or to be in the process of attaining a parliamentary democracy and a free market economy (only recently NATO officially accepted that Russia is a free market economy, as if such recognition were a matter of political decision and not of economic behavior). But this does not necessarily mean that they really have attained it. Quite the contrary, the evidence shows that some democracies are deteriorating, and that some democracies are really not democracies in the full sense of that concept, even if they are politically accepted as such. Great differences are found between some free market economies and others, and a great variety of policies are approved to obviate the free market and to mask protectionist and monopolistic or oligarchic markets instead. The evidence of the increasing inequalities among countries and within countries should not be neglected in this context.

The first hypotheses that will be tested in this research is that there is a clear relationship between economic, political and cultural systems in the world today, in the sense that high levels of economic development are directly related to democratic political systems, and that both are directly related to a particular value system that may be labeled as "post-modern." But, related to this hypotheses, it is also proposed that, even if we accept the existence of a general trend for social systems to adopt free market economy and parliamentary democracy, great differences remain in levels of economic and political development among countries around the world. Similarly large differences are also found in value systems, though there is also a growing trend towards isomorphism in this realm, as a consequence of the increase in exchanges and communications among countries around the world, facilitated by developments in transportation and communication technologies. The reduction of the cost and time of travel have brought a reduction of social distance, facilitating and even encouraging mass population movements, just as the increasing ease of communication among individuals favor human contacts, exchange of ideas, and therefore the homogenization of cultural and value systems on a world wide basis. Very important differences in the realm of values and cultural systems persist, and in some cases new social movements attempt to counteract "globalization" not only of economic institutions but also of value systems.

In contrast to Fukuyama's hypotheses of convergence in political and economic systems because of globalization, Huntington (1996) has proposed an opposite hypothesis about the existence of seven great cultural systems or civilizations: Confucian-Chinese, Japanese, Hindu, Islamic, Western, Latin American and African. How he arrives at seven such civilizations, and not at fourteen, five or thirty is not fully explained: It depends on what dimension one selects to classify reality. Thus, if one classifies living organisms in two classes, mammals and non-mammals, whales and humans would be in the same category, but apart from being mammals there seem to be no other traits that would justify putting whales and humans in the same basket. The basis for Huntington's classification seem to include religious, linguistic, historical and geographical criteria, and his argumentation lead to some confusion, so that some authors interpret him as referring to nine civilizations (the additional two being the Orthodox and the Buddhist) (Norris & Inglehart 2002). Huntington's thesis has two main assumptions: first, that the civilizations he defines are internally relatively homogeneous around one or more of the dimensions used for classifying them (religion, language, etc.), and that each such civilization is distinctively different from other civilizations. Second, that because civilizations are different, they will necessarily conflict or "clash" with each other. Huntington seems to overlook the fact that the countries that he considers parts of one civilization, Western Europe, have been fighting each other for centuries, and that the last of those wars took place only seventy years ago. Huntington's main propositions have been widely discussed and criticized from a sociological perspective (Höfert & Salvatore 2000; Haller 2002; Norris & Inglehart 2002), but also from an ideological-strategic-military perspective (del Valle 2000). The fact that Huntington takes religion and other cultural dimensions as the basis for classifying civilizations makes it possible to try to confront his assumptions on internal homogeneity and external differentiation through the valuable data on social and cultural values provided by the World Values Surveys. [1]

According to Inglehart (1977, 1990 and 1997), there is a general trend in value change that seems to be at least two-fold, from scarcity or survival values to self-expression values, and from traditional values to rational-secular values. This hypothesis has been tested and verified broadly and widely by Inglehart and others. This change in values seems to be universal, though at different levels, providing a gradient of societies along a continuum from societies which are still very close to the survival-scarcity pole, while others are very close to the self-expression-security pole, and another gradient where some societies can still be classified as traditional while others can be classified as rational-legal, following the Weberian terminology. Furthermore, the level a society has attained in those two axes seems to be related to the degree that its political institutions have developed towards a parliamentary democracy, as well as to the degree that it has attained a certain level of economic development. Inglehart has extensively reported on the high positive relationship between the economic, the political and the cultural systems (Inglehart 1999, 2001).

But, though findings have unequivocally shown some clustering of societies among those dimensions, they do not exclude a great degree of variation within the groups that may be constructed. Once more, one should not forget that reality does not come classified, but that researchers classify reality through a set of categories that are arbitrarily defined, though on the basis of arguments derived from theory. Accepting the existence of certain groups of societies that share particular set of values does not necessarily imply that they should "clash" with each other. Haller (2001) has rightly described how societies may have positive and friendly relations, or negative and conflictual relations, based on equal or different levels of socio-economic development and/or similar or different cultural systems.

---

[1] The WVS data that are used here are the officially approved datasets for the 1995 wave (WVS1995_V2_1.sav) and the provisionally approved version for the 2000 wave (WVS2000_V3.sav), by the World Values Survey Association, as well as the EVS provisional version for the 1999 wave (EVS99#03.sav) (Halman 2001).

The hypothesis that will be tested here is that, though there seems to be a general trend in value change along the lines defined by Inglehart, there are great differences among countries and world regions with respect to the extent to which change along the lines described above has taken place. Furthermore, it will be argued that variation within civilizations, to use Huntington's terminology, is greater than among civilizations, an assertion that was established by Stein Rokkan (Merrit & Rokkan 1966) many decades ago when referring to within-country or between-country differences. Not only that, but it will also be argued that differences in value systems within individuals in a society and differences among societies derive from socio-economic differences more than from so called regional or civilization groupings.

Since a great part of Huntington's book is devoted to the future "clash" between the Western Christian World versus the Islamic Civilization, it may be relevant to mention that political events during the past years have shown that some Islamic societies have been considered as "good" allies by the Western alliance (Bosnia, Kosovo, Azerbaijan, Chechnya, Kuwait, Saudi Arabia, Morocco, and most especially Turkey), while others have been defined as "evil" (Afghanistan, Iraq, Iran, Palestine, Somalia, Yemen, Syria or Pakistan). An alternative hypothesis might be that the cleavages between and among societies are based more on their socio-economic than on their "cultural" differences, something that seems to explain great and significant value differences within some of the usually accepted groupings of societies.

A final hypothesis to reject Huntington's assertion about the clash of civilizations is that when individuals move from more traditional and less developed "civilizations" to societies that are more developed and post-modern, they tend to diverge from the value system prevalent in their original culture and to adopt the values of the receiving society, because value systems are instrumental for individuals to better adapt to their natural and social environment (Hawley 1986; Díez-Nicolás 1982).

The Relationship between Economic, Political and Cultural Systems

Inglehart has verified the hypotheses that economic, political and cultural systems are related in several of his most recent writings (Inglehart 1997, 1999, 2001; Norris & Inglehart 2002). We replicate that test here, using GNP per capita to measure a country's economic level, the Human Development Index (HDI) to measure human development, Freedom House ratings on civic liberties to measure democratic development, and the difference between the proportions of post-materialists and materialists, using the common four items scale developed by Inglehart [2] for 81 societies. As expected, all correlation coefficients were very strong and statistically significant at the .01 level: the correlation between GNP and Post-materialism is .66, HDI-Post-materialism (.56), and FHR-Post-materialism (.46), with the FH ratings inverted so that higher values indicate higher ratings of civic liberties. Additionally, GNP-HDI (.82), GNP-FHR (.69) and HDI-FHR (.70) correlations are also very high and statistically significant. Clearly, countries with higher economic levels, with higher social well-being levels, and with more democratic forms of government show higher levels of modern (self expression) values. This finding is not new. It validates once more Inglehart's scale for measuring value change, something that by itself has been a great contribution to the explanation of social and cultural change. The reason to examine these findings here, is that they sometimes lead to the ideological misconception that the world is converging towards similar economic and political (and eventually cultural) systems, in the sense that Fukuyama seems to have pretended, similarly to Kahn and Wiener's optimistic predictions of "economic development for all in the year 2000" (Kahn & Wiener 1967).

Quite on the contrary, differences in GNP per capita between societies are increasing, not decreasing — as was predicted after the first oil crisis of 1973 (Council on Environmental Quality and Department of State 1980; Díez-Nicolás 1980; United Nations 1987). Thus, in 1963 the GNP per capita in the richest world region (North America) was 40 times higher than in the poorest region (using the standard UN definition of world regions), and the economic and social policies during the following decade resulted in a certain decrease of between-regions inequalities (in 1973 the richest region had 39 times the GNP per capita of the poorest region). But after the 1973 oil crisis, between-countries economic inequality increased continuously, so that by 1983 the ratio was 51 times, by 1991 it was 91 times, and by 2000 it was 108 times. The Human Development Report

---

[2] The data have been collected for the 81 individual countries included either on the 1995 and/or the 2000 WVS waves or the 1999 EVS wave. The most recent data file for each country has been selected, so that 17 belong to the 1995 WVS wave (with a total of 25,147 cases), 31 belong to the 1999 EVS wave (with a total of 37,704 cases), and 33 belong to the 2000 WVS (with a total of 50,398 cases). The Freedom House ratings were chosen for the period 1997-98, even though data for later years were available, to match the period 1995-2000 covered by the surveys. For similar reasons, GNP and HDI country data were taken from PNUD, Human Devolopment Report, 2001, and the data refer to 1999, though there is a later edition for 2002. Measurement of post-materialism has been based on the four items scale more widely used (maintain order in society, participation in important political decisions, fight raising prices and defend freedom of expression), in which the first and third items measure materialist values, and the second and fourth items measure post-materialist values.

for 2002 provides even more spectacular comparisons between the richer and the poorer countries. The Human Development Index series from 1975 to 1999 also shows increasing, not decreasing, differences between countries. The Freedom House ratings show a less clear pattern, probably due to the fact that many countries have adopted the "formal" appearance of parliamentary democracies, though hiding sometimes non-democratic regimes, and to the fact that their index has a much shorter variation between the highest and the lowest values. As for the change in values, Inglehart has shown that there seems to be a predominance of change towards more post-materialist values in most societies, though the data for 2000 show some opposite trends in some parts of the world, and more specifically in Latin America.

Are Civilizations Significant Units for Sociological Analysis?

In order to test Huntington's hypotheses, WVS countries have been grouped along the lines of the seven civilizations he defined, taking also into consideration some of his own sub-divisions, and others that have been used by Norris and Inglehart (2002). Considering that some of the "civilization clashes" also involve the old division between the Western and Eastern empires deriving from the breakup of the Roman Empire, reinforced by the separation of Roman Catholics and Orthodox churches, and the division between Catholic and Protestant Europe, as well as the apparent distinctiveness of Anglo-Saxon countries from the rest of Western countries, the 81 countries for which WVS data were available have been grouped into twelve World regions.[3]

To test Huntington's argument regarding the internal homogeneity of civilizations and their distinctiveness with respect to other civilizations, the three objective indicators reported above (GNP, HDI and FHR), have been used for the 81 countries grouped into 12 world regions. We find

---

[3] The twelve regions and the countries they include are the following: Anglo-Saxon (5): Britain, USA, Canada, Australia and New Zealand. West European Catholic (11): France, Italy, Netherlands, Belgium, Spain, Ireland, Switzerland, Portugal, Austria, Luxembourg and Malta. West European Protestant (7): West Germany, Denmark, North Ireland, Norway, Sweden, Iceland and Finland. East European Christian (10): Hungary, Poland, Czech Republic, East Germany, Slovenia, Lithuania, Latvia, Estonia, Croatia and Slovakia. European Orthodox (14): Belarus, Bulgaria, Romania, Grece, Ukraine, Russia, Moldavia, Georgia, Armenia, Serbia, Montenegro, Macedonia, Bosnia and SrpSka. Latin America (10): Mexico, Argentina, Puerto Rico, Brazil, Chile, Peru, Venezuela, Uruguay, Dominican Republic and Colombia. Islam (11): Pakistan, Turkey, Azerbaijan, Bangladesh, Indonesia, Albania, Egypt, Morocco, Iran, Jordan and Algeria. Sinic-Confucian (4): South Korea, China, Taiwán and Vietnam. Japan (1). India (1). African Sub Saharan (5): South Africa, Nigeria, Zimbabwe, Tanzania and Uganda. Others (2): Philippines and Israel.

that the differences between regions with the highest and the lowest values in each of them, as measured by the ratio between the two figures, are often smaller than those found comparing the countries with the highest and lowest values within each region. Thus, the West European Protestant region had a GNP per capita 8.8 times that of African sub-Saharan countries, a HDI 1.8 times higher, and a FHR 2.0 times higher than that of the same African region. But the ratios between the highest and lowest value of individual countries with respect to GNP in the African sub-Saharan and the Sinic-Confucian regions, or with respect to FHR in the Eastern Orthodox, the Islamic, the Sinic-Confucian and the African sub-Saharan regions, are larger. Besides, the ratio between the highest and lowest values in those three indicators, disregarding regions, was 85 times when comparing the GNP per capita of Luxembourg and Tanzania, and 40 times when comparing the FHR of many western countries and that of China. These findings by themselves not only show that differences between countries and regions with respect to their degree of economic and political development continue to be very large, but they also show that within-region differences may be greater than between-regions differences.

Apart from these macro-economic and macro-political indicators, Huntington's thesis has been tested at the micro- or individual level. To this effect, some questions from the values-surveys studies were selected to measure religious and political attitudes, as well as other questions that would measure personal well-being, social capital, and attitudes toward the role of women. The selection of these questions was based, apart from theoretical considerations (Norris & Inglehart 2002), on other more pragmatic grounds regarding possibilities for comparison. In fact, a section of this paper will compare the attitudes of migrants into Spain from different world regions, with the attitudes of the populations in their countries of origin, and with the Spanish population as the receiving society. While the data for countries of origin and the receiving country were drawn from the 1995-2000 surveys, the data regarding migrants were obtained from a survey on migrants into Spain in 2001. Some relevant questions from the WVS questionnaires were included in that survey. Thus, the comparative analysis of migrants' values with those of the populations in their regions of origin and in Spain include the following variables:

- Personal Well-being: Happiness and satisfaction with one's life.
- Social Capital: Freedom of choice and control of one's life, and interpersonal trust.
- Support for Democracy: Opinion on how good or bad it would be to have a government based on a Strong leader, the decisions of Experts, the Army, or a Democratic system.

- Religiosity: Importance of God in one's life and getting comfort in religion.
- Role of Women: Opinion on whether women need to have children in order to be fulfilled.
- Post-materialist or Post-modern values: Difference in the percent of R's who are categorized as post-materialist or materialist in the 4 item values scale developed by Inglehart.

The following analysis is based on more than 113,000 interviews in 81 different countries that represent more than 80% of the world's population in the five continents and all of the main "civilizations" or cultures, showing very different levels of economic and political development, as has been shown above. The differences among regions were in the expected direction, showing that Anglo-Saxons, West Europeans (both Catholic and Protestant) and Latin Americans are more satisfied with their life and are happier than the rest. Anglo-Saxons and West European Protestants, and to a certain degree also Latin Americans, Sinic-Confucians and Japanese show higher values on social capital indicators than citizens from other regions (though Latin American show a very low degree of social trust). Religiosity is more prominent in Islamic, African sub-Saharan and Latin American societies, and a more traditional attitude towards the role of women also predominates in Islamic and European Orthodox societies as well as in India. Democracy is considered almost unanimously as the best form of government in all regions, but a government based on a strong leader who has not to struggle with a Parliament, or based on the rule of the armed forces is considered good relatively more in Latin American and Sinic-Confucian countries. Finally, post-materialist values predominate exclusively in Anglo-Saxon societies, while materialist values predominate in all other regions, and very remarkably in European Orthodox, Islamic and Sinic-Confucian societies, as well as in India.

To simplify the analysis below, only one indicator from each dimension has been chosen. Satisfaction of life and happiness are highly correlated (.47), but the former has been used because its scale provides greater variation. Interpersonal trust has been preferred to freedom of choice and control over one's life because it is the most common indicator of social trust used in the literature (Putnam, Leonardi & Nanetti 1993), and because the latter is better correlated with life satisfaction and happiness (.42 and .25 respectively) than with trust (.05), which suggests that it is probably a better indicator of social well-being than of interpersonal trust. The correlation between the importance of God in one's life and getting comfort from religion is very high (.72), but the former has been selected because it is based on a ten point scale while getting comfort is a dichotomous variable. The four indicators on forms of government are highly correlated, but the one

Table 1
Attitudinal indicators by Cultural Regions, 1995-2000*

	Anglo-Saxon	West European Catholic	West European Protestant	East European Christian	European Orthodox	Latin American	Islamic	Sinic-Confucian	Japan	India	African sub-Sahara
N=	(7,380)	(14,698)	(7,208)	(11,378)	(17,430)	(16,027)	(21,193)	(3,975)	(1,362)	(2,002)	(8,197)
Personal Well-Being:											
Satisfaction with life (mean on scale 0-10)	7.64	7.56	7.89	6.31	5.00	7.71	5.80	6.44	6.48	5.14	5.55
% Very Happy	36	32	35	12	9	33	20	24	28	25	44
Social Capital:											
% Most people can be Trusted	38	30	51	22	22	14	29	38	40	39	14
Freedom of choice and Control of one's life (mean on scale 0-10)	7.65	6.87	7.40	6.51	5.94	7.66	5.92	7.29	6.00	5.65	6.60
Religiosity:											
Importance of God in one's life (mean on scale 0-10)	6.43	6.31	5.34	5.49	6.63	9.12	9.45	5.41	5.02	7.60	9.38
% Get Comfort in Religion	54	56	47	47	58	60	91	32	24	79	92
Role of Women:											
% Women need Children	19	40	31	58	76	41	78	63	44	82	66
Political Attitudes:											
% Strong leader is good or very good	23	24	16	23	41	44	27	43	24	43	28
% Government of Experts is good or very good	41	42	39	64	53	59	47	52	47	46	50
% Army rule is good or very good	6	4	3	5	14	25	27	36	2	14	21
% Democratic system is good or very good	81	87	91	79	74	83	82	80	80	68	87
Post-materialism:											
% Post-materialists	24	19	14	8	5	14	7	6	9	2	7
Difference in % post-materialist/materialist	+17.1	-2.3	-4.5	-24.7	-40.2	-5.8	-32.6	-32.8	-7.1	-36.7	-28.8

* See notes 3 and 4 for explanation on the origin of the survey data and the distribution of the 81 countries into cultural regions.

that measures favoring democracy has been rejected precisely because of the high consensus on supporting that kind of government in all countries. Instead, favoring a government based on a strong leader has been preferred for three reasons: it shows greater variation; it is highly correlated with preference for army rule (.36) and experts making decisions (.31); and it is the indicator that is more ighly (and negatively) correlated with favoring democracy (−.21). Women need children was the only indicator on attitudes towards the present social role of women, and therefore was selected.

A test that provides reassurance on the selection of these indicators was its relationship with the indicator that supposedly measures the change of values, that is, Inglehart's four items scale on post-materialism (Inglehart 1977, 1990, 1997; Díez-Nicolás 2000). The indicator (difference between the percent of respondents who show post-materialist values and the percent who show materialist values, disregarding the central category of mixed values) shows high and statistically significant (.000 level) correlations with life satisfaction (.14), interpersonal trust (.07), importance of God in one's life (−.08), women need children (−.19) and favoring strong leadership (−.10). It may be added that its relationship to favoring democracy is the same (but of opposite sign) that to favoring strong leadership. All relationships were in the expected direction.

Regional comparisons on the selected five attitudinal indicators seem to mask, once more, very high within-region differences, even higher than between region differences, as may be seen in some examples reported in Table 2. Thus, the ratios between the highest and the lowest values of regions in four selected attitudinal indicators have been compared with the ratios obtained between the highest and lowest values of countries within each region. Since Huntington has placed a great emphasis on religion as one of the most important basis for confrontation between "the West" and Islam, it may be interesting to underline that, though Islamic countries show an average of 9 points on a scale 0 to 10 points, the same importance is also attached to God in one's life in Latin American and African sub-Saharan societies, though they do not seem to be labeled "fundamentalists." Besides, the average for that item is 8.5 in the U.S., 9.2 in Malta, 8.4 in Poland, 8.6 in Romania, 9.6 in the Philippines, and over 9.0 in all African sub-Saharan and most Latin American countries, though that doesn't seem to worry.

The data provides further evidence to question Huntington's assumptions of internal homogeneity of "civilizations" or "cultural regions" and external differentiation with respect to other regions. The importance of God in one's life within the Anglo-Saxon group, for example, varies from 8.5 in the U.S. to 4.9 in Britain, while citizens of Islamic, African sub-Saharan, and Latin American countries attribute an equal importance to God in their lives.

Table 2

Between-regions and within-regions ratios of the highest over the lowest value of some attitudinal indicators, 1995-2000*

	Ratios of Highest to Lowest Values in:			
	Life satisfaction	Freedom of choice and own life's control	Importance of God in one's life	Difference of % post-materialist and materialist
Between regions (highest/lowest):	**1.6**	**1.4**	**1.9**	**2.0**
Within regions (between countries, highest/lowest):				
Anglo Saxon	1.1	1.1	1.7	1.1
West European Catholic	1.2	1.2	2.1	1.7
West Eruopean Protestant	1.1	1.1	1.8	1.4
East European Christian	1.4	1.2	2.7	2.0
European Orthodox	1.7	1.4	1.7	1.9
Latin American	1.3	1.2	1.4	1.4
Islamic	1.5	1.6	1.4	2.2
Sinic-Confucian	1.1	1.1	1.1	1.5
African sub-Saharan	1.8	1.2	1.1	1.2

*Japan and India, two countries that are treated as single-country cultural regions, are not included here because they have no within-region differences. The "Others" category (that includes the Philippines and Israel) are also excluded because they do not constitute a region.

At this point it seemed necessary to verify whether or not the concept of civilization or world region is a good predictor of values, and to establish what is its explanatory value in comparison with other potential explanatory variables. To this effect a regression (OLS) model was constructed in such a way that its results could be easily compared with those found by Norris and Inglehart (2002) in their comparison of the West and Islam, where they conclude that these two regions differ more regarding issues that relate to gender equality and sexual liberalization than to issues concerning democracy.

The five indicators previously selected were taken as dependent variables, and the same explanatory variables were included in the five regression models. Similarly to Norris and Inglehart, some macro-variables (contextual, societal) seemed necessary, and the three that were discussed in the first part of these paper were selected, that is, GNP per capita, Human Development Index and Freedom House Ratings, to measure the levels of economic, social well-being and democratic development. The high correlations among the three indicators, and of each one of them with the average post-materialist measure (four items scale) for each country and region have already been reported and commented. It must be noted that Norris and Inglehart did not include in their model GNP per capita as one of their development control variables, in spite of the fact that Inglehart has repeatedly shown its very high relationship with value change.

Another group of control variables at the micro-level include gender, age, educational level attained, family income and religiosity.[4] These five variables were also included in Norris and Inglehart's comparative analysis of the West and Islam.

Finally, the type of societies variable includes the twelve groups of countries that have been already defined. The main difference with respect to Norris and Inglehart's grouping is that Anglo-Saxon countries have been considered separately from the West, on the assumption that they differ significantly especially with respect to religious beliefs and practice. Besides, West European countries have been divided into those that are predominantly protestant or catholic. On this same line, the dummy variable for type of society was the Anglo-Saxon countries, instead of the West European.

The full regression model for the five dependent variables is presented in Table 3. But the effect of each group of explanatory or control variables

---

[4] Gender was measured through the proportion of female respondents as dummy variable, males being the omitted category. Age was measured in single years. Education was measured through a nine points scale (1 = low, 9 = high). Family income was measured through a ten deciles scale (1 = low, 10 = high), and religiosity was measured through a five points scale (1 = low, 5 = high).

Table 3

Explanation of Social and Political Values by groups of control variables*

	Satisfaction with life				Interpersonal Trust				Importance of God				Women need children				Favor Strong Leader			
	B	St. Err.	Beta	Sig.	B	St. Err.	Beta	Sig.	B	St. Err.	Beta	Sig.	B	St. Err.	Beta	Sig.	B	St. Err.	Beta	Sig.
Developmental variables:																				
GNP per capita	.0	.00	.18	.000	.0	.00	.09	.000	-.0	.00	-.14	.000	-.0	.00	-.05	.000	-.0	.00	-.21	.000
Human Development Index	1.4	.17	.07	.000	.0	.03	.02	.068	.3	.17	.01	.122	-1.0	.03	-.27	.000	1.4	.07	.18	.000
Freedom House Ratings	-.0	.00	-.06	.000	.0	.00	-.13	.000	.0	.01	.01	.133	.0	.00	.12	.000	-.0	.00	-.04	.000
Socio-demographic variables																				
Sex (female)	.0	.02	.01	.001	-.0	.00	-.01	.006	.6	.02	.09	.000	-.0	.00	-.01	.064	-.0	.01	-.00	.215
Age	-.0	.00	-.02	.000	.0	.00	.03	.000	.0	.00	.04	.000	.0	.00	.09	.000	-.0	.00	-.01	.000
Education	.0	.00	.02	.000	.0	.00	.04	.000	-.0	.00	-.02	.000	-.0	.00	-.07	.000	-.0	.00	-.08	.000
Religious practice	.1	.01	.06	.000	.0	.00	.02	.000	.8	.01	.40	.000	.0	.00	.04	.000	.0	.00	.01	.003
Family income	.2	.00	.16	.000	.0	.00	.08	.000	-.0	.00	-.05	.000	-.0	.00	-.03	.000	-.0	.00	-.08	.000
Type of Society 1:																				
West European Catholic	.0	.04	.00	.944	-.0	.01	-.06	.000	-.3	.04	-.03	.000	.2	.01	.16	.000	-.0	.02	-.00	.379
West European Protestant	.3	.04	.03	.000	.2	.01	.09	.000	-1.1	.04	-.08	.000	.2	.01	.08	.000	-.2	.02	-.05	.000
East European Christian	-.3	.05	-.04	.000	-.1	.01	-.07	.000	-1.4	.05	-.14	.000	.3	.01	.21	.000	-.2	.02	-.05	.000
Orthodox European	-1.7	.06	-.22	.000	-.14	.01	-.11	.000	-.6	.06	-.07	.000	.5	.01	.34	.000	.4	.02	.13	.000
Latin American	1.0	.05	.14	.000	-.2	.01	-.18	.000	1.2	.05	.13	.000	.2	.01	.15	.000	.3	.02	.10	.000

*Variables are defined in notes 3, 4 and 5. The omitted variable in Type of Society is Anglo-Saxon countries. All R^2 are significant at .000.

Table 3
(Continued)

	Satisfaction with life				Interpersonal Trust				Importance of God				Women need children				Favor Strong Leader			
	B	St. Err.	Beta	Sig.	B	St. Err.	Beta	Sig.	B	St. Err.	Beta	Sig.	B	St. Err.	Beta	Sig.	B	St. Err.	Beta	Sig.
Type of Society 1:																				
Islamic	-.7	.06	-.10	.000	-.0	.01	-.06	.000	1.3	.06	.17	.000	.4	.01	.34	.000	-.0	.02	-.02	.036
Sinic-Confucian	-.4	.06	-.02	.000	-.0	.01	-.01	.022	-1.8	.07	-.09	.000	.5	.01	.17	.000	.6	.03	.10	.000
Japan	-1.1	.07	-.05	.000	.0	.01	.01	.025	-1.7	.08	-.06	.000	.5	.02	.09	.000	.0	.03	.01	.014
India	-.7	.08	-.04	.000	.1	.02	.04	.000	-.9	.08	-.04	.000	.2	.02	.08	.000	.8	.04	.10	.000
Sub-Saharan African	-.6	.07	-.06	.000	-.2	.01	-.12	.000	.5	.07	.04	.000	.2	.01	.08	.000	.0	.03	.01	.214
Others	.2	.09	.01	.090	-.2	.02	-.06	.000	.7	.09	.03	.000	.5	.02	.11	.000	.6	.04	.06	.000
(Constant)	4.5				1.3				5.1				1.9				1.7			
Adj. R² (developmental var.)	.09				.03				.17				.13				.05			
Adj. R² (socio-demogra. var.)	.04				.02				.31				.04				.02			
Adj. R² (type of society var.)	.16				.05				.27				.16				.08			
Adj. R² (control var. only)	.13				.05				.36				.16				.07			
Adj. R² (control var. + type)	.20				.08				.44				.21				.11			

has been calculated separately and jointly. Thus, it may be noticed that the type of society explains by itself a greater degree of the variance in life satisfaction, interpersonal trust, women need children and strong leadership than the macro- or micro-level control variables, but the socio-demographic variables explain a greater degree of the variance of the importance of God in one's life. Obviously, this is due to the contribution of religious practice (its individual standardized regression coefficient is .40) among the socio-demographic independent variables. But it must be also remarked that the development variables (GNP, HDI and FHR) explain almost as much a proportion of the variance on each of the five dependent variables as the type of society. As a matter of fact, GNP per capita contributes more to the explanation of life satisfaction, importance of God and favoring strong leadership than the other two development variables, and it is certainly one of two or three variables, of all the variables in the model, that contributes more to the explanation of the variance in any of the five dependent variables. At the individual level, family income is also the socio-demographic variable that contributes more to the explanation of life satisfaction, interpersonal trust and (negatively) to strong leadership. The relationship between the development variables and type of society is very high, for which reason the additional contribution of socio-demographic variables to the total adjusted R^2 is never higher than .02. The same result is true if religion is included as another micro-level (individual) variable (using seven categories and catholic as the dummy variable for comparison of results. Its additional contribution to the total R^2 is usually none or .01, probably because predominant country religion has been used as one of the criteria to define types of society. It seems, therefore, that individual socio-demographic variables, including one's religion, make a smaller contribution to the explanation of life satisfaction, interpersonal trust, importance of God in one's life, attitude towards women being in need of having children, and rejection of strong leadership as an acceptable form of government, when type of society and three macro-level measures of economic, social and political development are controlled. These results confirm very strongly the findings of Norris and Inglehart using a very similar model, though they do not compare the separate contribution of macro- and micro- control variables. It must be added, nevertheless, that when their regression models are used (that is, removing GNP per capita, collapsing Anglo-Saxon, West European Protestant and West European Catholic into a West category, and using this as the omitted variable, and removing Japan and India as separate categories, including them in the Other category), the total R^2 for each of the five dependent variable changes very little or not at all. More specifically, it doesn't change at all with respect to life satisfaction, it loses .01 with respect to importance of God in one's life, agreement that women need to have children and with favoring strong leadership, and it diminishes .02 with respect to interpersonal trust.

Norris and Inglehart's model, however, was intended to compare mainly the West and Islam with respect to political attitudes and attitudes towards gender equality and sexual liberalization. The model presented here was intended to verify the hypothesis that Huntington's classification of societies into seven civilizations is an artifact, and that country differences within the said civilizations may be very significant. While it is true that Norris and Inglehart find significant differences between the West and Islam, the results of the analysis presented here demonstrates that Anglo-Saxon countries differ significantly from West European Protestant and West European Catholic countries (and also from other groups of countries). More specifically, the data demonstrate that citizens of Anglo-Saxon countries, once three development variables and five socio-demographic variables are controlled, are significantly less satisfied with life, show lower interpersonal trust, give more importance to God in their lives, agree less with the idea that women need to have children, and support strong leadership more than citizens of West European Protestant countries. Besides, they show significant more interpersonal trust, they give more importance to God in their lives, and they agree less in the need of women to have children than citizens of West European Catholic countries. The West is not an homogeneous entity, as well as other groupings of countries are not either. And the results seem to be consistent with five different dimensions of attitudes. It seems to be true that the country of residence of individuals (and not necessarily the world region) continues to be the best predictor of individual's attitudes in international comparative research (Deflen & Pampel 1996).

It seems appropriate to underline the fact that citizens in Anglo-Saxon countries give a greater importance to God in their lives than citizens of countries that have been here labeled as West European Protestant and Catholic, East European Christian, European Orthodox, Sinic-Confucian, Japan, and India. They attribute less importance to God only when compared with citizens of Latin America, Islam and African sub-Saharan countries, and also less than citizens of the Philippines and Israel. The clash of civilizations that Huntington foresees seems to be dependent not only on the presumed religious fundamentalism of individuals in Islamic countries. If the clash is going to occur at all, it will probably depend on other more important variables, and maybe on the religious fundamentalism of other countries and religions.

Nevertheless, the data suggest that the three groups of control variables that have been used in this analysis explain almost half of the variance in the importance given to God by individuals around the world, much more than they explain in the other four dependent variables. One might be led to believe that this is due to the inclusion of religious practice among the socio-demographic variables. But when this variable is removed from the regression model the total R^2 is reduced from .44 to only .31, a proportion that, nevertheless, is still double than the variance explained for life satisfaction and the agreement with the need of women to have children.

The Importance of the Social Context

A final argument to refute the "clash of civilizations" hypothesis refers to effect of geographical mobility, and more specifically of international migration, in the attitudes and value system of people. Data from a sample survey among immigrants into Spain carried out in November 2001 (Díez-Nicolás & Ramírez-Lafita, forthcoming) provide the opportunity to compare them with the populations of their world region of origin and with the receiving Spanish population with respect to certain items of the WVS-EVS surveys that have been analyzed above. The three main groups of immigrants into Spain come from Latin America, Arab-Islamic countries (and more specifically from Morocco) and from sub-Saharan Africa. East European immigrants are more recent and smaller in numbers, though growing (Díez-Nicolás & Ramírez-Lafita 2001a). A first survey was conducted in 2000 (Díez-Nicolás & Ramírez-Lafita 2001b), but only in the 2001 wave were some WVS questions included in the questionnaire. Both surveys were conducted with 250 immigrants in each of the five regions of Spain having the largest number of immigrants (Madrid, Cataluña, Valencia, Andalucía and Canary Islands), and in each region the four main groups of immigrants (grouped according to region of origin) were proportionally represented in the sample. For this paper only the three main groups, representing more than 80% of the total sample, have been selected: Latin Americans, Islamic-Arabs (the great majority of them Moroccans) and sub-Saharan Africans.

The main hypothesis to test was that immigrants tend to adopt the values of the receiving society as an instrumental response to facilitate their social integration. An annual survey on the attitudes of Spaniards towards immigrants has shown that they favor the integration of Latin Americans more than that of any other group of immigrants, though they express their desire for all groups to integrate into Spanish society. They also believe that Latin American immigrants are more capable of integration, that they show a greater interest in integrating themselves, and that they acknowledge to have achieved integration more fully than other groups of immigrants (Díez-Nicolás & Ramírez-Lafita 2001a). The first survey conducted among migrants in 2000 showed that migrants themselves perceived Latin Americans as the group with more facilities and interest to be integrated into Spanish society and as the group that had achieved integration more fully (Díez-Nicolás & Ramírez-Lafita 2001b). A comparison of attitudes of migrants and Spaniards with respect to migration policies and problems has shown a greater degree of coincidence than expected, as the surveys conducted in 2001 have confirmed (Díez-Nicolás 2002).

On the basis of theses results, it was expected that Latin American immigrants would exhibit attitudes and values closer to the receiving Spanish population, while sub-Saharan Africans were expected to differ more from Spaniards, with Islamic-Arabs more or less on the middle. And it was further hypothesized that all three groups of immigrants would exhibit attitudes and values that were closer to those of Spaniards than to those of the populations of the world region from which they came.

The first hypothesis seems to be confirmed for the most part. In all but two of the eleven comparisons that may be made with the data in Table 4 attitudes of Latin American immigrants are closer to those of Spaniards than attitudes of Islamic-Arab or sub-Saharan African immigrants. The two exceptions refer to interpersonal trust, lower among Spaniards than among Latin American and Islamic-Arab immigrants, and to rejection of army rule, an option rejected by Islamic-Arab immigrants in lower but closer proportion to Spaniards, equally rejected by sub-Saharan African immigrants, and slightly more rejected by Latin American immigrants, probably because a significant proportion of them migrated to Spain to escape from military rule in their countries of origin. However, in five out of the eleven comparisons sub-Saharan African migrants are closer to Spaniards than Islamic-Arab immigrants. This is especially the case with respect to the two religious items, the agreement on the need of women to have children (very much related to religious beliefs), and to favoring the army rule, and it suggests that Islamic-Arab immigrants (mainly Moroccans) tend to maintain their original cultural values, especially those that refer to religion, more strongly than sub-Saharan African immigrants, who come from a greater variety of countries and a less homogeneous culture.

As for the second hypothesis, it is clear that Latin American immigrants' attitudes are closer to those of Spaniards than to the Latin American populations from which they come in nine of the eleven items that have been compared in Table 4. The comparison is more complex when it refers to Islamic-Arab immigrants and Spaniards. They are closer to Spaniards with respect to the political items, but they are closer to their populations of origin with respect to religious and family (influenced by religion) items.

Table 4

Comparison of some attitudinal indicators among Immigrants into Spain by region of origin, and Nationals of the same regions of origin and Nationals of Spain, 1995-2000*

	Spain	Latin American Immigrants	Latin American Nationals	Islamic Immigrants	Moroccans	Islamic Nationals	African sub-Saharan Immigrants	African sub-Saharan Nationals
N=	(1,209)	(261)	(16,027)	(238)	(1,251)	(21,193)	(117)	(8,197)
Personal Well-Being:								
Satisfaction with life (mean on scale 0-10)	6.98	6.72	7.71	5.41	5.86	5.80	5.17	5.55
% Very Happy	20	14	33	7	22	20	11	44
Social Capital:								
% Most people can be Trusted	33	40	14	37	22	29	33	14
Freedom of choice and Control of one's life (mean on scale 0-10)	6.72	7.03	7.66	5.48	6.13	5.92	5.42	6.60
Religiosity:								
Importance of God in one's life (mean on scale 0-10)	5.83	6.93	9.12	7.74	9.93	9.45	7.03	9.38
% Get Comfort in Religion	52	63	60	90	99	91	85	92
Role of Women:								
% Women need Children	45	42	41	69	72	78	42	66
Political Attitudes:								
% Strong leader is good or very good	16	11	44	21	13	27	10	28
% Government of Experts is good or very good	28	29	59	26	51	47	15	50
% Army rule is good or very good	6	2	25	9	10	27	4	21
% Democratic system is good or very good	87	86	83	65	69	82	51	87

* Countries included in Latin American, Islamic and African sub-Saharan countries are defined in note 4. Data for immigrants come from ASEP Data Archive, and are part of a survey conducted with a sample of 750 immigrants in Spain in November 2001. Data for Spain and Morocco are part of the 2000 WVS survey as described in notes 2 and 3.

However, it must be underlined that even though Islamic-Arab immigrants seem to be closer to the values of their populations of origin in most items, they show a clear divergence in some of them (even religious items), approaching the values of Spaniards. On the other hand, since most Islamic-Arab immigrants come from Morocco, it has been possible to compare their attitudes with those of the Moroccan sample in the 2000 WVS wave in Table 4. This comparison suggests that Islamic-Arab immigrants (mainly Moroccans) diverge more from Moroccans than from the Islamic populations in the WVS surveys with respect to all but four items. This divergence is especially notable with the two religious items (to the point that they are closer to Spaniards than to Moroccans in the importance attached to God in their lives) and with respect to the rejection of a government based on a strong leader or experts, but immigrants seem to be closer to Moroccans with respect to their favoring the a democratic political system (and in their small support to army rule). As for the sub-Saharan African immigrants, their attitudes are closer to those of Spaniards in all but three of the eleven comparisons.

It must be also remarked that the three groups of immigrants are significantly less satisfied with their lives and less happy than their counterparts in their regions of origin and than Spaniards. This is easy to understand, inasmuch as migration produces a lot of strain and sacrifice, and even if in the long run migrants attain a better standard of living than in their country of origin, it always produces in the individual a sense of unhappiness for having been forced by circumstances to abandon their original family, social and cultural environment. Besides, perhaps because of comparisons with their country of origin, they show greater interpersonal trust not only than their fellow countrymen in their regions of origin, but even a little more than Spaniards in the case of Latin American and Islamic-Arab immigrants. Finally, it may be observed that immigrants tend to be closer to their cultural origins with respect to religious and family attitudes, though even in this case there is a clear change towards the attitudes of the Spanish receiving population, but they are already closer to Spaniards' attitudes with respect to political issues, and very significantly so with respect to their rejection of a government based on a strong leader that doesn't have to care about a Parliament.

A regression OLS model (see Table 5) has also been used with the same selected five dependent variables that have been used to compare world regions above.[5] In this case, the three development control variables have been omitted, since it would be difficult to measure their influence

---

[5] The only differences with respect to the socio-demographic variables used for comparing world regions refer to education, measured in this case through a seven points

on immigrants' attitudes, because those of the receiving country would be constant and those of the regions of origin would have the same values for immigrants from each region and the nationals from the same region. The groups that have been compared are, therefore, the three groups of immigrants and the three regions from which they come as dummy variables, plus the residual category of other immigrants and other nationals. Spain has been the omitted variable for comparison.

It may be noticed that socio-demographic variables explain almost as much of the total variance in each of the five selected values variables than the type of society variable, and in the case of the importance of God in one's life, even more. The explanation is the same that the one offered before, the inclusion, among the socio-demographic variable, of an item measuring religious practice, that by itself has the greatest contribution (.42) to the total explained variance. The important conclusions to derive from these analysis, however, are that, when gender, age, education, religious practice and family income are controlled, all immigrants and nationals (except Latin American) are significantly less satisfied with their lives than Spaniards, a finding that is coherent with the high positive relationship mentioned above between the three development variables and life satisfaction. All immigrant groups exhibit a significantly higher interpersonal trust than Spaniards, while Spaniards show significant more interpersonal trust than Latin American and sub-Saharan African nationals (though this difference is not significant with respect to Islamic nationals). All immigrant and national groups give significant greater importance to God than Spaniards (except sub-Saharan African and other immigrants). Islamic-Arab and other immigrants, as well as all national groups, show a higher agreement with the statement that women need children than Spaniards, though the opposite seems to be true with respect to sub-Saharan African immigrants. And Latin American and other immigrants are less supportive of a government based on a strong leader that the receiving Spanish population, though Spaniards are less favorable to strong leadership than the nationals of Latin America and Islamic countries.

Finally, in Table 6, immigrants (as the omitted variable in each of the three regression OLS models) have been compared with Spaniards and nationals (as dummy variables) to test the significance of their differences when the same set of socio-demographic variables are controlled. It seems possible to conclude that Latin American immigrants are less satisfied with life than their counterparts in Latin America and than Spaniards, they agree more with women being in need of having children than their

---

scale (1 = low, 7 = high) and age, measured through age groups (1 = 18-29 years; 2 = 30-49 years; 3 = 50-64 years; and 4 = 65 years and over).

Table 5

Explanation of Social and Political Values by groups of control variables, Immigrants into Spain and Nationals from three World Regions*

	Satisfaction with life				Interpersonal Trust				Importance of God				Women need children				Favor Strong Leader			
	B	St. Err.	Beta	Sig.	B	St. Err.	Beta	Sig.	B	St. Err.	Beta	Sig.	B	St. Err.	Beta	Sig.	B	St. Err.	Beta	Sig.
Socio-demographic variables																				
Sex (female)	.0	.02	.01	.000	-.0	.00	-.01	.000	.6	.02	.09	.000	-.0	.00	-.02	.000	-.0	.01	-.01	.044
Age	.0	.01	.00	.263	.0	.00	.02	.000	.0	.01	.03	.000	-.0	.00	.06	.000	-.0	.00	-.03	.000
Education	.0	.01	.01	.054	.0	.00	.02	.000	-.0	.01	-.03	.000	-.0	.00	-.09	.000	-.0	.00	-.07	.000
Religious practice	.0	.01	.04	.000	.0	.00	.00	.175	.9	.01	.42	.000	.0	.00	.08	.000	.0	.00	.03	.000
Family income	.2	.00	.19	.000	.0	.00	.10	.000	-.0	.00	-.05	.000	-.0	.00	-.05	.000	-.0	.00	-.09	.000
Type of Society 1:																				
Latin American Immigrants	.0	.24	.00	.739	.1	.04	.01	.001	1.4	.23	.02	.000	-.0	.05	-.00	.287	-.3	.11	-.01	.008
Islamic Immigrants	-1.2	.23	-.02	.000	.1	.04	.01	.002	.8	.22	.01	.000	.1	.04	.01	.006	-.1	.11	-.00	.288
African sub-Saharan Immigrants	-1.6	.30	-.02	.000	.3	.06	.02	.000	.2	.29	.00	.531	-.2	.06	-.01	.007	-.2	.17	-.00	.319
Other Immigrants	-.6	.29	-.01	.047	.2	.05	.01	.000	-.0	.28	.00	.976	.1	.06	.01	.013	-.4	.13	-.01	.005
Latin American Nationals	.7	.09	.10	.000	-.2	.02	-.15	.000	2.9	.08	.31	.000	.0	.02	.02	.125	.44	.04	.16	.000
Islamic Nationals	-1.2	.09	-.18	.000	-.0	.02	-.01	.465	3.1	.08	.40	.000	.3	.02	.25	.000	.0	.04	.03	.036
African sub-Saharan Nationals	-1.3	.09	-.12	.000	-.2	.02	-.10	.000	2.2	.09	.19	.000	.2	.02	.09	.000	.0	.04	.00	.795
Other Nationals	-.5	.09	-.10	.000	-.0	.02	-.02	.233	.7	.08	.11	.000	.0	.02	.10	.000	.2	.04	.09	.000
(Constant)	5.8				1.2				3.3				1.5				2.4			
Adj. R²(socio-demogra. var.)	**.04**				**.02**				**.31**				**.04**				**.02**			
Adj. R²(type of society var.)	**.05**				**.02**				**.24**				**.04**				**.02**			
Adj. R²(socio-demogra.+type)	**.09**				**.04**				**.41**				**.07**				**.03**			

* See end notes 4 and 6 for definition of variables. The omitted variable in the regression OLS model for Type of Society is Spain. All R^2 are significant at .000.

Table 6

Explanation of Social and Political Values by groups of control variables, Immigrants into Spain and Nationals from three World Regions*

	Satisfaction with life				Interpersonal Trust				Importance of God				Women need children				Favor Strong Leader			
	B	St.Err.	Beta	Sig.	B	St.Err.	Beta	Sig.	B	St.Err.	Beta	Sig.	B	St.Err.	Beta	Sig.	B	St.Err.	Beta	Sig.
Socio-demographic variables																				
Sex (female)	.0	.02	.02	.000	.00	.00	-.01	.002	.5	.02	.07	.000	-.0	.00	-.02	.000	-.0	.01	-.00	.292
Age	.0	.01	.03	.000	.0	.00	.03	.000	-.1	.01	-.04	.000	.0	.00	.03	.000	-.0	.00	-.02	.000
Education	.0	.01	.03	.000	.0	.00	.03	.000	-.2	.01	-.08	.000	-.0	.00	-.11	.000	-.0	.00	-.06	.000
Religious practice	.0	.01	.00	.187	-.0	.00	-.02	.000	1.1	.01	.51	.000	.0	.00	.12	.000	.0	.00	.01	.081
Family income	.2	.00	.19	.000	.0	.00	.10	.000	-.0	.00	-.06	.000	-.0	.00	-.06	.000	-.0	.01	-.09	.000
Latin Americans																				
Nationals	1.5	.02	.21	.000	-.2	.00	-.12	.000	1.4	.02	.15	.000	-.14	.00	-.09	.000	.32	.01	.11	.000
Spaniards	.8	.09	.03	.000	.0	.02	.01	.064	-1.4	.09	-.04	.000	-.16	.02	-.03	.000	-.15	.04	-.01	.000
(Constant)	4.8				1.2				5.2				1.7				2.5			
Adj. R²	**.08**				**.03**				**.33**				**.05**				**.03**			
Socio-demographic variables																				
Sex (female)	.0	.02	.01	.000	.0	.00	-.01	.020	.5	.02	.08	.000	-.0	.00	-.02	.000	-.0	.01	-.01	.091
Age	-.0	.01	-.01	.010	-.0	.00	.05	.000	-.0	.01	-.02	.000	.0	.00	.06	.000	-.0	.00	-.04	.000
Education	.0	.01	.00	.114	.0	.00	.04	.000	-.0	.01	-.04	.000	-.0	.00	-.09	.000	-.0	.00	-.07	.000
Religious practice	.0	.01	.04	.000	-.0	.00	-.04	.000	1.0	.01	.49	.000	.0	.00	.08	.000	.0	.00	.02	.000
Family income	.2	.00	.18	.000	.0	.00	.10	.000	-.0	.00	-.06	.000	-.0	.00	-.05	.000	-.0	.00	-.09	.000
Islamic																				
Nationals	-.9	.02	-.13	.000	.0	.00	.06	.000	1.8	.02	.23	.000	.2	.00	.17	.000	-.1	.01	-.05	.000
Spaniards	.4	.09	.01	.000	.0	.02	.01	.000	-1.2	.09	-.04	.000	-.0	.02	-.02	.000	-.2	.04	-.02	.000
(Constant)	5.5				1.1				4.6				1.6				2.6			
Adj. R²	**.05**				**.02**				**.36**				**.07**				**.02**			

Table 6
(Continued)

	Satisfaction with life				Interpersonal Trust				Importance of God				Women need children				Favor Strong Leader			
	B	St. Err.	Beta	Sig.	B	St. Err.	Beta	Sig.	B	St. Err.	Beta	Sig.	B	St. Err.	Beta	Sig.	B	St. Err.	Beta	Sig.
Socio-demographic variables																				
Sex (female)	.0	.02	.01	.000	-.0	.00	-.01	.000	.5	.02	.07	.000	-.0	.00	-.02	.000	-.0	.01	-.00	.108
Age	.0	.01	.00	.606	.0	.00	.04	.000	-.2	.01	-.05	.000	.0	.00	.04	.000	-.0	.00	-.03	.000
Education	.0	.01	.02	.000	.0	.00	.02	.000	-.2	.01	-.07	.000	-.0	.00	-.12	.000	-.0	.00	-.06	.000
Religious practice	.0	.01	.05	.000	-.0	.00	-.01	.000	1.1	.01	.52	.000	.0	.00	.10	.000	.0	.00	.03	.000
Family income	.2	.00	.18	.000	.0	.00	.10	.000	-.0	.00	-.06	.000	-.0	.00	-.05	.000	-.0	.00	-.09	.000
Africans sub-Sahara																				
Nationals	-.8	.03	-.08	.000	-.1	.01	-.07	.000	.2	.03	.02	.000	.0	.01	.01	.045	-.2	.01	-.05	.000
Spaniards	.5	.09	.02	.000	.0	.02	.01	.006	-1.6	.09	-.05	.000	-.1	.02	-.03	.000	-.2	.04	-.02	.000
(Constant)	5.2				1.2				5.3				1.7				2.6			
Adj. R²	**.04**				**.02**				**.31**				**.04**				**.02**			

* See notes 4 and 6 for definition of variables. The omitted variables in each of the three regression OLS models are the Immigrants from Latin America, Islamic countries and African sub-Saharan countries respectively. All R² are significant at .000.

national counterparts and Spaniards, they show higher interpersonal trust, give more importance to God, and favor less strong leadership than their national counterparts, but they give less importance to God and favor strong leadership significantly more than Spaniards.

Islamic-Arab (mainly Moroccans) are more satisfied with their life, and favor more strong leadership than their national counterparts, though they show less interpersonal trust, less agreement with women being in need of having children and give less importance to God than Islamic populations. In comparison with Spaniards, they are less satisfied with life, they show less interpersonal trust and they give more importance to God in their lives, agree more with women being in need of having children and support more strong leadership.

And finally, sub-Saharan African immigrants are more satisfied with life and show more interpersonal trust, but give less importance to God in their lives and favor more strong leadership than their national counterparts, and they are less satisfied with life and show less interpersonal trust, but give more importance to God, agree more with the need of women to have children, and support more strong leadership, than Spaniards.

Therefore, on the basis of available data, the two hypotheses regarding the change of their values cannot be rejected, that is, that immigrants tend to adopt the values of the receiving population, in this case the Spanish population, at the same time that they diverge from the values of their original populations, and that Latin American immigrants, because of greater facilities for integration due to common language, religion and culture, adopt the values of Spaniards more fully than immigrants of Islamic or sub-Saharan African origin. Besides, the evidence seems to support the conclusion that adoption of new values is easier with respect to political-democratic values and slower, but showing intensive and significant change, with respect to religious values. This finding suggests that communication, especially interpersonal communication, may facilitate the knowledge, and consequently the adoption, of new postmodern values by the populations of more traditional societies. But this conclusion contests, once more, Huntington's views of civilizations or cultures as internally homogeneous and externally predetermined to "clash."

Summary of Results

This paper has attempted to present empirical evidence to refute Fukuyama's thesis of the end of history and Huntington's thesis of the "clash" of civilizations. The data that have been presented and analyzed above support the initial hypotheses that, at the macro-level, there is a strong positive relationship between economic, political, social and cultural development, as measured by GNP per capita, Freedom House Ratings, Human Development Index and post-materialist values. However, this strong relationship is compatible with the observation of very large and even increasing inequalities with respect to the level of development reached by countries and world regions in each of the mentioned dimensions. Even though free market economy and parliamentary democracy seem to be the only economic and political models at present for all societies, countries are far from having reached the same level of development in their economic, their social well-being, their civic liberties and their value systems. Consequently, the world seems to be far away from the end of history.

Furthermore, the evidence seems to confirm that within-world regions variation may be larger than between-world regions in the four mentioned dimensions, and that the concept of "civilization" or "world region" as an homogeneous entity cannot be accepted uncritically. Thus, the West has been divided into Anglo-Saxon, West European Catholic and West European Protestant blocks for analytical purposes, and the data have clearly shown significant differences between Anglo-Saxon countries and West European countries. Probably similar findings could be obtained for other presumed homogeneous world regions. The country seems to be still a better unit of analysis for explaining individual attitudes in international comparative research.

Nevertheless, the types of society defined as world cultural regions seem to have a significant explanatory power at the micro-level, that is, for individuals' attitudes, greater than the block of development and the block of individual socio-demographic control variables. But socio-economic differences among world regions (especially GNP differences) may explain differences in values in a similar and sometimes even greater degree than types of society or "civilizations" as Huntington defines them. And, at the micro-level, family income also seems to be the variable with greater explanatory power of individuals' attitudes. The internal homogeneity of "civilizations" is therefore questioned by empirical evidence.

Finally, regarding the effect of migration on changing people's values, it seems that migrants tend to adopt the values of the receiving society as an instrumental response to better adapt to their new social environment. This change is evident when comparing three groups of migrants into Spain (Latin American, Islamic-Arab and sub-Sahara African) on the basis of their attitudes to five different dimensions, both with respect to Spaniards and to nationals from their world regions of origin. Though the change is significant in all observed dimensions, it seems to be faster regarding political attitudes than regarding religious and family or related attitudes. And the change seems to be more fully accomplished among

Latin American immigrants than among Islamic or sub-Sahara African immigrants, as expected.

References

BECK, U.
1999   *World Risk Society*. New York: Blacwell Publishers.
COUNCIL ON ENVIRONMENTAL QUALITY AND DEPARTMENT OF STATE
1980   *The Global 2000 Report to the President*. Washington D.C.: Government Printing Office.
DÍEZ-NICOLÁS, J.
1980   "La España Previsible." *Revista Española de Investigaciones Sociológicas*, 12.
1982   "Ecología Humana y Ecosistema Social" in CEOTMA, *Sociología y Medio Ambiente*. Madrid: MOPU.
1995   "Postmaterialism and the social ecosystem" in Beat y Beatrix Sitter Liver (eds.), *Culture within nature*. Paris: UNESCO.
1999   "Industrialization and Concern for the Environment" en N. Tos, P. Ph. Mohler y B. Malnar (eds.), *Modern Society and Values*. Ljubljana: FSS y Mannheim: ZUMA. (Traducción al español en F. Cruz Beltrán y E. Gualda Caballero (comps.), Huelva: *Medio Ambiente y Sociedad*, Huelva: Universidad de Huelva.)
2000   "La Escala de Postmaterialismo como Medida del Cambio de Valores en las Sociedades Contemporáneas" en F. Andrés Orizo y J. Elzo, *España 2000, entre el Localismo y la Globalidad*. Madrid: Editorial SM.
2001   "Social Values, Social Change and Social Integration." Paper presented at the Fourth International Forum on Urban Poverty (IFUP), Marrakech: United Nations.
2002   "Las dos Caras de la Inmigración" in *Migraciones internas e intra-europeas en la Península Ibérica*. Santiago de Compostela: Servicio de Publicaciones de la Universidad de Santiago.
DÍEZ-NICOLÁS, J. & M.J. RAMÍREZ-LAFITA
2001a   *La Inmigración en España: Una Década de Investigaciones*. Madrid: IMSERSO.
2001b   *La Voz de los Inmigrantes*. Madrid: IMSERSO.
(forthcoming)*Las Dos Caras de la Imigración*. Madrid: IMSERSO.
DUNCAN, O.D.
1964   "Social Organization and the Ecosystem" in: R.E.L. Faris (ed.), *Handbook of Modern Sociology*. Chicago: Rand Mc Nally and Co.
FUKUYAMA, F.
1991   *The End of History and Last Man*. New York: The Free Press.
GIDDENS, A.
2000   *Runaway World*. London & New York: Routledge.
HALLER, M.
2001   "Europe and the Arab-Islamic World. A Sociological Perspective on the Differences and Mutual (mis-) Perceptions between Two Neighbouring Culture Areas." Paper presented at the First International Conference on Social Sciences and the Development of Society, Kuwait University, Kuwait.
HAWLEY, A.H.
1986   *Human Ecology. A theoretical essay*. Chicago: The University of Chicago Press.

HÖFERT, A. & A. SALVATORE
2000   "Beyond the Clash of Civilizations: Transcultural Politics between Europe and
            Islam" in A. Höfert and A. Salvatore (eds), *Between Europe and Islam: Shaping
            Modernity in a Transcultural Space*. Frankfurt: Lang.
HUNTINGTON, S.P.
1996   *The Clash of Civilizations and the Remaking of the World Order*. New York: Simon
            & Schuster.
HUTTON, W. & A. GIDDENS (EDS.)
2000   *Global Capitalism*. New York: New Press.
INGLEHART, R.
1977   *The Silent Revolution*. Princeton, N.J.: Princeton University Press.
1990   *Culture Shift*. Princeton, N.J.: Princeton University Press. (Translated into
            Spanish (1992): *El Cambio Cultural*, Madrid: CIS, Introduction by J. Díez
            Nicolás).
1997   *Modernization and Postmodernization*. Princeton, N.J.: Princeton University
            Press. (Translated into Spanish (1998): Modernización y Postmodernización,
            Madrid: CIS, Introduction by J. Díez Nicolás).
1999   "Postmodernization Erodes Respect for Authority, but Increases Support for
            Democracy" in P. Norris (ed.): *Critical Citizens: Global Support for Democratic
            Governance*. Oxford: Oxford University Press.
2001   "Public Support for Democratic Institutions: A Global Perspective," report
            prepared for Fundación para las Relaciones Internacionales y el Diálogo
            Exterior (FRIDE), Madrid.
KAHN, H. AND J. WIENER
1967   *L'An 2000*. Paris: Laffont.
LASSWELL, H.D.
1977   *Harold D. Lasswell on Political Sociology*. Chicago: University of Chicago Press.
MARX, K.
1904   *A Contribution to the Critique of Political Economy*. New York: International Library
            Publishing Co.
MERRIT, R.L. & S. ROKKAN (EDS.)
1966   *Comparing Nations, The Use of Quantitative Data in Cross — National Research*. New
            Haven: Yale University Press.
NORRIS, P. & R. INGLEHART
2002   "Islamic Culture and Democracy: Testing the Clash of Civilizations Thesis."
            Comparative Sociology 1(3): 235-263.
PARETO, V.
1921   *Transformazione della Democracia*. Corbaccio: Milano.
SHEARMUR, J.
1996   *Political Thought of Karl Popper*. London & New York: Routledge.
DEL VALLE, A.
2000   *Guerres contre l'Europe*. Paris: Editions des Syrtes.
UNITED NATIONS
1987   *Our Common Future*. UN Commission on Environment and Development, New
            York.
2002   *The Human Development Report*. New York: PNUD, UN.
WEBER, M.
1946   *The Theory of Economic and Social Organization*. Glencoe, IL: The Free Press.

Corruption and Democracy:
A Cultural Assessment

Alejandro Moreno[*]

There is strong evidence that corruption has a negative impact on economic development and on the emergence and survival of democratic institutions.[1] This article asks, "To what extent does permissiveness toward corruption reflect cultural factors? If so, how widely does cultural acceptance of corruption vary across societies — and have the publics of given societies become less tolerant of corrupt practices as a result of the global trend toward democratization?" Data from successive waves of the World Values Surveys help us to answer these questions.

Awareness of the negative impact that corruption has on economic development and democratization, has made the study of government transparency an increasingly important topic. Transparency International has done valuable work in measuring the level of corruption in public office, and publishing the results in the Corruption Perceptions Index (CPI). But corruption may reflect cultural factors, not just the actions of government officials, and measuring the extent to which ordinary citizens are willing to justify corrupt acts complements efforts to measure perceptions of government corruption. To what extent is cultural permissiveness toward corruption involved in these relationships?

Corruption can play an important role in political competition. In Latin America, for example, opposition electoral campaigns have benefited from exposing corrupt incumbents. Nonetheless, Latin American publics are, on the average, more permissive toward corrupt practices than most publics in Western Europe and East Asia. Consequently, fighting corruption becomes

---

[*] Instituto Tecnológico Autónomo de México, México City, Mexico.

[1] See for example Seymour Martin Lipset and Gabriel Salman Lenz, "Corruption, Culture, and Markets," in *Culture Matters: How Values Shape Human Progess*, L.E. Harrison and S.P. Huntington, eds. (New York: Basic Books, 2000).

one of the main tasks of newly democratic governments. In this sense, is democratization reducing corruption? More specifically, as democratic political attitudes become more widely shared, is permissiveness toward corruption decreasing?

Attitudes toward corruption vary cross-culturally. Most societies have a certain degree of permissiveness toward corruption, with some of them being more likely to justify corrupt practices than others. We will use an index of permissiveness toward corruption, based on citizen responses to survey questions, as an indicator of the extent to which corruption is considered acceptable in given societies. We find that attitudes toward corruption do indeed show a strong negative relationship to democratic attitudes. Permissiveness toward corruption is strongly and negatively correlated with support for democracy and with interpersonal trust, both of which are important components of a democratic political culture.

In newly democratic countries, corruption may be part of the inherited practices from old authoritarian regimes and governments have the task of fighting it. However, the publics of those countries may think that corruption continues under the new democratic governments. The following example illustrates this: In a poll conducted in Mexico in 2001, a year after the historic elections that ended 71 years of uninterrupted rule by one massively corrupt party, the PRI, 40 percent of respondents still agreed that bribes are necessary to deal with government authorities, whereas 57 disagreed. [2] This serves as an indicator of corruption in government, but, as mentioned earlier, perceptions of citizen corruption may be as important as the former. For example, 47 percent thought that most people in their country are corrupt, while 32 per cent believed most people are honest. This shows the other side of the coin, in which corruption not only is a problem of governing, but also a daily expectation among the mass publics. A combination of both is reflected in the following: there is a wide belief that if an honest person gets a job in public office, it is most likely that that person would become corrupt, according to 6 out of 10 respondents. On the contrary, 3 out of 10 Mexicans said that the person would remain honest despite his or her position. [3] This is very indicative not only of how people perceive the chances that public officials could be involved in acts of corruption, but also how they actually think that there are more corrupt than honest people. The question is to what extent mass publics are likely to justify acts of corruption in their daily lives.

This article analyzes data from the World Values Survey and European Values Survey (WVS/EVS), which includes 64 societies in 4 rounds of

---

[2] *Reforma* newspaper, October 30th, 2001.

[3] Ibid.

surveys conducted between 1981 and 2001. By constructing an index of permissiveness toward corruption, that is, the extent to which individuals tend to justify practices that are widely considered corrupt, I analyze the cross-national differences in such a measure and its relationship to indicators of a democratic political culture. We will examine how permissiveness toward corruption in given societies compares to their scores on the Corruption Perception Index, a poll of polls published by Transparency International.

Support for Democracy and Permissiveness toward Corruption

One expects stable democratic institutions and corruption to be negatively related, but is it solely the rule of law that prevents corruption? Or are support for democracy and permissiveness toward corruption enduring cultural traits, to some extent? Evidence from World Values Survey shows that these two variables are, in fact, strongly and negatively related, and that there is a great deal of cross-regional and cross-national variation in both.

The index of permissiveness toward corruption constructed for this article is a measure of culturally justifiable corrupt practices. The purpose is to assess how such a cultural trait varies among different countries and regions of the world, and how it has evolved through the last two decades. The index is based on individual responses to questions that address four issues: The extent to which individuals justify "claiming government benefits to which you are not entitled," "avoiding a fare on public transport," "cheating on taxes if you have a chance," and people "accepting a bribe in the course of their duties." Each variable was originally measured using a ten-point scale (where 1 = never justifiable and 10 = always justifiable), but an additive index summarized the responses into a five-point scale where 1 means respondents consider these acts as "never justifiable" and 5 as "always justifiable." The reason to simplify the additive scale into one with 5 points was to make it as comparable as possible to other constructed indexes of political and social attitudes, particularly support for democracy. Questions regarding the extent to which respondents justify acts of corruption are likely to be contaminated with social desirability biases: it may be hard to admit that such acts are justifiable. In the World Values Survey, about half of respondents, on average, placed their responses in the first category of the 10-point scale, meaning that the act referring to was hardly justified. Nonetheless, the additive index provides enough cross-national and cross-regional variance and it allows us to draw some conclusions.

As a note, the index of permissiveness toward corruption has a modest correlation with International Transparency's Corruption Perceptions

Index. Taking the results from the 2001 CPI and the ones derived from the 1995-2001 World Values Survey, the correlation with data from 58 societies included in both studies is −.32, meaning that relatively high scores on transparency (the CPI is measured in a scale where high scores mean less corruption) are associated with low levels of permissiveness toward corruption. In other words, countries that have higher levels of permissiveness toward corruption in the WVS tend to be those with less corruption in the CPI (though there are exemptions, as shown below). [4]

The five-point composite index of support for democracy is based on responses to 4 questions: whether "having a strong leader who does not have to bother with parliament and elections" is a good or bad way of governing the country, whether "having the army rule" is good or bad, whether respondents agree or disagre that "democracies are indecisive and have too much quibbling," and agree or disagree that "democracies aren't good at maintaining order." [5]

Figure 1 shows the average scores for each country in the scales of permissiveness toward corruption and support for democracy. The correlation between both variables is −.43, indicating that high support for democracy is associated with low citizen justification of corruption. Among the most supportive of democracy and least likely to justify corruption are Japan, Hong Kong, and the United States in the 1995 survey. However, while the Japanese stayed in a similar level on both scales by 2000, the American public expressed the same level of support for democracy, but its score on permissiveness toward corruption increased significantly between 1995 and 2000.

Some countries from Latin America experienced some movement from one survey to the next: Chile and Venezuela moved relatively in a similar fashion, but Mexico had a trajectory in the opposite direction. Venezuelans grew in both support for democracy and permissiveness toward corruption from 1995 to 2000. Chileans stayed in a similar level

---

[4] The results from both idicators were osberved in a scatter-plot and cases distribute relatively well along the negative regression line. There was only one extreme case, Bangladesh, which appears as one the most corrupt countries in the CPI and has the lowest score in permissiveness toward corruption in the World Values Survey. This country was left out of the analysis.

[5] The WVS questionnaire also includes two items on support for democracy that, with exception of Russia, have a relatively high level of support in most cases. Also, there is an item in which respondents agree or disagree that "in democracy, the economic system runs badly." The former were not included in the index, so the test on support for democracy could be a little less driven by social desibility biases towards democratic rule. The latter was excluded so the index would not be affected by perception of the current economic conditions in each country.

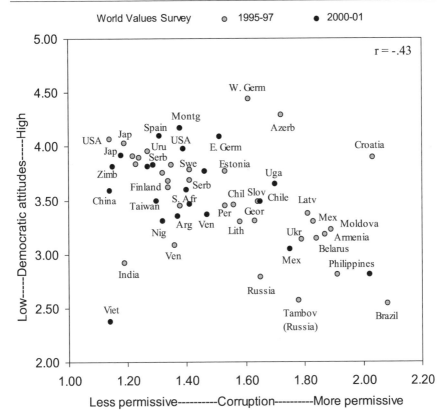

Figure 1.   Corruption Permissiveness and Support for Democracy.

of support for democracy, but extended their corruption permisiveness. Mexicans became slightly less likely to justify corruption, but also less supportive of democracy, as measured by the index. Uruguay is the Latin American country with the highest level of support for democracy and the lowest level of permissiveness toward corruption, followed by Argentina, which is significantly less supoortive of democratic rule and more likely to justify corruption. In contrast, Brazil has the lowest score on support for democracy and the highest one on permissiveness toward corruption.

In South Asia, the Philippines' trajectory is similar to the Chilean, with no movement in support for democracy and a broadening in their permissiveness toward corruption. Unlike Chileans, filipinos have a lower level of support for democracy and are much more likely to justify corruption acts. There are few cases among formerly Communist countries where trajectories in time can be assessed, but Serbia is one interesting exemption. The Serbs were the only ones that moved along the regression line, becoming less permissive towards corruption and more supportive of democracy in the last few years. Most of the societal average scores follow the negative-relation pattern, but there are some outliers: Both Thailand and India show low levels of permissiveness toward corruption, but also low scores on support for democracy. At the opposite end, Croatia scores highly on support for democratic rule, but also on permissiveness toward corruption.

The reason why trajectories in time are only shown for some countries in Figure 1, is that questions for the index of permissiveness toward corruption are included since the 1981-84, but the current questions of support for democracy have been included in the questionnaire since the 1995 wave. I will return to changes over time later, referring to the early surveys.

Due to the few of number of cases in some regions, it is hard to calculate cross-regional differences in support for democracy and permissiveness toward corruption. However, the data at hand allow us to have a good idea of how these two indexes vary across regions. Western democracies, for example, have the highest score on support for democracy (an average of 3.93 in the 5 point scale), as opposed to other regions of the world. The score for Western democracies was obtained from 12 surveys conducted between 1995 and 2001 in 9 countries, including two samples of the United States taken in 1995 and 2000. The second highest score in support for democracy is observed in East Asian societies (3.84), which includes China and Japan. Africa comes third, with an average of (3.51) resulting from Central Africa, Ghana, Nigeria and South Africa. Seventeen formerly Communist societies obtain a score of 3.50, higher than that of Latin America (3.41), and South Asia (2.91), this latter defined only by three countries: India, the Philippines, and Thailand. The Thai public is the one with the lowest score in support for democracy among all countries considered in the study.

Cross-regional differences in permissiveness toward corruption result in a somewhat different ranking: East Asian societies are the least likely to justify corruption (1.19), followed by Western democracies (1.33), and African societies (1.39). Many of the African countries score low in International Transparency's CPI, meaning that corruption is high. However, the few African publics included in the World Values Survey show that permissiveness toward corruption at the citizen level are lower than in other regions. For example, Nigeria is one of the most corrupt countries in the CPI, but scores relatively low in the index constructed with World Values Survey data. Rather than being contradictory, these opposing results may show the reality of high corruption in a country where it is culturally rejected, or may also reflect the social desirability effects mentioned above. Latin America and South Asia have higher levels of permissiveness toward corruption (1.53 and 1.57, respectively), but formerly

Communist societies have the highest average level of permissiveness toward corruption among all regions considered here (1.64).

In sum, corruption and democracy seem antagonistic, not just for the fact that democratic institutions increase government transparency, but also because permissiveness toward corruption at the citizen level is negatively related to support for democracy. Nonetheless, support for democracy as such is not an indicator of how democratic a country is. It reflects the extent to which democratic rule is massively accepted. In this section I have shown how such acceptance is related, generally, to rejection of morally corrupt practices. It is now the turn to assess how corruption permissivenes and interpersonal trust, an important component of a democratic political culture, relate to each other.

Trust and Corruption

It has been widely documented that social capital lubricates the functioning of democratic rule, and that interpersonal trust is a central component of social capital.[6] Scholarly work on the subject also shows that interpersonal trust is positively related to economic development and democracy.[7] From these propositions, we should expect that trust and corruption are also negatively correlated, which is what results from individual survey responses to the World Values Survey.

Figure 2 shows the countries's average positions on two scales: permissiveness toward corruption and interpersonal trust. Trust is represented by the percent of respondents who say that "most people can be trusted." The correlation coefficient between these two variables is $-.46$, indicating that, generally, more trusting societies also tend to be less likely to justify corruption. The relationship runs from highly trusting societies with relatively low permissiveness toward corruption, like Norway, Sweden and China, to generally distrusting and highly corrupt permissive societies like Brazil and the Philippines. Nonetheless, there are some societies where both trust and permissiveness toward corruption are low. Hong Kong and Puerto Rico are the best examples of low trust and low corruption. However, there are hardly any cases where both permissiveness toward corruption and trust are high. This indicates that corruption and trust simply do not go together in a positive way.

---

[6] See for example Francis Fukuyama, *Trust: The Social Virtues and the Creation of Prosperity* (New York: Free Press, 1995), and Robert Putnam, *Bowling Alone: The Collapse and Revival of American Community* (New York: Touchstone, 2000).

[7] Ronald Inglehart, *Modernization and Postmodernization* (Princeton: Princeton University Press, 1997).

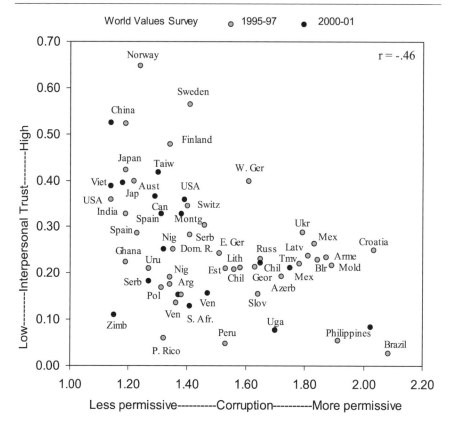

Figure 2.   Corruption Permissiveness and Interpersonal Trust.

There are trajectories over time in some countries that resemble those in Figure 1, which shows the scores for support for democracy and corruption. Serbia is a clear case where permissiveness toward corruption decreased in the last few years, but trust also decreases significanlty. The same happens in Mexico, but less significantly. On the other hand, Spain experienced moderate increases in both corruption permissivenes and trust. The difference is minimal, but China may be the case where trust increased and permissiveness toward corruption decreased in the last few years.

Again, regional differences are hard to asess with asymmetries in the number of cases. Nonetheless, the data at hand provide the following rankings. Western democracies have the highest level of trust, with an average of 43 percent. Norway and Sweden are the countries where more respondents say that, generally, you can "trust most people," 65 and 64 percent in the latest surveys, respectively. In comparison, 36 percent of Americans express trust, a smaller proportion than that observed in China, where slightly over 50 percent of Chinese said, both in 1995 and 2000, that you can trust most people. On average, East Asia's level of trust is about 37 percent. The lowest average level of trust is observed in Latin America (16 percent), which has a slightly lower average score than the ones obsereved in South Asia (19 percent) and Africa (17 percent). Only 3 percent of Brazilians, 5 percent of Peruvians, and 6 percent of Puerto Ricans say they generally trust most people, contributing to the fact that Latin American societies are, on average, the most distrusting of all. The highest level of interpersonal trust in Latin America was observed in Mexico in the 1995-97 survey, but it went down to 21 percent in 2000, below Dominican Republic in 1995 (25 percent), and Chile in 2000 (22 percent). Post-Communist societies have an average level of trust of about 23 percent. The highest is Montenegro in both of its surveys (30-33 percent) and the lowest is Slovenia in 1995: 16 percent.

In sum, permissiveness toward corruption is negatively related to support for democracy and to interpersonal trust. If we take the latter two variables as indicators of a democratic political culture, there is some evidence justifying corruption is culturally undemocratic. The question is whether the wave of democratization that has taken place since the mid-1970s has reduced the justification of morally corrupt practices among the mass publics. Th next section addresses this question by looking at the data gathered between 1981 and 2001 in both stable democracies and democratizing polities.

Changes in Permissiveness toward Corruption over Time

The *World Values Survey* offers the opportunity to compare the values and cultures of over 60 societies in a time span of two decades. However, not all the countries where the survey has been carried out have been consistently participants in every wave. This makes it difficult to assess how the index of permissiveness toward corruption has evolved both regionally and cross-nationally in a significant number of countries. Nonetheless, as the same set of questions about corruption have been asked in every single wave of the survey, from 1981 to 2000, it is possible to look at some of the general trends (See Table 1 in the Appendix).

Permissiveness toward corruption in Western democracies has remained about the same during the last two decades, even though there are some noticeable changes in particular countries. The United States is the most dramatic case. After dropping from 1.26 to 1.14 between 1990 and 1995, the score on the 5-point permissiveness toward corruption index increased to 1.39 in 2000. The score in West Germany also increased from 1990 to 1995, going from 1.41 to 1.61. In other countries, like Canada and Spain, the score on permissiveness toward corruption went down, meaning that there is a generally lower level of acceptance of corruption among those publics.

The average score of permissiveness toward corruption in East Asia, where corruption is less justified than anywhere else, according to the surveys, also reflects a reduction between 1995 and 2000. Particuarly, the decrease in the index is more noticeable in China. In contrast, permissiveness toward corruption increased in South Asia, particularly in India and the Philippines.

The most significant change in permissiveness toward corruption was observed in post-Communist societies between 1990 and 1995, when the score on the five-point index went up from 1.46 to .167. In this sense, the fall of Communism may have been a catalyst to greater acceptance of corruption in those societies. For example, the scores went up in Russia (from 1.45 to 1.65), Latvia (1.38 to 1.81), Lthuania (1.35 to 1.58), and even in East Germany (from 1.17 to 1.51), despite German reunification. After 1995, some countries seem to go in the opposite direction, though. The surveys conducted in Serbia and Montenegro in 2000 show a reduction of permissiveness toward corruption, but unfortunately we do not have recent data for other post-Communist countries to verify that the trend from the early 1990s has actually reversed.

The trend in Latin America shows some variations as well. The average regional score went down from 1.80 in three societies surveyed in 1990-1993, to 1.52 in 9 countries surveyed in 1995-1997. Then it slightly increased to 1.56 in three countries surveyed in 2000. Mexico is the only country where permissiveness toward corruption has systematically deacreased in the 1990s, when it experienced a deep political transformation and higher political competition. In Argentina, Brazil, Chile, and Venzuela, the average score on permissiveness toward corruption went up.

In sum, despite the relatively strong association between permissiveness toward corruption and democratic attitudes, particularly support for democracy and interpersonal trust, democratization does not seem to reflect a reduction in culturally unacceptable corrupt practices. During the early 1990s, permissiveness toward corruption increased in most post-Communist societies. In Latin America, several countries also showed a higher justification of corruption by the end of the decade than in the mid 1990s. Permissiveness toward corruption even increased in some advanced industrial societies, such as the United States. Besides its governmental dimension, as measured by the CPI, corruption has a cultural face in both stable and new democracies.

Conclusion

The acceptance of corrupt practices is culturally undemocratic. Democratic institutions are expected to diminish the possibilities of corruption in government, but there is also an expected relation between a democratic political culture and permissiveness toward corruption. The efforts to measure perception of government corruption are only one side of the coin. The other one centers on the extent to which mass publics are becoming more or less likely to tolerate or accept some sorrupt practices in society. Survey data from over 60 societies show that there is a negative relationship between permissiveness toward corruption and support of democracy, and between the former and interpersonal trust. However, the trend in the last two decades, when democratization took place in a significant number of countries from Latin America, South Asia, Africa and the post-Communist world, indicates that permissiveness toward corruption has not decreased significantly. In some cases it has even increased.

There are important cross-national differences in corruption permissivenes, which suggests that in some countries there is a wide cultural basis for the justification of corruption. The level of permissiveness toward corruption is higher in post-Communist societies, followed by Latin American countries, and South Asian publics. But the increase observed in the last decade is not exclusive of those societies. There is an observable increase in permissiveness toward corruption in Western democracies as well, including the United States.

Appendix

Table 1

Corruption Permissiveness by Region and Country, by year. (1 = Low and 5 = High in a 4-item composite index)

	1981-84	1990-93	1995-97	2000-01
Western democracies	**1.37**	**1.36**	**1.28**	**1.40**
Australia	1.43		1.22	
Austria		1.17		
Belgium	1.51	1.70		
Britain	1.39	1.26		
Canada	1.41	1.29		1.29
Denmark	1.23	1.19		
Finland	1.25		1.34	
France	1.83	1.69		
Iceland	1.28			
Ireland	1.47	1.32		
Italy	1.24	1.34		
Netherlands	1.40	1.33		
N. Ireland	1.28	1.22		
Norway	1.28	1.25	1.24	
Portugal		1.65		
Spain	1.43	1.43	1.23	1.31
Sweden	1.14	1.25	1.41	
Switzerland			1.40	
USA	1.26	1.26	1.14	1.39
W. Germany	1.41	1.41		1.61
East Asia	**1.22**	**1.14**	**1.23**	**1.16**
China		1.12	1.19	1.14
Japan	1.19	1.15	1.19	1.18
South Korea	1.25		n.a.	n.a.
Taiwan			1.30	
South Asia		**1.14**	**1.55**	**1.58**
India		1.15	1.19	
Philippines			1.91	2.02
Vietnam				1.14
Turkey		1.13	n.a.	n.a.
Ex-Comunist countries		**1.46**	**1.67**	**1.33**
Armenia			1.87	
Azerbaijan			1.72	
Belarus		1.72	1.84	
Bulgaria		1.33		
Croatia			2.03	
E. Germany		1.17	1.51	
Estonia		1.33	1.53	
Georgia			1.63	

Table 1

(Continued)

	1981-84	1990-93	1995-97	2000-01
Hungary		1.81		
Latvia		1.38	1.81	
Lithuania		1.35	1.58	
Moldova			1.89	
Montenegro			1.46	1.38
Poland			1.31	
Romania		1.32		
Russia		1.45	1.65	
(Moscow)		1.80		
Serbia			1.41	1.27
Slovenia		1.40	1.64	
Tambov			1.78	
Ukraine			1.79	
Latin America	**1.62**	**1.80**	**1.52**	**1.56**
Argentina	1.36		1.34	1.37
Brazil		1.56	2.08	
Chile		1.62	1.56	1.65
Dominican Rep.			1.35	
Mexico	1.88	2.23	1.83	1.75
Peru			1.53	
Puerto Rico			1.32	
Uruguay			1.27	
Venezuela			1.36	1.47
Africa	**1.48**	**1.42**	**1.30**	**1.39**
Uganda				1.70
Ghana			1.19	
Nigeria		1.42	1.34	1.32
South Africa	1.48		1.38	1.41
Zimbabwe				1.15

Source: World Values Survey, author's calculations.

General Index

abortion, 19, 20, 26, 28, 45
Abramson, P., 186n, 187
Abu-Zayd, Gehan, 93
Abuza, Zachary, 143
Africa, 13-4, 20-1, 26, 30, 37, 102
African immigrants, 253
  see also 'immigrant'
African National Congress, 185
Aharoni, Meir, 122
Aharoni, Sara, 122
Akhavi, S., 88
Al-Qaeda, 9
Albania, 60, 64
Almond, Gabriel, 41
Alter, Robert, 120
Anderson, Kym, 140
Arabic, 8
Arbuckle, J., 223
Arian, Asher, 121
army rule, 49
Aron, Ramond, 118
Ashkenazi, 131, 132
Atkinson, 185n
authoritarian societies, 31
authority orientation, 157, 166, 173
authority patterns, congruence in, 160
Azadarmaki, Taqhi, 69

Baker, Wayne, 8, 15, 39, 45, 51, 56, 102-
  3, 117, 140, 216, 221
Bangladesh, 25
Bank of Sweden Tercentenary Founda-
  tion, 2
Bar-Tal, Daniel, 121
Barne, Samuel, 106
Barzilay, Gad, 121
Bauer-Kaase, P., 187n
Beck, U., 236
Bell, Daniel, 118
Ben-Rafael, Eliezer, 120
Bin Laden, 9
Bosnia, 60, 64
Botha, PW, 184
Brazil, 95

Brechin, Steven, 119
Buddhist, 13
Bulgaria, 60, 64
Burkhardt, Ross, 108, 111
Byrne, B., 223

Carroll, Susan, 92
Catholic, 14, 38, 56, 103
  historically, 128
Caul, 92
Central Europe, 20, 21
Central European, 26
children, 76, 77, 150
  subnumber of, 76
China, 95, 141, 147, 150, 274
Chinese, 144
Chinese culture, 149
Chirot, D., 6, 9
Christian civilization, 35
Christian Democrat, 18
civic orientation, 216, 220, 223, 225-8,
  232
civilization, 37, 52, 63
civilization differentiation, 235
citizen satisfaction, 166
Clarke, H., 187n, 194
Clarke, T., 159, 168
clash of civilizations, 5-6, 29, 36, 235, 252
classless society, 236
cognitive mobility, 168
cohort, 28
Coleman, J., 55, 228
Comparing Cultural Values, 50
Communist, historically, 128
Confidence
  in government, 170
  in institutions, 170
Confucian, 103, 145
  teaching of, 149
Cong, Huyen Ton Nu, 149
convergence, 237
corruption, 265-6, 271, 275
  and democracy, 265
  and trust, 266, 271

impact on economic development, 265
permissiveness towards, 266-7, 269-70, 272-3, 276
Corruption Perception Index (CPI), 265, 267-8
Cox, M., 6
crime levels, 193
Crozier, M., 157
cultural barriers, 92
  change, 100
  conflict, 11
  factors, 109
  regions, 244
  values, 38

Dahrendorf, Ralf, 118
Dalton, Russell, 16, 139, 157, 159
Dark, K., 211
Dasgupta, P., 42n
Davenport, D., 187n
Davis, D., 87n
De Klerk, F.W., 185
Deflen, 251
democracies, 49
democracy, 17, 29, 40, 48, 62, 64, 91, 95, 99, 106, 111, 113, 157
  support for, 30, 51, 267, 269-70
democratic culture, 46, 50, 53, 62-3
  ideals, 17, 19, 20, 22, 29
  institutions, 112, 275
  performance, 17, 19, 20, 22
  satisfaction, 170-1
  stability, 160
  values, 8, 23
determination, 67
Diamond, Larry, 121
Diez-Nicolas, Juan, 235, 239-40, 245, 252
Dimaggio, Paul, 118
dissatisfaction with government, 166
divorce, 19, 20, 26, 28
Dogan, M., 213, 223
Dollar, David, 140
Dowley, K., 187n
Duch, R., 187
Duncan, O., 235
Durfee, M., 210
Dutt, N., 194

East Asia, 147, 150
  societies in, 151
Eastern European, 29
Easton, D., 168
Eckstein, Harry, 158, 160-2, 165, 168, 172
education, 151
efficacy, 44, 53
Egypt, 25, 69, 71, 79, 87, 95
Elon, Amos, 121
end of history, the, 236
English-speaking, 102
Esmer, Yilmaz, 35
Esposito, J. L., 6, 9, 88
European Values Surveys, 1, 36, 41, 266
Everts, Ph., 210, 221

faith, 67
family, 44, 60-1
  authority in, 162
  ties, 79
  values, 217, 231
  fatalism, 60-1
  fate, 59
Feinberg, Geoffrey, 12
Flanagan, S., 187n
Fox, J., 6
France, 95
freedom, 48, 64
Freedom House, 8, 94, 98, 99, 106, 107
  rating, 241, 261
Frenier, Mariam, 149
Friedman, S., 185n
Fuchs, D., 158, 173
Fukuyama, Francis, 41, 236-7, 240, 260, 271n
Fuller, Graham, 9
Fundamentalist, 73

Gallup, 11
Gammeltoft, Tine, 150
Gastrow, P., 194
gender equality, 5, 7, 11, 18-20, 26, 28, 31, 67, 91, 98-100, 106, 112-3
gender relation, 152
gender role, 150
Germany, 37
Gertler, Paul, 140
Giddens, A., 236
Giliomee, H., 185n

globalization, 235, 237
God, 43, 61
  importance of, 243, 248-9, 257-9
Greece, 25
Guha, Ramachandra, 119
Guiorossi, G., 173
Gurr, Ted, 6, 160-2, 168

Habib, A., 185n
Haller, M., 238
Halman, L., 39, 45, 55, 57, 215, 231
Halper, Jeff, 120
Hanelman, Don, 121
Harris, Marvin, 36
Harshav, Benjamin, 120
Hawley, A., 235, 239
Heaven, R., 43
Hell, 43
Henderson, R., 6
Herman, Tamar, 121
Herzog, Hanna, 120
Hindu, 13, 20, 26, 37-8, 56
Hickey, Gerald, 141
Hofert, A, 237
homosexual, 45
homosexuality, 19, 20, 26-7, 28, 46
Human Development Index, 15, 215, 241, 261
Human Development Report, 186
Hunter, Shireen, 9
Huntington, Samuel P., 5-10, 13, 18, 30, 36-7, 51-2, 55, 63, 102, 118, 120, 157, 237-9, 241-2, 260
Hutton, W., 236

immigrant, 255
  of Africa, 253
  of Latin America, 253, 260
immigrant groups, 256
India, 61, 65, 95
individual level values, 211
industrialization, 10
Inkeles, Alex, 45, 140
Inglehart, Ronald, 8, 10-1, 15, 18, 31, 36, 39, 43, 45, 51, 52, 54, 56, 62-3, 91, 102-3, 117, 119, 124-7, 130, 132-3, 140, 145, 157-9, 162, 184, 186, 186n, 188, 194, 198, 201, 212, 216, 221-2, 237-43, 245, 250-1, 271n

Institute of Human Studies in Vietnam, 155
International Relations, 210
interpersonal trust, 42, 58, 243, 248-9, 255-9, 272
Iran, 25, 69, 71, 79, 87
Ireland, 95
Islam, 7, 25, 29-31, 51
Islamic, 13-4, 18, 20, 26-7, 35-8, 54, 98
Islamic societies, 1, 19, 21, 30
Islamic publics, 5, 69
Islamic civilization, 35, 54, 239
Islamic countries, 69
Islamic-Arab immigrants, 255
Islamic-Arabs, 253, 260
Israel, 117, 119-123, 126, 128-130, 133
  society, 117, 119

Japan, 21, 95, 141, 147, 150
Japanese, 13, 20, 26, 37, 144
Jews, 121
job market, 85
Johnson, 185n
Jordan, 25, 69, 71, 79, 87
Jun, J., 159

Kaas, Max, 106, 158, 161, 187n
Kabuli, Naiz, 6, 9
Kahn, H., 240
Kanji, Mebs, 157
Karam, Azza, 92
Katriel, Tamar, 120
Katz, Elihu, 121, 124
Kenworthy, 92-3
Kepel, G., 88
Kerr, Clark, 117
Kiewiet, 190
Kimberly, Mancini, 149
Kinder, 190
King, D., 173
Klandermans, B., 191
Klingemann, H., 16, 21, 46, 47, 157-8, 162, 173
Korea, 147, 150
Kornberg, A., 168, 187n
Kotzé, Hennie, 183

Lapid, Y., 210
Lasswell, H., 235

Latin America, 13-4, 20-1, 26, 30, 37, 102, 274
Le, Thi, 140
leadership attitudes, 24
Lenin, 236
Lenz, Gabriel, 265n
Lerner, Daniel, 118
Levi, 124
Levinson, 124
Lewis, Bernard, 11
Lewis-Beck, Michael, 108, 111
Liberal theory, 210
Liebenberg, I., 185n
life satisfaction, 243, 248-9, 257-9
Limogi, Fernando, 108, 111
Lindberg, L., 212
Lipset, Seymour, 108, 265n
Litvack, Jennie, 140
Lockart, Greg, 144
Lodge, 185n
Lombard, Karin, 183
Lovenduski, 93

Macedonia, 60, 64
Maharaj, G., 185n
Malami, 92, 93
Mandela, Nelson, 185
marriage, 44, 77
marriage and family, 50, 53, 62
Marsh, A., 161
Martinez-Alier, 119
Maslow, Abraham, 186n
materialism, 45, 188, 195
Materialist values, 103, 105
Materialists, 45, 193, 197
materialist/post-materialist continuum, 199
materialist/post-materialist dimension, 183-4, 189, 199
Marks, G., 187n
Marx, Karl, 42, 235-6
McIntyre, C., 187n
membership, 144
Merrit, R., 239
Mexico, 266
Middle East, 8
Midlarsky, 8
Miller, Thomas, 12
Misztal, Barbara, 41

Moaddel, Mansoor, 69, 88
modernity, 40, 42, 50, 58, 60, 63
modernization, 10, 42-4, 53, 95, 97, 109, 111, 124, 130, 132-3
Moldova, 29
Moller, V., 191
Montenegro, 60, 64
Moodley, K., 185n
Moore, 12
Moreno, Alejandro, 265
Morocco, 25, 255
Morocan, 260
mother, 150
multi religion, 55
Muslim, 24, 40, 56, 83-4

national identity, 82, 217, 231
National Science Foundation, 2
nationalism, 71, 89
nationalist, 83-4
Nattrass, N., 191-2
Nevitte, Neil, 157, 160, 168
Newton, K., 158, 170, 173
Nguyen, Van Huyen, 141
Niedermayer, O., 217-8
Nigeria, 60, 64, 95
Nie, N., 159
non-Muslim, 4
Norris, Pippa, 8, 10, 11, 15-6, 18, 31, 36, 51-2, 54, 62-3, 91-3, 158-9, 168, 170, 173, 237-8, 241-2, 250-1
Nye, Joseph, 173

obedience, 78-9, 148, 162
Ohana, David, 121
Olivier, J., 191
O'Neal, J., 6
Ong, Nhu-Ngoc, 139
Orthodox, 13-4, 20, 26, 37-8, 56, 103, 111
societies, 24

Pakistan, 95
Pampel, 251
parent, 80
parental duty, 138
participation, 64
Pelassy, D., 213, 223
Peres, Yochanan, 121
personal well-beings, 244, 254

Pettersson, Thorleif, 39, 45, 55, 57, 209, 215-6
Pham, Minh Hac, 139, 149
Pham, Thanh Nghi, 139
Pham, Van Bich, 140, 147, 149
Pham, Xuan Nam, 149
Pharr, Susan, 16, 158
Philippines, 141, 144
political
    attitudes, 244, 254
    authority, 162-4
    leaders, 86, 97, 99, 105
political values, 11
    factor analysis of, 17
post-modern values, 118, 243
postindustrial, 10
postindustrial society, 118
postinernationalist theory, 210, 218, 228
Postmaterialism, 45, 200, 216-7, 220, 227, 240, 244
    index of, 232
Postmaterialist, 45, 188
Postmaterialist
    syndrome, 119
    values, 103, 105, 107, 108, 133, 168, 243, 261
pre-materialism, 195
pre-materialist, 197
pre-materialist
    needs, 192
    values, 191
pre-materialist/materialist continuum, 183-4, 189-90
pre-materialist/materialist dimension, 196, 200-1
Prezworski, Adam, 108, 111, 213
prostitution, 46
protest proness, 217, 220, 227, 232
Protestant, 14, 38, 56, 98, 102, 111
    historically, 128
Protestant ethic, 40, 41, 50, 53, 56, 63
Putnam, Robert, 16, 41, 55, 145, 158-60, 216, 271n
Pye, Lucian, 147

Quran, the, 59

Ramirez-Lafita, M., 252
Realist, 210, 228

Regev, Motti, 120
religion, 7, 37, 70, 71, 80
religiosity, 54, 58, 60, 61, 67, 72, 79, 243-44, 254
religious
    authorities, 30
    faith, 43
    leaders, 19, 20, 20
    leadership, 17, 22
    legacies, 5
    values, 217, 231
Rempel, M., 159
Rescher, N., 201
respect
    for authority, 148
    for others, 58
    for parents, 148
Reynolds, Andrew, 92, 96
Robert, H., 88
Roefs, M., 191
Rokkan, Stein, 239
Roman Catholic, 102
Roper Reports Worldwide, 12
Rosenau, J., 209-12, 218
Rotberg, R., 42n
Rule, Wilma, 92, 93, 96
Russett, B., 6
Russia, 29, 274

Said, 9
Salvatore, A., 238
Sapiro, Virginia, 92
satisfaction with government, 160, 165, 169
Scandinavia, 25
Scandinavian societies, 24
Scheingold, S., 212
Schlemmer, L., 185n
Secular-Rational values, 10, 39, 100, 101, 126, 128, 129, 130, 131, 216
secularism, 44, 53, 59, 60, 61
Seekings, J., 191-2
Selden, Mark, 139
Self-Expression values, 10, 39, 100-1, 104-5, 107, 110-1, 118, 126, 128-30, 132, 216-7
Serageldin, I., 42n
Seroussi, Edwin, 120
Sepharadi, 131, 132

sexual
  liberalization, 7, 11, 28, 31, 67
  tolerance, 45, 53-4, 60-2, 67
Shadid, 6, 9
Shamir, Michal, 121
Shamir, Jacob, 121
Shavit, Zohar, 120
Shaw, S., 185n, 194
Shearmur, J., 236
Shi, Tianjian, 143
signing a petition, 58
Silver, B., 187n
single economic system model, 236
single political system model, 236
Sinnott, R., 211
Sisk, T., 185n
Smith, David, 45
Sinic/Confucian, 13-4, 20-1, 26, 37
social capital, 40-1, 50, 53, 58, 63, 139,
    168, 217, 220, 227, 254, 271
  index of, 216, 232
social
  group network, 152
  network, 143, 153, 216
  relation, 139, 152
  trust, 145, 216, 243
societal convergence, 235
South Africa, 183-4, 188, 200-2
Southhall, R., 185n
Soviet Union, successor states, 108
Spaniard, 255-6, 260
Sprinzak, Ehud, 121
Squires-Kidron, Pamela, 120
Stehlik-Barry, K., 159
Stevensson, P., 173
strong leader, 19, 20, 49, 248-9, 257-9
strong leadership, 17, 20
sub-Saharan Africans, 253
survival needs, 118
Survival values, 10, 39, 100, 101, 104,
    105, 107, 110, 111, 124, 126, 128, 129,
    130, 132, 216
Swedish Agency for International Devel-
    opment, 2

Taiwan, 147, 150
Taliban, 9
Talmud, Ilan, 121
Tanzania, 61, 65

Teune, H., 213
Thayer, Carlyle, 144
tolerance, 47, 64
Traditional
  values, 10, 39, 100-1, 124, 126, 128-31,
    216-7, 223, 226, 231
  orientation, 216, 227-8, 231
Transparency International, 265, 267
Trinh, Minh-ha, 150
trust, 81, 146
  in government, 84, 85
  see also 'interpersonal trust'
Tucker, R., 6
Turkey, 25
Turley, William, 139

Uganda, 61, 65
Ukraine, 29
undesirable groups, 47
United Nations (UN), 209-10, 218-9, 221-
    2, 225, 228, 233
  confidence in, 219-20, 222-3, 233
  orientations towards, 213, 216-7, 221-
    2, 224
  vertical power structure of, 217, 224-5,
    232
United Nations Security Council, 218
U.S., 95

de Valle, A., 238
value shift, 183
Van Den Berg, 191
Van Zyl Slabbert, F., 185n
Vahanen, 215
veil, 86-7
Verba, Sydney, 41
Vietnam, 139-45, 147, 149-50, 152
Vietnamese, 144
Vloet, 231
Voll, 6, 9

Warren, Mark, 41
Watanuki, J., 157
Weber, Max, 56, 102, 118, 235
Weintraub, J., 216
Welzel, Christian, 31, 91, 162
West, 7, 8, 25, 29, 30, 31, 51
Western, 24, 27
Western

societies, 19, 21
Christian World, 239
Christianity, 9, 13, 20
civilization, 7
culture, 18, 73
democracy, 130
cultural invasion, 74, 88
Westle, B., 217-8
Wiener, J., 240
wife, 150
must always obey, 97
Wistrich, Robert, 121
Womack, Brantly, 144
women, 54, 60, 61
right of, 85
role of, 243-4, 254
in parliament, 94, 95, 96, 98, 109

political leadership of, 85
representation of, 92, 112
need children, 248-9, 257-9
Woods, D., 185n
World Bank, 139
World Values Survey, 1, 6, 36, 41, 69, 74-
5, 95, 100, 125, 144, 151, 158, 161,
183, 188, 209, 265-8, 270-1, 273
web sites of, 3, 12, 156
World Values Survey Association, 238n
working mother, 78

Yamamoto, Tadashi, 143
Yuchtman-Ya'ar, Ephraim, 117, 121

Zionist, 122
Zrubavel, Yael, 120

INTERNATIONAL STUDIES
IN
SOCIOLOGY AND SOCIAL ANTHROPOLOGY

66. LAUDERDALE, P. & R. AMSTER (eds.). *Lives in the Balance*. Perspectives on Global Injustice and Inequality. 1997. ISBN 90 04 10875 0
67. LOVEJOY, P.E. & P.A.T. WILLIAMS (eds.). *Displacement and the Politics of Violence in Nigeria*. 1997. ISBN 90 04 10876 9
68. JABBRA, J.G. & N.W. JABBRA (eds.). *Challenging Environmental Issues*. Middle Eastern Perspectives. 1997. ISBN 90 04 10877 7
69. SASAKI, M. (ed.). *Values and Attitudes Across Nations and Time*. 1998. ISBN 90 04 11219 7
70. SPERLING, J., Y. MALIK & D. LOUSCHER (eds.). *Zones of Amity, Zones of Enmity*. The Prospects for Economic and Military Security in Asia. 1998. ISBN 90 04 11218 9
71. NANDI, P.K. & S.M. SHAHIDULLAH (eds.). *Globalization and the Evolving World Society*. 1998. ISBN 90 04 11247 2
72. ARTS, W. & L. HALMAN (eds.). *New Directions in Quantitative Comparative Sociology*. 1999. ISBN 90 04 11411 4
73. ISHWARAN, K. (ed.). *Ascetic Culture: Renunciation and Worldly Engagement*. 1999. ISBN 90 04 11412 2
74. PATTERSON, R. (ed.). *Science and Technology in Southern Africa and East and South Asia*, 1999. ISBN 90 04 11413 0
75. ARTS, W. (ed.). *Through a Glass, Darkly*. Blurred images of cultural tradition and modernity over distance and time. 2000. ISBN 90 04 11597 8
76. GERRITSEN, J.W. *The Control of Fuddle and Flash*, A Sociological History of the Regulation of Alcohol and Opiates. 2000. ISBN 90 04 11640 0
77. LEE, W.C. (ed.). *Taiwan in Perspective*. 2000. ISBN 90 04 11849 7
78. LUMUMBA-KASONGO, T. (ed.). *Dynamics and Policy Implications of the Global Reforms at the End of the Second Millennium*. 2000. ISBN 90 04 11847 0
79. HARRIS, R. & M. SEID (eds.). *Critical Perspectives on Globalization and Neoliberalism in the Developing Countries*. 2000. ISBN 90 04 11850 0
80. HOWARD, G.J. & G. NEWMAN (eds.), *Varieties of Comparative Criminology*. 2001. ISBN 90 04 12245 1
81. NDEGWA, S.N. (ed.), *A Decade of Democracy in Africa*. 2001. ISBN 90 04 12244 3
82. JREISAT, J.E. (ed.), *Governance and Developing Countries*. 2002. ISBN 90 04 12247 8
83. KEITA, M. (ed.), *Conceptualizing/Re-Conceptualizing Africa*. The construction of African Historical Identity. 2002. ISBN 90 04 12420 9
84. BERG, R. VAN DEN, *Nyoongar People of Australia*. Perspectives on Racism and Multiculturalism. 2002. ISBN 90 04 12478 0
85. DOGAN, M. (ed.), *Elite Configurations at the Apex of Power*. 2003. ISBN 90 04 12808 5
86. SENGERS, G., *Women and Demons*. Cult Healing in Islamic Egypt. 2003. ISBN 90 04 12771 2
88. ZEGEYE, A. and R.L. HARRIS, *Media, Identity and the Public Sphere in Post-Apartheid South Africa*. 2003. ISBN 90 04 12633 3
89. INGLEHART, R. (ed.), *Human Values and Social Change*. Findings from the Values Surveys. 2003. ISBN 90 04 12810 7